Norton

Dominator

Other Titles in the Crowood MotoClassics Series

AJS	Mick Walker
Aprilia	Mick Walker
Ariel	Mick Walker
BMW Motorcycles	Bruce Preston
BMW – The Racing Story	Mick Walker
BSA Bantam	Owen Wright
BSA Pre-Unit Twins	Mick Walker
BSA Unit Singles	Matthew Vale
BSA Unit Twins	Matthew Vale
Ducati 4-Valve V-Twins	Mick Walker
Gilera	Mick Walker
Honda Gold Wing	Phil West
Honda Production Motorcycles 1946–1980	Mick Walker
Laverda Twins & Triples	Mick Walker
Matchless	Mick Walker
Moto Guzzi – The Racing Story	Mick Walker
MV Agusta Fours	Mick Walker
Norton – The Racing Story	Mick Walker
Royal Enfield	Mick Walker
Triumph and BSA Triples	Mick Duckworth
Triumph – The Racing Story	Mick Walker
Vincent	David Wright

Norton

Dominator

MICK WALKER

THE CROWOOD PRESS

First published in 2006 by
The Crowood Press Ltd
Ramsbury, Marlborough
Wiltshire SN8 2HR

www.crowood.com

British Library Cataloguing-in-Publication Data
A catalogue record for this book is available from the British Library.

ISBN 1 86126 844 0
EAN 978 1 86126 844 0

Acknowledgements

The task of compiling and writing *Norton Dominator – The Complete Story* was made that much easier thanks to the many good friends I am lucky enough to have in the great family of motorcycling. This, combined with my own experiences, both of riding and working on Norton machines over a long period, made this a pleasurable task.

The list of those good people who have helped in some way include: Sammy Miller, Peter Reeve, Vic Bates, Mick Hemmings, the late Jock West, Philippe Niels, Philip Tooth, Graeme Noonan, Bob McKeever, Andrew Kemp, the late Don Upshaw, The National Motorcycle Museum and Pooks Motor Bookshop.

Typeface used: Bembo.

Typeset and designed by
D & N Publishing, Lambourn Woodlands, Hungerford, Berkshire.

Printed and bound in Great Britain by The Cromwell Press, Trowbridge.

Contents

Introduction

The Norton Dominator series, which began in November 1948 with the arrival of the Model 7 five-hundred and ended in January 1970 when the last of the Mercury 650s was built, represents for many the very best in classic British bikes. Its importance can be appreciated when one considers that its engine ran on in the Commando series until 1978, thus giving a combined life span of some three decades – a figure unmatched by any other British twin, bar the Triumph.

The Dominator also marked my own entry into the world of motorcycling, albeit as a twelve-year-old, when I was taken pillion around the Norfolk village in which I grew up by a local man who had purchased a new Model 88 in 1955. Although at the time I knew little or nothing about motorcycles, the experience is still with me today, some fifty years later! This was not because the rider went at any real speed, but the thrill came from the purposeful looks of the machine and the exhilaration of being transported on what, for the time, was state-of-the-art engineering.

I now appreciate features such as the famed Featherbed frame, Roadholder forks and the Hopwood-designed ohv twin-cylinder engine, but back in the mid-1950s this meant little.

The first Dominators, the '7' and '88' were generally well-built machines, in a relatively low state of tune, and as smooth as any other 500cc-class vertical twin with a 360-degree crankshaft.

As time went by they gained alloy instead of cast-iron heads, raised compression ratios, followed by increases in engine displacement to 597cc (1956), 646cc (1961) and finally 745cc (1962). With these increases in compression ratios and engine sizes also came increased vibration levels, with the 750 Atlas being the worst offender. Ultimately Norton built the Commando, with a new frame featuring Isolastic mountings (to combat the vibes), twin carbs and an alloy chaincase. Finally, in 1973 came the 850 (829cc, actually). But the Commando story is outside the remit of this book and, to my eyes at least, the Dominator/Atlas Featherbed-framed bikes represent the zenith reached by Norton with their ohv vertical design.

Many good people assisted me in the *Norton Dominator* project, illustrating just how many enthusiastic, knowledgeable and helpful folk there are in the classic motorcycle scene.

Mick Walker, Wisbech, Cambridgeshire
January 2006.

1 Origins

For more than 100 years the name Norton has stood for one of the very top marques in the history of the motorcycle. And unlike very many of the prestige British firms, Brough and Vincent excluded, the Norton name actually stood for its founder.

James Lansdowne Norton was born in the city of Birmingham in 1869, the son of a deeply religious cabinetmaker and woodcarver. But the 'junior' Norton's talents were to be in an entirely different direction from that of his father, except for his equally devout Christian faith. From an early age his great love was mechanical engineering and, as if to prove his potential, the young James demonstrated this in no small measure by constructing, at the age of twelve, a working model steam engine!

On leaving school at fifteen years of age, Norton was apprenticed as a toolmaker and was soon involved in the manufacture of cycle chains. When he was nineteen, however, he contracted rheumatic fever very seriously; despite sailing to New York aboard one of the new ocean-going liners on his doctor's instruction that 'the sea trip will do you good', his health never fully recovered. His subsequent continuing poor health aged him prematurely, which is why J.L. Norton was known as 'Pa', even while still a relatively young man.

Establishing the First Business

In 1898, at the age of twenty-nine, Norton established his first business, supplying components for the thriving bicycle trade. Known as the Norton Manufacturing Company, the new enterprise was based in Bromsgrove Street, Birmingham. That same year he married Sarah at the local Salvation Army Citadel.

Norton's first connection with motorcycles came from an informal club for local enthusiasts of this fledgling mode of transport, which was just beginning to take hold as the twentieth century beckoned. The club's meetings were held in the Norton Manufacturing Company headquarters, and it was here that he first voiced his plans to design and build his own motor-assisted bicycle.

These ideas, however, were to be put on the back burner following contact with Charles Riley Gerrard, the British importer of the French Clément engine. At that time the French were world leaders in the design of the newly created internal combustion engine, even though it was German engineers who had carried out the first experiments. Gerrard and Norton teamed up, with the Norton company initially building frames for Gerrard.

The Energette

Called the Energette, the first real Norton came in November 1902. Like so many other early machines, this was little more than a conventional pedal cycle with an engine 'clipped' on the front downtube of the frame. Displacing 143cc, the Clément engine was a four-stroke with an overhead exhaust valve and what was known as an 'automatic' inlet valve, meaning that it was sucked open and fresh fuel mixture entered the cylinder as the piston descended. It could be supplied with belt or chain drive and with either single or two-speed gear. Quite why the Energette name was chosen remains something of a mystery. Very few were actually built, although at least one example was used for reliability and speed trials.

Next the company moved from Bromsgrove Street to Bedford Street. The motorcycle business increased and a range of machines was introduced over the next few years, including a larger-engined version of the Energette powered by a twin-cylinder Swiss Moto Reve engine.

In typical pioneering spirit it should be pointed out that James Norton himself often competed in various competitive events, including trials and eventually racing. There is no doubt that this experience provided him with a greater understanding of his products than would otherwise have been possible.

But things were not easy, and it was not until early 1906, when he launched a range of Peugeot-engined machines, from a 330cc single up to a massive 985cc v-twin, that business finally began to prosper.

A Racing Debut

Norton made a major breakthrough in 1907, the year of the inaugural Isle of Man TT (Tourist Trophy) series, an event that was to bring undreamt of success for the still little-known marque. Their sole entry was a 'semi-works' effort, with a local Birmingham rider, Harold Rembrant Fowler (more commonly known today as Rem Fowler), on his own Peugeot-engined Norton, with personal assistance from James Norton.

The Fowler motorcycle, powered by a 690cc (76 × 76mm), 45-degree v-twin Peugeot engine, produced a maximum speed in excess of 60mph (100km/h). Lubrication was by a hand-operated pump and was of the total loss type. The only modification from standard was the fitment of stronger springs for the automatic inlet valves, increased in poundage from 4 to 8. The Peugeot-engined Norton weighed in at 182lb (82.5kg).

Surprisingly, this was the first ever race for both machine and rider! In fact, prior to the start, no one thought for a moment that the combination had any hope of winning, as there were full factory entries from the likes of Matchless and Triumph, both of whom were far better established than Norton and had riders of the calibre of the Collier brothers, Jack Marshall and Frank Hulbert, all superstars of their day.

But against all the odds, not only did Fowler and Norton emerge victorious in the twin-cylinder class (the race being divided into separate categories for singles and twins), but the combination also set the fastest lap of either class with a speed of 42.91mph (69km/h). This was almost a minute quicker than the best single-cylinder time (Harry Collier, Matchless). There is little doubt that if Fowler had not been forced to make numerous stops (including no fewer than six plug changes), he would also have recorded the fastest race average for the 158-mile (254km) event. As it was, this honour went to the single-cylinder class victor, Harry Collier.

The Unapproachable Norton

Even though he had just won the TT, James Norton was not entirely happy with the Peugeot engine. As soon as he returned to Birmingham he set about designing two new engines. The first was a 724.8cc (76 × 80mm) v-twin, in effect an updated Peugeot v-twin. The second, however, was an entirely original effort – the first Norton single-cylinder power unit designed 'in house'. It displaced 475cc (82 × 90mm), had both valves mechanically operated, a front-mounted magneto, pedaling gear and belt final drive.

As the first decade of the twentieth century came to a close, James Norton decided to race in the TT himself – a surprising decision as he was then over forty years of age and in poor health. He also broke new ground by becoming the very first to ride a single-cylinder Norton around the Isle of Man course. Sadly his debut was not capped with success, as he was forced to retire.

'The Unapproachable Norton' advertising slogan was coined by James Norton at this time to describe his machines. Except for the 1907 TT victory, however, the marque's main claim to fame was that its founder rode his own products, which endeared him to the British public. He was also viewed as a real gentleman rather than simply as a factory boss.

In November 1910, *The Motor Cycle* carried news of a forthcoming Norton that was to mark an important milestone in the Birmingham company's history: 'The new 1911 Norton single and the TT model will be of the long-stroke type, the dimensions being 79 × 100mm. This is to come within the 500cc limit.' The actual displacement was 490cc and this, together with the dimensions, was to become a Norton trademark, being retained on one model or another until as late as 1963.

Bankruptcy

In August 1912 Norton moved from Floodgate Street to Sampson Road North. The old 'Manufacturing' firm had gone bankrupt, and had only been saved by R.T. (Bob) Shelley, a well-known Birmingham businessman of the era, who had bought it at auction. Shelley realized the potential of James L. Norton himself, and engaged him as joint managing director; Walter (Bill) Mansell, one of Shelley's right-hand men, was installed as financial director.

So why had Norton failed? The answer is very simple: James Norton had no interest in the financial side of things; all he really cared about were his beloved mechanical creations, his family and friends – plus his religious beliefs. You could not have found a more unlikely businessman. But Shelley appreciated that James Norton was in essence the company's biggest asset: a brilliant creative engineer, a knowledgeable and keen motorcyclist and, most of all, adored by the press and public alike. What better figurehead could one wish for?

O'Donovan and the Brooklands Special

Besides the Isle of Man, the other major racing circuit of the era was Brooklands in Surrey. Situated between Weybridge and Byfleet, it was the first purpose-built motor-racing circuit in the world, being opened in June 1907. It measured some 3 miles (5km) in length, and was an amazing feat of construction, with steeply banked corner sections. From 1912 until the outbreak of the First World War, Brooklands was also the scene of many Norton triumphs. Names such as Percy Brewster, Jack Emerson and Daniel O'Donovan all helped to put the Norton name on the Brooklands map.

O'Donovan was R.T. Shelley's brother-in-law and had quit the German NSU company (a big name in Britain during this period) to join Norton. He first appeared at Brooklands with a Norton in August 1913, and from then on not only won countless races and broke endless records, but also gained a reputation for being a Norton tuner of great skill. Later, during the early 1920s, he was Norton's racing team manager. For his tuning prowess Daniel O'Donovan was given the nickname 'Wizard'.

Another connection with the Surrey speedbowl was a sporting side-valve single known as the Brooklands Special. The development of this motorcycle was keenly supported by O'Donovan and other riders. Priced at £60, each engine carried a certificate stating that it had officially exceeded a speed of 65mph (105km/h) for one lap of the Brooklands circuit. From this evolved the Norton legend known as 'Old Miracle', a bike reputedly used by O'Donovan to test some one thousand engines, and with which he set more than 120 world records.

Daniel O'Donovan (with Rex Judd in the chair) in 1915, after setting the world record of 82.85mph (133.33km/h) over 1km at Brooklands on his side-valve Norton single.

Expansion

In May 1916 Norton moved again, this time to Phillip Street, Aston, Birmingham, a much larger site than the old Sampson Road North works, and near the main R.T. Shelley headquarters. Norton were by now busily engaged on wartime contracts, producing munitions instead of motorcycles, a situation that continued until hostilities finally ended in November 1918.

Early in 1920 Norton moved from Phillip Street to an address that would come to represent the company and be famous the world over: Bracebridge Street. This location was ideal, as it backed on to the main R.T. Shelley works, where many of the components were manufactured. Bracebridge Street was to remain Norton's home for the next forty-three years.

The 1920s was to be a vital decade in the history of the marque, both for series production and racing. And at Norton the two were more interlinked than at any other mainstream motorcycle manufacturer. Despite its record-breaking achievements, Norton had struggled to repeat its 1907 TT success. So when the team's side-valve models simply did not come up to standard in the 1921 Isle of Man races, James Norton decided to embrace a new approach: he would abandon the long-running side-valve formula and adopt the more technically advanced ohv (overhead valve) design.

Rex Judd at Brooklands with his 1921 Isle of Man 490cc side-valve Norton single.

Model 18

This was to emerge as the Model 18. The first of Norton's ohv engines employed a modified side-valve bottom end and retained the company's by now traditional long-stroke 79 × 100mm bore and stroke dimensions, thus displacing 490cc. The first machine made its public bow at Brooklands on 17 March 1922. Daniel 'Wizard' O'Donovan was in charge, with Rex Judd as the rider, and James Norton in attendance.

Judd's fastest run on the new ohv Norton was timed over the flying kilometre at 98.76mph (158.93km/h) – a new British record. Not only this, but Judd averaged 89.92mph (144.68km/h) for two runs in opposite directions, which was a new world record.

Originally O'Donovan was not in favour of changing from the proven side-valve layout to the new and untried ohv format. Even though he had been responsible for the newcomer's preparation and its Brooklands debut, he was none too sure of its prospects. But the Wizard became far more positive after Rex Judd had taken the records, since the speeds were a significant improvement over the side-valve's times.

The big riding names for Norton during the early 1920s included Vic Horsman, Graham Walker, Noel Brown and Duggie Brown (no relation), plus the Ulsterman Jimmy Shaw. Daniel O'Donovan looked after the works riders, while Graham Walker was responsible for the Norton privateers. James Norton was design chief and 'commanding officer' of the race effort. O'Donovan also continued his record-breaking activities, both solo and with a sidecar attached.

At first the Model 18's biggest problem was its poor handling. For example the frame on the original racing models had come from the existing side-valve 16H model, with the top frame tube kinked to accommodate the taller ohv engine. So it was perhaps to be expected that problems arose: quite simply the new engine's capabilities far exceeded those of the cycle parts. At Brooklands these deficiencies were not really tested, but they certainly were on the much more demanding Isle of Man course, with Norton experiencing several crashes during the 1922 TT series.

As for the 1923 TT, although Norton didn't win (Douglas did), they did take the manufacturer's team prize (second, fifth and seventh). As a private entry Graham Walker came home fourth; he also finished runner-up in the first ever Sidecar TT, with George Tucker in third place.

1924 – A Year of Ups and Downs

In the following year, 1924, fortunes were mixed. For several years James Norton had suffered from serious rheumatism. His health deteriorated until, in 1922, his doctor diagnosed bowel cancer. Although he was then given only weeks to live, he actually carried on working and fighting the disease. Another blow was the loss of Graham Walker, competitions manager at Norton since 1919, who at the end of 1923 moved to Sunbeam.

Walter (Bill) Mansell reassessed the organization and, with James Norton's health steadily declining, decided that the firm needed a technical man, someone with acumen and ability to solve problems as they arose. This led, in March 1924, to the arrival of Walter Moore. Not only was he to take over the design reins, he also became the race team manager and soon told Mansell, in no uncertain terms, that, although the engine was suitable, 'the brakes were unsuitable and the oiling system out of date'.

Walter Moore had three months before the TT, so he concentrated upon what he viewed as the Model 18's weakest features: the rear brake and the lubrication. He soon discovered that the braking problem could not be improved using existing motorcycle industry practice and turned his attention to the car world – via Ford technology. The latest Model T was equipped with 8in (205mm) drums. As these were readily available, he ordered a quantity to be fitted to the Model 18's rear wheel. Next he uprated the lubrication system by using Best and Lloyd pump assemblies. These were probably not the complete answer, but, together with the improved stopping power, it was a start.

At the 1924 Isle of Man TT the revitalized Model 18 scored Norton's first TT victory since Rem Fowler's in 1907 – the first for seventeen years! This came in the sidecar event, with the winner George Tucker passengered by Moore himself; the two men had known each other since the time both lived in Bristol, when Norton's new race chief worked at the nearby Douglas works. The winning Tucker/Moore outfit featured a 588cc version of the Model 18 engine, since the rules allowed sidecars up to 600cc.

A couple of days later Alec Bennett made it two wins for Norton with victory in the Senior (500cc) TT. Bennett's average speed of 61.64mph (99.18km/h) was the first TT to be ridden at more than 60mph (96km/h) race speed. The Norton rider also set a new course lap record of 63.75mph (102.57km/h).

This was a truly great week for James Norton. After all his years of endeavour he was able to return to Birmingham with two trophies, and the rejoicing in the city was without equal, before or since, such was his popularity. The following year, however, James Lansdowne Norton died at his home in Sampson Road, Birmingham on 21 April 1925.

Overhead Camshaft

The period following his death was marked by major change for the Norton company. The big news for 1926 was the arrival of a young Dubliner, Stanley Woods, and what a debut it turned out to be, as he won no less an event than the Senior TT on his Model 18. For the fourth year in succession, Norton won the coveted Maudes Trophy. At the TT Woods was not a full-time employee, but joined later that year. Besides his racing, the Irishman was the Norton representative in the north of England.

The 1924 Senior TT-winning Model 18 ohv machine with, from left to right, James L. Norton, Alec Bennett and managing director Bill Mansell.

Next, in 1927, came the Walter Moore-designed CS1 (Cam Shaft 1), which was Norton's first overhead cam engine, or at least the first to see the light of day. Moore's new engine retained Norton's traditional 79 × 100mm bore and stroke dimensions. The crankcases, flywheel, con-rod, piston and barrel were all based upon Model 18 components. But instead of a pair of timing gears on the offside of the engine, there was a straight-cut bevel gear arrangement driving a vertical shaft that ran up to the cylinder head. Another set of bevel gears transmitted the drive to the single overhead camshaft. A notable feature was that the magneto was now mounted behind the engine, the first time this more practical location had been employed on a Norton-engined bike. Also new was the frame, which switched from the old 'diamond' layout to a cradle type. As the name implied, the new frame was of a full 'cradle' design, with a single front downtube that ran into twin tubes under the engine's crankcase. This frame was also used on the 1927 ES2 ohv model, and modified versions were employed on production roadsters until the 1950s. But although it was exceptionally strong, it was also very heavy.

Alec Bennett won his second Senior TT for Norton (he had also won on a Sunbeam in 1922) on the new CS1 in June 1927 at a record average speed of 68.41mph (110.07km/h).

The following year Moore created the CJ1 (Camshaft Junior 1), displacing 348cc (71 × 88mm), but 1928 was not to be a good year for Norton, and things didn't get much better in 1929. This resulted in Moore leaving the Birmingham company and going to work for NSU in Germany in July 1929. He was to stay there for over a decade, only returning to Britain when war was about to be declared during the summer of 1939.

The Carroll-Craig Engine

After Moore's departure two men reshaped Norton's fortunes. These were Joe Craig (who had previously worked at the company, but had fallen out with Moore) and Arthur Carroll, a young designer.

The first prototype Carroll-Craig engine was mounted in a CS1-type cradle frame and displayed on the company's stand at the London Olympia Show, which opened in November 1929. The 'new' engine retained the previous engine capacities and bore and stroke dimensions – 490cc (79 × 100mm) and 348cc (71 × 88mm) – but did abandon four notable features found on the Moore design: the reciprocating oil pump; the oil-tight cambox; the crankshaft magneto drive; and the splined vertical shaft. This actually made the Carroll-Craig engine far closer to those of their rivals Velocette than Moore's CS1/CJ1 series.

Unfortunately, the new engines were introduced in the same month as the New York stock market crash, which was to lead to the Great Depression that blighted the world during the early 1930s.

Besides Craig and Carroll, another important design figure at this time was Edgar Franks, who was largely involved with the series production roadster. He was later to take charge of Manx production racer development before, at the end of the 1950s, moving to Ambassador as design chief.

Norton works star Jimmy Guthrie at Quarter Bridge on his way to victory in the 1936 Senior TT.

The Start of a Decade of Success

Although Norton did not win the Senior TT in 1930, the new overhead cam engine came good in the 1931 event, taking five of the top six places. Not only this, but the winner, Tim Hunt, also won the Junior event. This was the start of a decade of success for the Bracebridge factory. As related in my book *Norton: The Racing Story* (Crowood Press, 2002), Norton not only dominated the Senior TT, except for victories by Moto Guzzi in 1935 and BMW in 1939, but also European Grand Prix racing.

Compared with companies such as BSA, AMC (AJS and Matchless) and Triumph, however, Norton's series production was not very large. When one realizes, for example, that the company sold fewer than 4,000 bikes in the year from October 1934 to October 1935, one could well ask how the massive racing budget was paid for?

The answer is also of relevance to the 1940s and 1950s and is quite simple. The money came from trade support, including Castrol, Amal, Lodge, BTH, Pratts, Dunlop, Ferodo and Renold, to name just some of the brands that supported the Norton effort. Although the words 'corporate sponsorship' had yet to be coined, this is precisely what it was.

Start of the 1938 500cc German Grand Prix at the Sachsenring: Norton riders Harold Daniell (5) and Freddie Frith (4) are on the front row. For much of the 1930s Norton dominated international racing.

Patient Development

Unfortunately Carroll was to die young during the early 1930s. This made Joe Craig very much the race supremo during Norton's years of glory, both before and after the Second World War, although in many ways this was to be to the detriment of innovation and sales in the showroom.

Probably the biggest technical change, at least for the Norton works racers during the 1930s, was the end of the road for the rigid frame, when the first of the rear-springing, plunger-framed bikes made their debut in the spring of 1936. The era of the famous 'Garden Gate' chassis had arrived.

The rigid cradle frame (as created by Walter Moore) had served Norton well, but technology was pressing ahead, so Craig and his team went 'Garden Gate' with the works racers from 1936 onwards. But it was not altogether the end of the rigid-framed Norton line, as the side and overhead-valve roadsters were thus equipped for several years more, as were the overhead camshaft International series (the latter having the cost option of a plunger frame from 1938).

Besides its Grand Prix racers, Norton also built a range of sv, ohv and ohc production roadsters, including this top-of-the-range 490cc International camshaft single.

War Bikes, Rather Than Racing Bikes

At the end of 1938 Norton decided to withdraw from racing. According to the official line this was 'to concentrate upon series production'. But this was not for the civilian market; instead it was to satisfy military contracts that the company's director, Gilbert Smith, had negotiated with the British government.

Behind the scenes things had not gone Norton's way since their star rider, Jimmy Guthrie, had been killed near the end of the German Grand Prix at the Sachsenring in July 1937. Even though Harold Daniel won the 1938 Senior TT and set a new lap record of more than 90mph (145km/h) – a speed that was to last until the late 1940s – Norton did not enjoy a very successful season in 1938. The team now faced a strong challenge from BMW, NSU, DKW, Velocette and Gilera.

In addition Joe Craig quit to join rivals BSA. 'Why BSA?', everyone asked. Again the answer concerned racing: BSA had plans to continue racing. The outbreak of war on 1 September 1939 changed all that. It also proved that Gilbert Smith and Norton had made the right decision.

The war effectively stopped civilian production and racing for six long years. During this time Joe Craig switched from BSA to AMC in Woolwich (where he was involved in the design of the Porcupine five-hundred racing twin).

Back at Norton things were busy. Besides building a reputed 100,000 WD 16H side-valve singles, there was also time for 'development work' that would ultimately benefit peacetime production. An example of this came in January 1944 when the Bracebridge Street concern took out a clutch of patents for a totally new design of front fork assembly. This was the work of Jack Moore, who had taken over prototype work from Edgar Franks.

As described later in Chapter 13, during the immediate postwar period there were considerable management changes at Norton, at both boardroom and senior management levels. The principal subject of this book, the Dominator series, was to kick off with the Model 7 (*see* Chapter 2) at about the time these new appointments arrived on the scene, including of course the Model 7's designer, Bert Hopwood.

At the 1947 Belgian GP the top three riders in the 500cc race were all Norton-mounted: in first place was Harold Daniell (2), second was Artie Bell (4) and third Ken Bills (6).

Australian rider Ken Kavanagh with his newly purchased five-hundred 'Garden Gate' plunger frame Manx Norton, circa *1949.*

2 Model 7

The famous Dominator series was introduced with the launch of the Model 7 in November 1948, on the eve of the London Earls Court Show. However, this was far from being Norton's first twin-cylinder machine.

This honour went to the Peugeot v-twin engined models, produced by James L. Norton in the first decade of the twentieth century including, of course, Rem Fowler's 1907 TT winning machine (*see* Chapter 1). This TT success put Norton firmly in the public eye, and for the 1908 model year Norton offered their own v-twin engine. After few examples were produced, however, the Norton-engined v-twin was dropped in favour of a range of single-cylinder bikes.

Wartime Prototypes

It was not until 1944 that Norton produced a 500cc side-valve parallel twin in response to a British War Office request for a new 'standard motorcycle for military service'. Issued by the department's Standardization Committee, this had to be either a 500cc sv or 350cc ohv twin. Since the Bracebridge Street factory had been

The first Norton twin of the 1940s was this experimental model built to compete for a military contract that eventually went to the Triumph TRW.

the largest supplier of military motorcycles during the conflict, Norton had high hopes in the contest, although rivals from BSA, Douglas, Royal Enfield and Triumph were ranged against their design. Eventually Triumph was awarded the contract, with its TRW side-valve five-hundred twin.

In the context of this book, however, Norton's military prototype is important and calls for details of its main design features. These included cast-iron cylinder block and head (both one-piece assemblies), single Amal carburettor, siamesed exhaust (exiting on the offside), rigid frame, single seat, carrier and pannier frame (a combined assembly), battery/coil ignition and telescopic front forks.

Besides the vertical twin outlined above, Norton also built a 1096cc side-valve v-twin sidecar combination. This was designed as a replacement for the Big 4 single, and was constructed in the period 1940–41. Power came from a bought-in JAP v-twin engine. Triumph and Sunbeam built similar prototypes, but all were discarded with the arrival of the American Jeep.

Postwar Prototypes

In the immediate postwar era (1945–47) two vastly different designs were put forward before the definitive Norton twin, which was to emerge as the Model 7 (Dominator).

The first of these, with an inline engine and similar to the Sunbeam S7/S8 series, was drawn up by Edgar Franks during 1945–46, but the design was dropped as too 'revolutionary' after being presented to the board of directors.

The other project was far more conventional and was the work of J.E. (Jack) Moore (no relation to the earlier Norton designer, Walter Moore). This was an overhead-valve engine featured twin camshafts (like the Triumph), with the cylinder head retaining bolts passing through the barrels and down into the crankcases. As for the heads and barrels, these were manufactured in cast iron, with separate aluminium rocker boxes. The whole assembly was housed in cycle parts from the ES2 and International single-cylinder models of the period: a cradle frame with single front downtube, telescopic front forks and plunger rear suspension. Today little is known of the design – or

How the Dominator might have looked had Norton accepted Jack Moore's design.

its ultimate fate – but it definitely didn't reach the production stage and was taken no further.

Hopwood Arrives

One reason why the Jack Moore ohv vertical twin was stillborn was because Herbert (Bert) Hopwood, formerly with their rivals Triumph, joined Norton as chief designer on 1 April 1947. As Hopwood later wrote:

> When I moved to Norton Motors in Bracebridge Street, Birmingham, as Chief Designer I was quite shocked to learn that neither Gilbert Smith, the Managing Director, nor Joe Craig, the Engineering Director, had taken the courtesy to inform the incumbent head of design that such a change was being introduced!

It seems, however, that the incumbent, Jack Moore ('a first class engineer and a highly skilled designer'), certainly didn't bear a grudge since, as Hopwood continued, 'We became good friends and colleagues as time went on and I forever will be indebted to him for his loyal help in the difficult times for me which were to follow.' The same could not be said of Moore's view of Gilbert Smith, which Hopwood described as 'quite angry'.

Since there was no office for Hopwood, 'Jack immediately offered to move out of his but I would have none of it and told him that it was obvious that we needed the help of the other, so we compromised by sharing.' This 'office' was meagre in the extreme, being only 8 feet square. Hopwood described the situation thus: 'We managed to get two drawing stands inside, with the pair of us sitting back to back, each supporting the other, a strange set up but the only one possible.'

Hopwood also painted a graphic view of the Bracebridge Street factory, saying:

> Not even during the wartime blitzes did I have to work under such difficult conditions; the whole Norton building was such a slummy shambles sandwiched with machines and parts, and men and vermin, in a noisy and dirty conglomeration, that a space such as mine did not seem too bad. After all, it was reasonably quiet and did not let in all that much rain!

Ninety Per Cent Racing, Ten Per Cent Product

Bert Hopwood (and Jack Moore), however, faced an even bigger problem since, as he described, 'the company's design engineering activity had been of the order of ninety per cent racing and ten per cent product activity.' Joe Craig was responsible for this policy, which was to lead to problems between the two men during Hopwood's relatively short stay at Norton. The politics behind this are fully described in Chapter 13, but suffice to say Bert Hopwood was to have a strained relationship with both his Managing Director and Engineering Director.

The Model 7 Arrives

It was perhaps only natural that Hopwood's experiences at Triumph were evident in the design of his twin for Norton: 'I started the design of a 500cc ohv twin cylinder machine immediately and my experience at Triumph of excessive cylinder head overheating problems made me determined to improve the air flow conditions.'

When the Model 7, the first of the Dominator series, made its public bow, it was thus perhaps not surprising that, as *The Motor Cycle* (11 November 1948) commented:

> Departing from their long standing practice of marketing singles only, Norton Motors Ltd are announcing a high-performance 497cc (66 × 72.6mm) ohv vertical twin. Cooling of the engine has been particularly studied: finning is generous, and the clever geometry of the cylinder head and barrel block provides for a good flow of air through numerous passages.

The centre of the newly introduced Model 7 was its 497cc (66 × 72.6mm) ohv vertical twin-cylinder engine, designed by Bert Hopwood. It made its debut in November 1948 on the eve of the London Earls Court Show.

Hopwood and Moore had worked together on the design for almost eighteen months since the former's arrival at Norton, and the finished product was to continue in production in updated form for some three decades. As the Commando it was destined to outlive every other British vertical twin save the Triumph, testament to the value of their initial work.

Engine Design

It was the engine and the gearbox that were new, rather than the cycle parts, which utilized existing Norton components. With a design priority of top-end cooling, Hopwood had ensured there was an airflow between the cylinder barrels themselves, between one combustion chamber and the other, transversely between the bores and the pushrod housings, and transversely between the inlet and exhaust valves.

In addition, the exhaust ports were, as one journalist of the day described, 'in extremely well-ventilated positions'. In plain view this meant the port axes of the new twin converged towards the induction tract, with a total angle of 50 degrees. Thus, in layman's terms, the exhaust ports were widely spaced and, as *The Motor Cycle* described, 'the cylinder head as it were opens its arms wide to the incoming flow of air.' This also

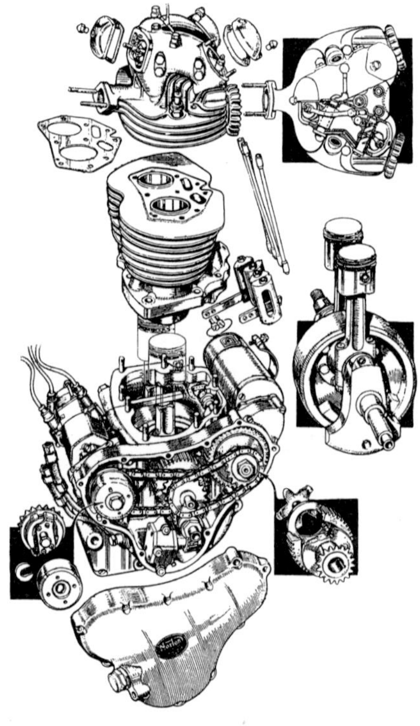

The original Model 7 engine with single, integral manifold. The exhaust ports were widely splayed to assist cooling, whilst all four pushrods were at the front of the cylinders due to the single camshaft. The crankshaft was of the built-up type with a central flywheel.

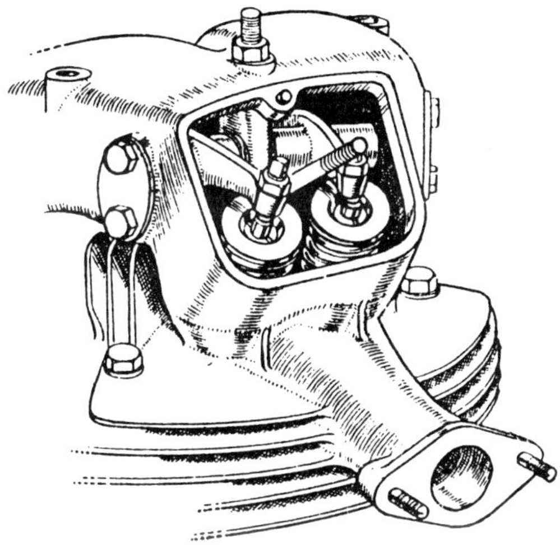

The first batch of Model 7s featured this integral inlet manifold. The single access cover, held on by one stud, gave access to both inlet valves.

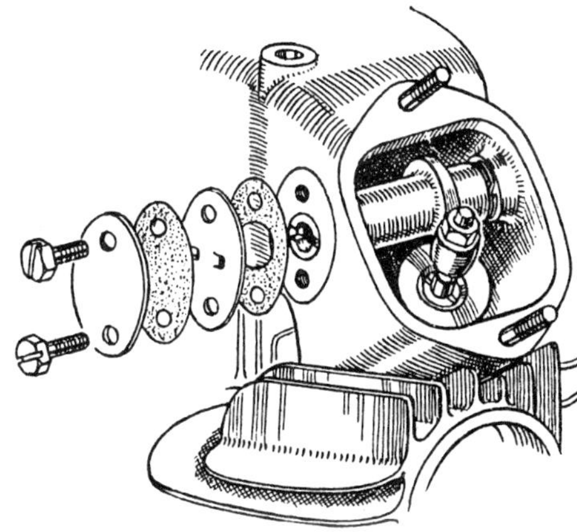

Tappet and rocker spindle details.

meant that the inlet side of the head was extremely compact. It should be explained that on the prototypes and very early production engines the head incorporated an integral manifold, whereas from then on the inlet ports were connected by a separate aluminium induction manifold for the single Amal carburettor.

The valves were set at a total angle to each other of 58 degrees. Also the valves (made of Silchrome) were more upright than in many designs, thus allowing shallow combustion chambers to be employed. Inner and outer coil valve springs were specified. Manufactured of cast iron, the one-piece cylinder head featured an integral rocker box. Two separate aluminium covers were employed to provide access to the exhaust rockers, but only one (of a different shape) for the inlet rockers. Tappet adjustment, by the conventional screw and locknut method, was provided at the end of each rocker arm.

The quartet of rocker shafts featured flange-shaped ends and were a light press fit in the rocker box. Each flange was pulled up to its flat face by a pair of ¼in (6mm) pins.

A pair of cast-in pushrod tunnels sloped downwards through the front section of the cylinder head and cylinder barrel assemblies, terminating near the base of the latter in large-diameter tappet housings. Each tunnel contained a pair of pushrods, these tappets being of the cast-iron car type with chilled rubbing surfaces. Each pair formed a complete circle, with each half circle, forming a single tappet, moving independently of the other. No tappet guides were provided (Hopwood considered these unnecessary). Instead the tappets operated directly in the cast-iron cylinder block casting. At the summit of the tappets and pushrods were small cups that retained oil and thus aided mechanical quietness. This was particularly notable, since the Norton singles of the period were not renowned for this attribute – in fact they were just the reverse!

At the top of the rocker box was a single fixing for the engine torque stay (head steady), which ran rearwards to the top frame tube.

A one-piece copper-asbestos cylinder head/barrel joint gasket was employed, whilst the head was secured by ten holding-down bolts, three of which took the form of inverted

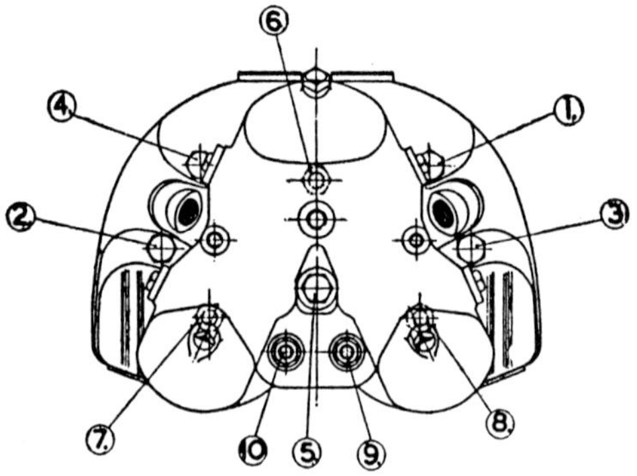

Correct order of tightening down the cylinder head nuts and bolts of the Norton twin engine.

cylinder head studs, protruding in a downward direction and fastened by nuts. As *The Motor Cycle* commented: 'There are generous air spaces between the bores, and transversely between the bores and the pushrod housings, which are thus isolated.'

The cylinder barrel was spigoted into both the head and the crankcase, the latter being of the conventional British vertically split configuration and manufactured in light aluminium. The barrel was retained to the crankcase by seven ⅜in and two ⁵⁄₁₆in diameter studs.

In order to accommodate a central holding-down stud, the crankcase was split slightly off-centre. The timing chest was contained within the offside (right) section of the crankcase. On the nearside (left) of the cases were the attachment points for the primary chaincase cover.

Both main bearings were 72 × 30 × 19mm, with a ball race on the timing side, a roller on the drive side.

The crankshaft was a three-piece design, with a central cast-iron flywheel sandwiched between a pair of toughened, forged crank halves, featuring bobweights. Half a dozen ⁵⁄₁₆in bolts held the assembly together. According to official Norton sources, 'Accuracy in the relationship between the crank members is maintained by a large diameter central dowel.'

The connecting rods and their split end-caps were of forged RR56 aluminium. Each con-rod had a phosphor-bronze small-end bush. As for the big-ends, these were of the plain car-type variety, steel-backed Micro-Babbit shell bearings.

The pistons were flat-topped and manufactured of Lo-Ex aluminium-alloy. Two compression rings were employed together with a single oil scraper. The pistons were retained by circlips, with fully floating gudgeon pins. A lowly 6.7:1 compression ratio reflected on the equally low octane of the fuel available, a feature of the immediate postwar era. This was an area that received constant revision over the following years as the quality of petrol improved. The original November 1948 launch ratio, however, did provide smooth running, a quality that later examples of the Dominator series were to steadily lose as higher compression and increases in engine size eroded the pleasant nature of the original power delivery.

Another feature of Hopwood's twin was its timing gear. On the crank mainshaft was a pinion, which meshed with a gear wheel that ran at half engine speed on a 'dead' shaft located in the crankcase. On this same shaft, side-by-side and integral with the gear wheel, were two sprockets. One of these sprockets drove the automatic advance and retard magneto (located at the rear of the cylinder barrel) through a ⅜in pitch chain. It is also worth noting that a slight adjustment could be made by moving the magneto. The other sprocket provided a fixed-centre drive forward via a slightly wider ⅜in pitch chain to the single camshaft. This camshaft carried a spring-loaded fibre wheel, which formed a slipping clutch drive to the Lucas dynamo (the latter located at the front of the engine). It should be explained that 'slip' only occurred on inertia overloads.

As for the camshaft, as explained above, this featured four lobes (one per valve), and ran in widely spaced phosphor-bronze bushes.

In his design Hopwood incorporated a mechanical engine breather, situated in the camshaft. In order to create enough energy and thus fling off heavy particles of oil, the middle of the camshaft was increased in diameter. This middle section was drilled radially with four holes leading to the main drilling in the camshaft. Keyed at the end of the camshaft was a spring-loaded valve with ports that matched up with stationary ports in the crankcase. Thus, at all engine speeds the breather opened on the downstroke of the pistons, while the ports were closed on the upstroke. From the stationary ports, the air and mist exited out of a specially drilled area of the rear of the crankcase.

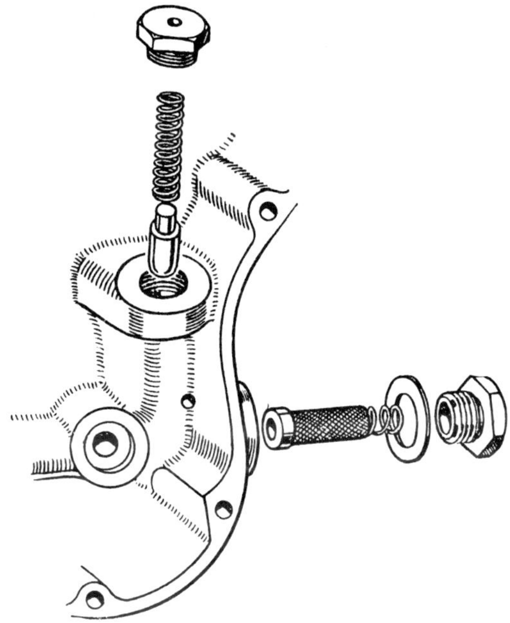

Pressure relief valve for lubrication system, simple but effective.

Lubrication

Lubrication followed conventional British practice with its dry sump/separate oil tank configuration. Driven by a worm screwed onto the mainshaft, the gear-type double-action pump (of Norton's own design) forced oil via a nozzle, sealed by a tapered rubber member, into a horizontal drilling in the timing cover. From here the oil passed to a compartment situated on the centre line of the engine in the timing cover. This chamber was equipped with a spring-loaded synthetic rubber oil seal. With the timing cover in place, the protruding end of the crankshaft fitted neatly into the oil seal within the chamber. Lubricating oil then passed under pressure through drillings in the crank members and continued to the big-ends.

Pressure was released by a substantial piston-type valve, this being connected to the horizontal drilling in the timing cover. At a predetermined pressure, the piston in the valve described above was lifted, allowing the oil into the timing chest. From there the oil returned via another drilling to the centre of the engine at the rear, and thence passed direct to the sump. This meant that cylinder lubrication bias was completely avoided. Oil released under pressure from the big-ends provided the main lubrication for the cylinder walls and pistons.

At the same time, via an internal drilling in the crankcase, the scavenge side of the pump picked up oil from the sump, returning it to the tank, which was positioned below the rider's saddle on the offside of the machine.

On the return pipe, next to the oil tank, was a bypass that carried oil up a pipe attached to the seat tube of the frame and into a T-section that distributed oil to a banjo on each side at the top of the rocker box. From these banjo unions, the lubricant passed through oilways direct to the hollow rocker spindles, each of which featured a dual scroll for distribution purposes. The oil then drained from the lowest points in the rocker box back to the crankcase, via the pushrod tunnels on the exhaust side of the engine, and on the inlet side via another oilway.

A New Gearbox

Besides the engine, the other important feature of the new twin was its gearbox. 'New' is not quite the correct word, as in reality it was a development of the earlier 4-speed footchange 'box that Norton had produced for many years, and which itself was derived from the even earlier Sturmey-Archer assembly. However, unlike the one it replaced, the latest gearbox was much more modern in appearance, being known as the 'Laid-down' type. This was because the earlier assembly had been upright, whereas the laid-down one featured an oval casing, gear position indicator and shorter pedal movement.

The new gearbox layout owed much to the factory's works racers, as *The Motor Cycle* pointed out:

> The gear train bears a close relationship with that used on the famous 'works' racing machines. Gear-shifting occurs in the usual way through a cam plate integral with an operating pinion that meshes with a transfer quadrant. Pivoting co-axially with the cam plate, this quadrant carries at its other end a cylindrical housing drilled parallel to the quadrant pivot and machined back on the outside to form a 'claw'. Inserted in this housing is a knuckle pin or T-member, of which the head is free to rotate in, or slide across, the 'claw' of the quadrant, which is free to operate through a cast vertical slot in the inner cover of the gearbox. Carried by the outer cover of the box is the foot-change pawl and ratchet mechanism operated by the short-movement positive-stop lever.

While the basis of the Norton ratchet and pawl indexing system (as the factory called it) was retained, the ratchet plate of the new assembly now featured an extension boss to the rear of its spindle into which the tail of the knuckle pin located with the ability to slide or rotate in the boss. Thus, as *The Motor Cycle* went on to describe: 'There is a fully universal

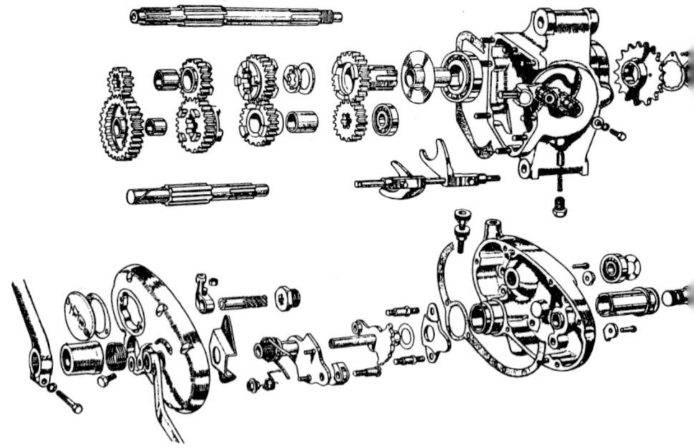

Also new was the 'laid-down' Norton-made 4-speed foot-change gearbox. Based on the old pre-war Sturmey-Archer design, it was tidied up for use on the Model 7 by Hopwood.

A 1949 model showing several features, including single downtube frame, separate valve adjustment covers on the exhaust side, front-mounted dynamo, pressed steel primary chain cover and chrome-plated fuel tank.

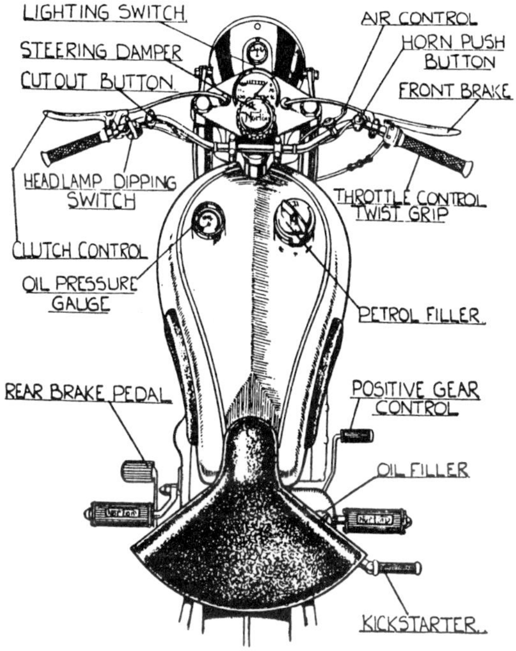

Model 7 control layout from the factory handbook.

motion between the operating lever and the cam plate.' This meant that the original Norton external linkage and loss of motion were obviated – and the foot-change lever spindle was now carried by fully lubricated, substantial-sized phosphor-bronze bearings. As for (solo) gear ratios, these were as follows: 14.9, 8.85, 6.05 and 5:1.

In an age when grease was still employed by some manufacturers to lubricate their gearboxes, Norton employed oil. This could be replenished via a hole revealed by removing the clutch adjustment cover. There was also a level plug.

The gearbox was mounted in the following manner: rigid extensions at the rear of the engine mounting plates were utilized as a clamping medium for the top gearbox support, whereas the offside (right) carried a simple, but robust and accessible, primary chain adjuster.

In order to prevent friction and ensure clutch action was made easier, the withdrawal pushrod was operated by a small-diameter, multi-start worm, this being carried by an additional outrigger bearing. A simplex primary chain was specified, with the clutch being a three-spring affair, with a vane-type shock absorber (in the clutch body) and $\frac{5}{8} \times \frac{1}{14}$in final drive chain completing the transmission.

As for the electrics, these were the conventional period-type, 6 volts, a rear-mounted magneto (Lucas, or in a few early instances, BTH), while at the front of the crankcases there was a Lucas dynamo (retained by a strap). The ammeter and switch for the system were mounted in a purpose-made console in the rear of the headlamp shell, while an oil pressure gauge was recessed in the front nearside (left) of the fuel tank.

The Cycle Parts

The Model 7's frame was based on that already in service on the ohc International and ohv ES2 500cc singles. It was not exactly the same, however, as has often wrongly been quoted. For example, the rear of the frame had been strengthened by transferring the seat and chainstay cross-members nearer to the plunger rear suspension; this form of suspension was a standard fitment on the new twin.

Essentially the frame was a single front downtube cradle type, with rear springing by plungers that have been described as having 'been lightened and tidied on their appearance after the war.' At the front was a pair of the latest hydraulically damped 'long' Norton forks, which underneath the outer covers were external stanchions ('external' in regards to being outside fork legs, but not obviously the covers!).

It is also worth noting that alternative fork springs were specified, colour-coded red for solo machines and yellow for sidecars. The forks needed 7 fluid oz of oil, compared with

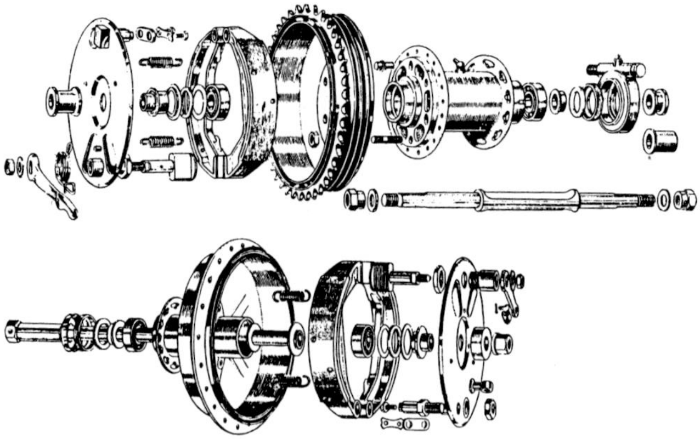

Front and rear wheel hubs from the early Model 7. The rear was quickly detachable, the sprocket being integral with the drum.

the 5 fluid oz of the later 'short' Roadholder forks. A mechanical friction-type steering damper was provided, this being given a knurled bakelite knob above the steering head column.

The Motor Cycle described the mudguards as being of 'deep-section semi-Gothic design'. The rear assembly detached from a point near the seat stays; there were also convenient lifting handles, formed by the rear mudguard stays. The rear guard also featured a flared lip to its tail portion (the type of styling cue Hopwood had learned from his old boss at Triumph, Edward Turner).

Also new was the fuel tank, which at 3¾gal (17ltr) was larger than that found on the singles, and also of a different style. The tank narrowed at the rear, to suit the rider's knees (there were rubber knee pads, inscribed with the Norton logo).

The oil tank contained 7 pints (4ltr), while other equipment included a single sprung saddle, Dunlop tyres (a ribbed at the front and a 3.50 × 19 studded rear), a single Amal Type 76 1in carburettor, a centre stand and a large toolbox. The 7in (180mm) single-sided SLS drum brakes were standard (ES2) Norton components.

The Earls Court Show

The first time the public got to see the new Norton twin in the metal, as it were, was at the London Earls Court Show, which was officially opened by Field Marshal Bernard Law Montgomery at 11am on Thursday 18 November 1948 and ran through to 10pm on Wednesday 24 November. This show was enormously popular: more than 70,000 visitors attended on Saturday 20 November alone!

The Motor Cycle Show Report, dated 25 November 1948, commented: 'There were so many exhibits of exceptional interest on the Norton stand that it is difficult to know which to mention first. Probably the vertical twin

This photograph of a 1949 model year bike shows features such as telescopic front forks, centrally mounted speedo between the fork legs, headlamp and handlebars.

deserves pride of place, because it is new.' The report continued: 'With its large petrol tank, semi-gothic mudguards and clean power-unit, the new twin is a good looking machine.'

But of course it was Norton's sporting successes that held centre stage, with *The Motor Cycle* stating:

> Bell's TT-winning Norton was on view, and also for those who liked looking at machines that had given battle, was Jack Williams' International Six Days' Trial machine, still coated with its Italian mud. The crowds seemed very pleased that real Italian mud could be seen and touched on an Earls Court exhibit!

In its issue for 25 November 1948 *Motor Cycling* had this to say:

> One of the new Model 7 500cc 'Dominator' vertical twin models was finished in a blue-grey metallic sheen enamel. Such a break with traditional Norton black, red and silver caused much discussion, but everyone agreed that, whatever 'ensemble' was adopted, the machine possessed a most attractive appearance, its price is £170.

By way of comparison, the AJS Model 20 Springtwin was £165, the BSA A7 £140, the Matchless Super Clubman £167, the Royal Enfield 500 Twin £155 and Triumph's best-selling Speed Twin £142. Even the high performance Tiger 100 was 'only' £152. This made the new Norton the most expensive of all the British five-hundred vertical twins.

Although the Model 7 had been launched to considerable press and public acclaim at

Tank top of a 1949 machine with the oil pressure gauge and filler cap.

Earls Court in mid-November 1948, this did not mean that it went on sale at the same time. As explained in Chapter 1, the reasons for this centred around the hostility shown by Norton's Engineering Director, Joe Craig, towards the new twin's designer, Bert Hopwood. In fact the newcomer didn't go into production until *after* Hopwood had left in spring 1949 to join BSA that May.

But besides Hopwood's departure, the new twin also had the combined problems of high cost (as shown above) and a high dry weight, compared to the opposition, of 413lb (187kg).

A Sound and Worthy Design

Whatever the merits of the disagreement between Hopwood and Craig, the fact remains that the new Norton twin's overall design potential made it a sound, worthy design that was to stand the test of time better than the vast majority of its competitors. The reason for this is hinted at in an article entitled 'Crankshafts for Vertical-Twins' published in the 3 February 1949 issue of *The Motor Cycle*. In this detailed analysis of the various designs, the Norton assembly was described as: 'Altogether a sound job, such as might be expected from the Norton factory.'

Another reason for choosing the Norton twin came from a comprehensive four-page story entitled 'European Journey' penned by Arthur Bourne, Editor of *The Motor Cycle*, which was published in the magazine's 28 April 1949 issue. The main purpose of this arduous 2,000 mile (3,200km) journey was to tour seven countries and to visit the main German factories, including BMW. Details of the various factory visits then continued in *The Motor Cycle* over the following three weeks.

Many of the roads encountered were snowbound, particularly in Switzerland and Austria. Arthur Bourne used a pre-production prototype and, as he commented,

> I gather that a different cylinder head design is being standardized on the production models, a design that reduces pinking and gives improved low-speed torque. With the low-octane petrols which were the general rule, I could have made use of a manually operated ignition control; as it was, the gear pedal had to be used a lot – either this or genteel wafting of the twistgrip throttle was needed.

But Bourne was particularly impressed with what he described as 'magnificent handling'. He enlarged on this by saying: 'That the general handling of the new twin is excellent has already been remarked upon, it is an exceptionally manageable mount. It is also comfortable.' However he did point out: 'Of course, on some of the wavy continental roads, damping of the plunger-type rear suspension would have helped to stop any bouncing-ball effect.' In addition, he criticized the bike saying:

> It was a curse not having a prop-stand, and the central stand was far from easy to operate; particularly when all the luggage was weighing down the tail, the stand also clattered on rough roads. The brake and clutch levers were on the heavy side, though to my surprise my left wrist, which is not very strong, did not tire.

Reliability, however, was notably good, Bourne commenting:

> No oil was needed for the oil tank. Even the brakes were not adjusted except that there was the automatic taking up of the rear brake consequent upon the one adjustment of the back chain. At the finish of the journey in seven countries the only obvious faults were a rear chain that needed adjustment and some side-play in the rear-wheel bearings of the far-from-new machine – the speedometer showed over 21,000 miles [33,800km] when I took over. It is true, of course, that the machine was carefully groomed before the start but could one hope for greater reliability? Considering the conditions –

all the snow, ice, war-scarred roads and vile surfaces in general – the makers have reason to preen themselves.

Because of fuel shortages in Europe at the time, a particular eye was kept on consumption, with Bourne telling readers 'On the first leg of the journey, a total of 4 gallons and 20 litres – 8.4 gallons – sufficed for 531 miles. Thus, the consumption, with fairly hard driving, worked out at just over 63 mpg.'

Although the fabled editor of the *Blue 'Un* (the term often used to describe *The Motor Cycle* at the time) was able to get his hands on one of the new Model 7s, this was not the case for the British public, as during the first few months of production every available machine went for export.

And so prospective UK customers could only read about the new Norton twin, not actually own one. An early road test appeared in the 8 December 1949 issue of *The Motor Cycle*. The test carried the sub-heading 'An Attractive Machine With Outstanding All-round Performance: Exceptional Standards of Smoothness and Flexibility', and began in the same enthusiastic vein:

With its high standards of mechanical quietness, excellent low-speed torque and smoothness, and rip-snorting top-end performance, the Norton 497cc parallel twin in the Dominator sets a new criterion in its class. When it was started from cold the engine of the test machine was barely audible above the slow, even chuff from the exhausts. Even after it had been driven as hard as possible for four hours, the engine was as quiet as it had been at the beginning, and it would still idle perfectly slowly with complete reliability.

In fact the tester went on to say that the 'engine's low-speed torque is one of its most attractive features ... It proved so good, in fact, that it gave the impression that the engine was bigger than a 500cc and a "woolly" one at that.'

Mean maximum speeds in the gears were recorded as follows: 1st 34mph (54.7km/h), 2nd 61mph (98.2km/h), 3rd 84mph (135.2km/h) and top 92mph (148km/h); the standing quarter mile was achieved in 17.4 seconds, a terminal speed of 79mph (127.1km/h).

But it was not just the recorded maximum speeds that caused favourable comment, as the tester went on to explain:

An enchanting feature, however, was that the machine could be driven for as long as was wanted at 80–85mph [129–137km/h] without giving any hint of stress. No oil leaks were apparent from either engine or gearbox. The exhaust pipes did not discolour, even slightly, at the ports. An engine with better balance than that of the Dominator it is difficult to imagine. At low speeds the engine was beautifully and unobtrusively smooth.

Handling

The tester was no less enthusiastic when it came to its on-road characteristics:

As would be expected from any Norton, the handling of the Dominator at speed was sheer joy. Fast bends and corners could be taken cleanly at speed in the classic manner. There was always that 'on rails' feeling – even when the model was heeled over at seemingly impossible angles. Straight-ahead steering was of the quality that allowed the machine to be steered hands off at any speed between 20 mph and 90 mph. Only once was the damper used. That was when a long, downhill straight, clear of side turnings or obstructions, was taken on full throttle, the machine attaining 97 mph. The surface was bumpy and without the damper there was a tendency to yawing.

As for low speeds, this was proclaimed 'equally good', but with the following proviso: 'In the initial stages of the test a slight roll was apparent at low speeds. It disappeared however, after the adjustment of the steering head bearing had been eased. Thereafter the model could be ridden feet-up at the slightest crawl.'

However, the front and rear suspension did have rather hard characteristics: '... Comparatively little comfort is provided at low speeds on poor road surfaces ... At speed on the open road, however, the suspension comes into its own and allows pot-holes to be taken hands off, or when the model is heeled over, without allowing the machine to get the slightest bit out of hand.'

Close-up of the Model 7's front end with Roadholder forks, 7in (178mm) brake and 3.00 × 21 Avon Speedmaster tyre.

Although, according to the tester, 'When used seriously together the brakes provided excellent stopping power', he went on: 'In the early stages of the road test the front brake was poor. It improved as it bedded down, but never quite came up to the recognized Norton standard.' It was also 'unduly heavy in operation'.

The 1949 Model 7

Engine	Air-cooled, ohv twin with vertical cylinders, cast-iron head and barrel, two main bearings, 360-degree, 3-piece crankshaft, split con-rods and shell big-end bearings, chain-driven magneto (rear) and dynamo (front), coil valve springs, vertically-split aluminium crankcases
Bore	66mm
Stroke	72.6mm
Displacement	497cc
Compression ratio	6.7:1
Lubrication	Gear pump; dry sump
Ignition	Magneto, 6-volt
Carburettor	Amal 76 1in
Primary driver	Simplex chain
Final drive	Chain
Gearbox	4-speed, positive stop, foot-change
Frame	Cradle; single front downtube
Front suspension	Oil-damped telescopics
Rear suspension	Plunger
Front brake	7in single-sided drum, SLS
Rear brake	7in single-sided drum, SLS
Tyres	3.00 × 21 front, 3.50 × 19 rear
Wheelbase	56in (1,422mm)
Ground clearance	5.5in (140mm)
Seat height	30.6in (777mm)
Fuel tank capacity	3.75gal (17ltr)
Dry weight	413lb (187kg)
Maximum power	29bhp @ 6,000rpm
Top speed	90mph (144.8km/h)

The Norton Engine Explained

In the 24 November 1949 issue of *The Motor Cycle*, by which time Bert Hopwood had left the company, E.A. Sitwell interviewed Norton designer Jack Moore about the Dominator engine project. The first question was straightforward: 'What in your opinion are the advantages of a twin cylinder engine for motor-cycles?'. Moore replied:

> A twin gives better torque and, because of its lighter reciprocating ports, can be run at higher rpm than a single of the same capacity. Moreover, a twin pulls better at low speeds, is easier to silence and gives better acceleration. Improved vaporization can be obtained with a twin such as ours, compared to a single, owing to the fact that two pistons pull, so to speak, at the same main jet. You see, this double pulling of the jet causes a more constant depression on the carburettor, and consequently a smaller choke can be employed.

And why a vertical, parallel twin? 'Advantages of the vertical, parallel twin,' replied Jack Moore, 'are good cooling for both cylinders, easier carburation, compactness, pleasing appearance, rigidity and ease of manufacture.'

As far as balance was concerned, Moore's view was:

> I think it is understood that the total weight of reciprocating parts in a 500cc vertical twin is likely to be lower than the total weight of reciprocating parts in a single of the same capacity. For instance a vertical twin usually has light-alloy con-rods, and a shorter stroke ... Therefore, although the theoretical balance is identical in practice there are lower inertia forces in the twin for a given rpm with consequent smoother running. In balancing the engine, the aim should be to make the reciprocating and rotating parts as light as possible relative to the flywheel mass, in order to achieve smoothness at high rpm. This has been our aim with the Norton twin.

Crankshaft

When questioned why Norton had gone for a built-up crankshaft and flywheel assembly, Moore's answer was 'Simplicity of manufacture,' going to further explain: 'We think that, with a really high-efficiency engine, forged crank cheeks are desirable and this dictates the building up, since it would be impracticable to use a forged one-piece crankshaft and flywheel assembly because of the excessive machining that would be required after forging.' Jack Moore could of course have said, as Steve Wilson did almost 35 years later:

> Norton's financial condition and antiquated production machinery meant that their existing manufacturing techniques and components would have to be used, whether they were ideal or not. Thus Hopwood (assisted of course by Moore) would have preferred a one-piece crank, die cast cases and an alloy head and barrel, but had to settle for a built-up crankshaft, sand casting and an iron top end.

But of course, at the time neither the public nor even the press knew of Norton's problems, as detailed elsewhere in this book, which were to result in the takeover a few years later in 1953.

So what material was used for the Dominator crankshaft? 'The shaft is made of manganese-molybdenum and has toughened journals. We use this material because of its high tensile strength, which is about 65 tons per square inch.' And the flywheel? 'Cast-iron – an entirely suitable material, and more than strong enough for the job, especially since a flywheel is intrinsically strong in section.'

Finally, at the end of the interview *The Motor Cycle* asked Jack Moore for a few 'instruction book details'. Here is what the Norton engineer provided:

Magneto timing: Set, in the fully advanced position, at 31 degrees before tdc (top dead centre).

Valve timing: Exhaust opens 57.5 degrees before bdc (bottom dead centre) and closes 22

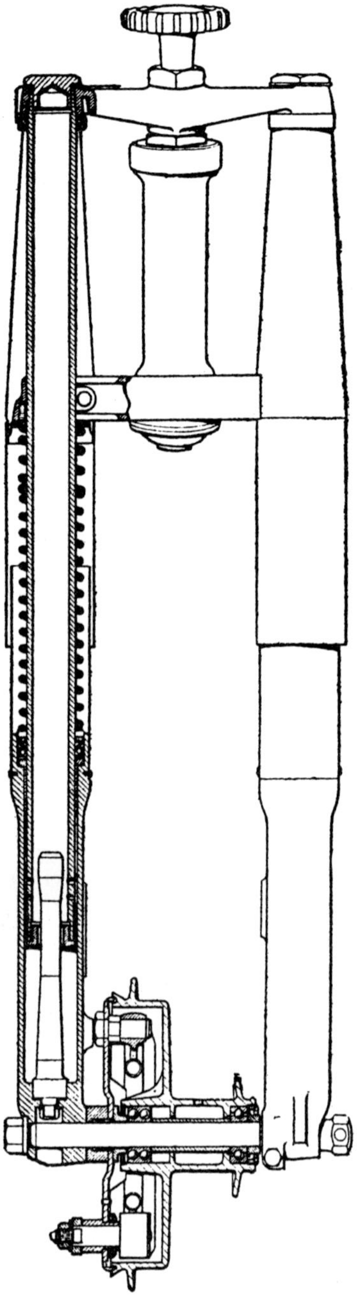

A part-sectional view of the hydraulically controlled telescopic forks fitted to the Model 7.

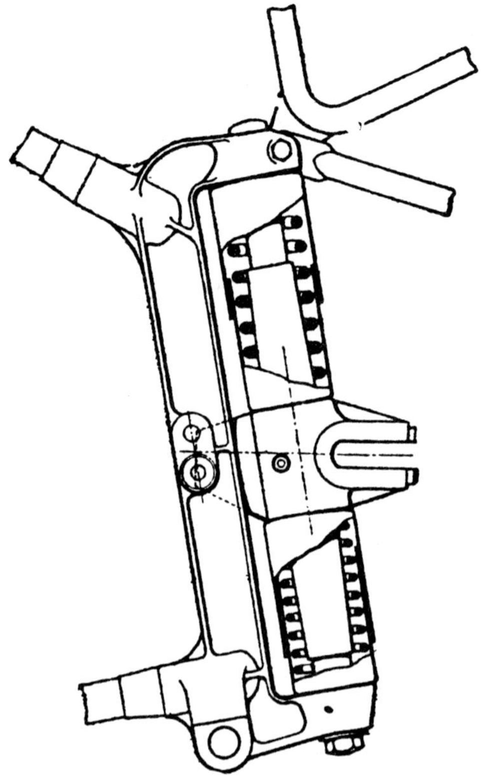

Norton plunger-type springing of the early Model 7 series, first used on the works racers back in 1936.

degrees after tdc. Inlet opens 22 degrees before tdc and closes 57.5 degrees after bdc. It is necessary for the valves to be timed with the tappet clearance set at 10 thousand (*not* the working clearance) when cold, because of the quietening curve ramps on the cams. Final working tappet clearances when cold are 3 thousand for the inlet and 5 thousand for the exhaust.

Updating the Twin

In its early years the twin, in the shape of the Model 7, was to remain largely unchanged. However, even as early as the 1950 model year, announced in mid-October 1949, there were small alterations.

One change – or, in reality, addition – was introduced on the Model 7 for the 1950 season: a prop-stand. According to Norton sources: 'Whereas, the prop-stand on the trials mount (the 500T ohv single) hinges from the nearside chain-stay, that on the other models is hinged at the front engine plate and can, therefore, be operated by a normally-seated rider.' The centre stand of the twin was retained but, advised Norton, 'to be used only when work was being carried out on the rear when the prop-stand is intended as the primary parking stand forthwith.'

Finish for the 1950 model year on all Norton models, including the Model 7 twin, was the traditional black silver and chromium. The price on 13 October 1949 was listed as £174, making a total with UK purchase tax of £220 19s 8d.

On the subject of colour schemes – the polychromatic blue finish referred to earlier in this chapter was mentioned again, this time in March 1950 when *The Motor Cycle*'s George Wilson used just such a Norton twin and Swallow Jet 80 sports sidecar for the grand occasion of the London Lord Mayor's Show and was then co-opted for family wedding duties!

The 1951 Model Year

The next development in the Model 7's evolution occurred in early November 1950, when the 1951 Norton model range arrived.

Together with certain other touring models there was a new front brake. Still of 7in (180mm) diameter, the design of this assembly had seen, according to *The Motor Cycle*, 'great care' taken to ensure maximum rigidity, light weight and, it was said most important of all, 'efficient sealing against the ingress of water'. Cast steel was employed for the drum, which was riveted to the wheel hub, the back plate being a die-cast aluminium component. There were also die-cast alloy brake shoes, which operated on individual steel fulcrum pins, one of which was riveted to the back plate, the second being extended through and, with a flat

A fleet of Model 7s delivered to the Norwegian police authorities for patrol work in Oslo, circa *1950.*

November 1950 advertisement for the 1951 Model 7 twin.

milled on each side, located in the lower fork leg as a brake reaction stop. Tab washers secured the bolts holding the shoes in place on the fulcrum pins.

The waterproofing measures included the lip of the brake drum featuring a groove machined on its edge, into which fitted the inner lips formed on the aluminium back plate. This, overlapping the outer periphery of the drum by approximately ⅛in (3mm), was one lip, while a second fitted neatly into the groove on the drum. Any water making its way past the initial overhang was unlikely to get past the second seal. Operation was by a heavy-duty Bowdenex cable, and adjustment was provided by a threaded cable stop on the backplate.

The price of the Model 7 remained unchanged. In mid-1951, due to a nickel shortage, the fuel tank finish went from chrome to an all-silver paint job. Likewise some machines were built with silver-painted, instead of chrome-plate, wheel rims but still with a centre red lining. This policy of deleting chromium was not just to be found at Norton, but throughout the British motorcycle industry at this time.

The Model 7 gained a younger, more sporting brother during 1952 in the shape of the export-only Dominator 88, which employed the race-developed Featherbed frame (*see* Chapter 4). At the same time the Model 7's timing cover was given the small oval Norton badge, as on the new 88.

The First Major Revision

In early October 1952 the 1953 model year Norton range was announced, and with it came the first major revision of the Model 7.

For the 1953 season, both the new Dominator 88 and the established Model 7 were to have pivoted fork rear suspension, rather than the plunger-type suspension featured since the introduction of the Model 7 some four years earlier. The Model 7 shared its new suspension and single downtube frame with the latest 490cc ohv ES2 single. The front section of the frame was largely unchanged. *The Motor Cycle* describing the revised frame thus:

> To accommodate it, the rear portion of the standard cradle frame has been redesigned. From the lug at the top of the seat pillar, two tubular stays extend to the rear for a short distance, then curve downward, substantially parallel with the seat tube, to meet the frame members which provide the bottom anchorage for the gearbox. Located near the bottom of the rear stays are forwardly projecting lugs which carry the pivot bearings for the fork. Bolted to the lugs is a fabricated steel bracket which links the lugs of the gearbox plates.

Although referred to as a pivoted-fork at the time, a more appropriate term used to describe the rear fork was 'swinging-arm'. Its welded tubular construction owed much to the McCandless technology employed for the famous Featherbed frame. The Model 7's swinging-arm pivoted on Silentbloc bushes, which required no maintenance. Fork movement was controlled by hydraulically damped telescopic spring legs which, at their summit, were attached to brackets welded to the frame at either side.

A major advantage of the new suspension was appreciably greater wheel movement – 3½in (89mm) more than was possible with the plunger springing. Another facet was that the pivot centre was less than 3in (76mm) behind the final-drive sprocket centre; and the variation of chain tension was what *The Motor Cycle* described as 'microscopic'. The wheelbase was the same as it was with plunger springing, namely 54½in (1,384mm).

Also new was the rear mudguard, described as 'a very wide deeply valanced rear 'guard'. The rear section of this mudguard was hinged (to ease rear wheel removal). Raising the hinged portion was achieved simply by the withdrawal of two bolts. There were also what were referred to as side lifting handles, which provided additional support for both sections of the mudguard.

There was also a newly designed toolbox, fitting neatly into the angle of the rear frame on the nearside (left). The lid was secured by a captive screw, described as a 'half wing nut'. As *The Motor Cycle* said: 'The scheme (which was employed during the war) is ingenious since, if the screw is not adequately tightened and therefore tends to loosen, the weight of the wing when it reaches "bottom dead centre" prevents further spontaneous unscrewing.'

New Silencers

Featured in the 1953 model year Nortons (the twins, plus the ES2 single) were new silencers, the side elevation being described by *The Motor Cycle* (dated 2 October 1952) as being: 'somewhat like an elongated pear – albeit a flattened pear!' Forever after these have been referred to as the 'pear-shaped' silencers.

Internally the new silencer was divided into three compartments, separated by two perforated plates. The integral outlet pipe extended forward to meet the foremost plate, and it featured two sets of holes – one set on each side of the second plate. Hence, as *The Motor Cycle* said: 'three compartments communicate with the outlet pipe through a multiplicity of holes.' Norton claimed that this set-up gave more efficient silencing with slightly less absorption of engine power.

Improved Rocker-Box Lubrication

On both the Model 7 and new Dominator 88, for the 1953 season Norton had improved the rocker-box lubrication. A spring-loaded ball valve had been put in the oil return pipe to ensure an adequate supply of oil to the rocker gear. In addition, as described in Chapter 4, the Dominator 88 (then known as the de Luxe) had been without an oil-gauge from its launch earlier in 1952. This lead was now adopted on the Model 7, which also had no pressure gauge for 1953. As for the price, this had increased to £187.

During spring 1953 came news that Norton were being 'acquired' by AMC (Associated Motor Cycles), which already controlled Matchless, AJS, James and Francis-Barnett. However, as will be fully covered in Chapter 13, this was not to be a marriage made in heaven.

Testing the Swinging-Arm Model 7

Although early 1953 Model 7s retained the plunger-frame models' 21in front wheel, by the time *The Motor Cycle* tested an example of the new swinging-arm machine, this had been reduced to 19in – even though the tyre section remained at 3.00.

As before, the engine came in for considerable praise: 'Throughout the engine's speed range, power delivery was commendably smooth. There was virtually no vibration period to dictate cruising speed. In town, the engine was quite happy at 30mph [48km/h] in top gear and would accelerate smoothly from that speed.' As for starting the Model 7's engine: 'No knack was called for whether the engine was hot or cold. A cold start required closure of the air lever and light flooding of the carburettor, a first-kick response was assured.'

As for performance, the mean maximum speed recorded in the official test session was 84mph (135km/h); however, 'Weather conditions were rather unfavourable.' A one-way, 'top gear speed in excess of 91mph [146km/h] was recorded with the rider wearing storm coat and waders.'

The gearbox was described as:

> a joy to use ... Engagement of bottom gear from neutral, with the engine idling, was noiseless. The clutch was sweet to operate and very positive in its take up of the drive. Neutral selection from bottom or second gear was simple. Movement of the gear pedal was light and short. Clean, silent and instantaneous changes, in either direction, could easily be made between any pair of gears. The ratios themselves are well chosen.

Racing Ancestry

Even though it didn't have the race-derived Featherbed frame (this being reserved for the more sporting Dominator 88), the new Model 7 still received praise for its handling prowess: 'As befits a machine with a successful racing ancestry, the suspension, steering and roadholding were outstandingly good.'

The tester described the bike as 'an extremely safe machine to ride ... At all speeds within its compass, the machine could be heeled over confidently almost regardless of surface irregularities. On fast or slow bends a chosen line could be held easily, with the assurance that no drifting whatsoever would occur.' However, it was noted that: 'On slow and medium-pace bends the prop stand grounded rather easily.'

The characteristics of both front and rear springing were described as 'exemplary'. Together 'they provided not only a high degree of physical comfort for the rider, but also uncommonly good roadholding under all conditions.'

After some 1,000 miles (1,600km) of what was described as 'hard riding', the tester noted that the:

> engine, gearbox and chaincase remained reasonably oil tight ... Only the slightest discolouration of the exhaust pipes had taken place close to the ports ... An unusually wide rear mudguard and a deep-side rear chainguard played a major part in keeping the rear end of the machine reasonably clean in use.

Criticisms

Like all motorcycles of its era, the swinging-arm Model 7 was not without criticism, notably an 'oil-tank filler cap which cannot be fully opened owing to the proximity of the dual seat, and the chaincase oil level plug, which is almost impossible to remove without first detaching the left-hand exhaust system.'

Another weakness, and one which had bugged the earlier plunger-frame machine, concerned the brakes. Although the tester rather too kindly described them as 'adequate for all occasions', he went on to say: 'It was felt, however, that they were not quite up to the high standard of the rest of the machine ... A good deal of pressure on the lever was required to obtain the best results from the front brake.'

Finally, very early on in the test the riding position – and adjustment – came in for

The 1953 Model 7

Engine	Air-cooled, ohv twin with vertical cylinders, cast-iron head (alloy from 1955) and barrel, two main bearings, 360-degree, 3-piece crankshaft, split con-rods and shell big-end bearings, chain-driven magneto (rear) and dynamo (front), coil valve springs, vertically-split aluminium crankcases
Bore	66mm
Stroke	72.6mm
Displacement	497cc
Compression ratio	6.7:1 (6.8:1 from 1955)
Lubrication	Gear pump; dry sump
Ignition	Magneto, 6-volt
Carburettor	Amal 76 1in (376 Monobloc from 1955)
Primary drive	Simplex chain
Final drive	Chain
Gearbox	4-speed, positive stop, foot-change
Frame	Cradle; single front downtube
Front suspension	Oil-damped telescopics
Rear suspension	Swinging arm
Front brake	7in (8in from 1954) single-sided drum, SLS
Rear brake	7in single-sided drum, SLS
Tyres	3.25 × 19 (some early 1953 machines had 3.00 × 21) front; 3.50 × 19 rear
Wheelbase	54.5in (1,384mm)
Ground clearance	6.5in (165mm)
Seat height	30.6in (777mm)
Fuel tank capacity	3.75gal (17ltr)
Dry weight	420lb (190kg)
Maximum power	29bhp @ 6,000rpm
Top speed	90mph (144.8km/h)

A December 1953 advertisement for the 1954 Model 7. New that season was a more powerful 8in (200mm) front brake. The swinging-arm frame, new silencers and restyle had arrived a year earlier.

unfavourable comment, the tester even going as far as saying: 'The relative position of seat and footrests was rather too close, resulting in some leg cramp on long rides.' Although it was possible to lower the footrests and adjust brake and gear pedals, this resulted in the brake pedal, in operation, fouling the prop stand, whilst the gear pedal 'assumed a less effective angle.'

On the test bike, the rider gained a 'considerable, though temporary, improvement' by raising the dual seat 'an inch or so on its slotted mountings.' However, this was only temporary 'because the forward mounting would not long remain in the raised position on bumpy roads.'

Yet even with these deficiencies *The Motor Cycle* described the 1953 Model 7 as: 'A Race-bred Machine with Excellent Suspension, Hair-line Steering and Smooth Power Output.'

Improved Braking

Although now overshadowed by the new Dominator 88, the Model 7 continued to be offered for three more years, and in mid-1953, when the 1954 Norton model was announced, it received a major improvement, with the fitment of a much better front brake.

As *The Motor Cycle* (17 September 1953) reported: 'Developed originally for the Dominator twins raced at Daytona, the new standard 8in (200mm) front brake has produced a rise in braking efficiency of greater magnitude than that which it might be anticipated would result from a 1in increase in brake diameter.'

A 25 per cent addition in brake lining area had been realized, resulting, Norton claimed, 'in a considerable reduction in the average rate of wear.' However, by far the most important fact was that the new front stopper provided real braking performance. Now, it wasn't simply adequate, but powerful.

After the full cable adjustment had been taken up to compensate for wear of the linings, what *The Motor Cycle* described as 'a further measure of adjustment' could be achieved by removing the operating arm and turning it over before replacing it on the cam spindle (in other words the reverse side of the arm now being on the outside). This additional adjustment was possible owing to the fact that the axis of a rectangular slot which located the operating arm on the spindle was at an angle to the centre-line of the arm.

The brake shoe plate was a substantial die-cast alloy affair, while the hub followed conventional Norton built-up construction, with a cast-iron shell spigoted and riveted to a malleable cast-iron brake drum. This assembly was supported by a pair of ball-race bearings and a knock-out spindle.

A Tester's Opinion

The Motor Cycle was able to report that a member of its staff: 'had the opportunity to gain experience with this type of brake earlier in the year when fitted to a Dominator prepared for Daytona, and more recently as fitted to the standard Dominator twin.' Reference to 'the standard Dominator' meant in reality a Model 7, because by now Norton referred to both the 7 and the 88 as Dominators, the former being the Standard, the latter the de Luxe.

As *The Motor Cycle* went on to say:

> The result was the same in each case. As felt at the control lever, the brake was moderately light in operation. Even if the lever was squeezed hard at speeds over 80 mph [129km/h], the braking was smooth and nicely progressive; when the speed dropped below 40 mph, which the brake would ensure in a commendably short distance, a loud squeal was evoked from the front tyre, but with the adjustment correct, the wheel would not lock (surface, dry tarmacadam). As the brake possesses non-fade characteristics, it should be of particular value where a Norton machine is used in conjunction with a sidecar.

This statement was made in the light of the new brake being specified for not only the twins, but also the 490 and 596cc singles, in both ohv and side-valve guises.

It is also worth recalling that Norton had also seen fit to equip its production racing Manx models with a twin-leading shoe brake for the 1954 season. But the new 8in brake found on the roadsters was still SLS operation.

Except for the new front stopper, the Model 7 remained unchanged; but the price was now £194 basic, or, with UK purchase tax, £233 8s.

When the 1955 range was announced in mid-September 1954 the Dominator 88 had been given full-width light alloy wheel hubs, but the Model 7's front and rear brakes remained single-sided components.

Alloy Heads

The 'Standard' Dominator, however, had been updated for the new 1955 model year, most notably with the use of light alloy heads for both twins.

The design of the new heads was virtually identical to that of the outgoing cast-iron component, and the compression ratios remained unchanged. The purpose of the change was not only to reduce weight, but, as *The Motor Cycle* reported, it 'increased ability to withstand hard driving, rather than enhanced maximum performance.'

Next the Model 7 had received a new, redesigned and contoured dual seat, which was supposed to provide more comfort and to blend with the general lines of the machine.

Another change was a switch to the newly introduced Amal Monobloc carburettor (Type 376). At 1in (26mm) the size remained as before, but in the UK specification bikes, at least, the main jet size had increased from 170 to 240, although the slide cutaway remained at 3½.

Other changes were polished fork sliders, a boxed-in rear number plate, built-in horn button and modified handlebar; the latter, together with the redesigned seat, was intended to improve the riding stance. The price remained unchanged.

The Model 7 was finally axed from the range at the same time as the introduction of the larger displacement (597cc) Dominator 99 in September 1955. This in turn was to lead to what was in effect the Model 7's replacement, the Model 77. Both these models are fully covered in Chapter 6.

The era of the ever larger twin-cylinder Norton had begun.

3 Featherbed

A major factor in Norton's postwar success – and length of production life – was the legendary Featherbed frame, which made its debut on the 88 (*see* Chapter 4) and which actually owed its existence originally to the Norton Grand Prix racing effort, rather than series production roadster models.

By the end of the 1949 racing season (the first year of the FIM's World Championship series) it had become patently obvious to all concerned with Norton's quest for racing honours, from team manager Joe Craig downwards, that something drastic was needed if the Bracebridge Street factory was to stand any real chance of winning the 350 or 500cc titles the following year.

Norton works rider Geoff Duke aboard the new McCandless-framed Featherbed 500cc single on his way to victory in the Senior TT, June 1950. Duke also broke the lap record held by Harold Daniell since 1938.

At that time Norton were still relying on the ancient 'Garden Gate' plunger frame, which had first been introduced during the mid-1930s. By the standards of 1949/50 this was not only lacking in handling and ground clearance, compared to the latest swinging-arm designs, but was also far too heavy.

Strangely, the answer to the Birmingham company's prayers was destined to come not from within, but from the back streets of Belfast, across the Irish Sea.

Back in 1944, whilst the war was still raging, *Motor Cycling* carried a two-page spread detailing how a well-known twenty-nine-year-old Irish racer, Rex McCandless, had created an interesting new frame design and rear-wheel suspension system, which had been in the process of development in Ulster over the previous couple of years. In fact, as long ago as 1942 *Motor Cycling*'s Belfast correspondent, who was then serving in the Royal Air Force, had visited the magazine's London offices and talked with 'immense enthusiasm' of a new type of suspension that a couple of his fellow countrymen had been 'playing around with'. One of these was McCandless and the other Artie Bell, who in 1939 was just beginning to attract factory interest as a rider who was showing true potential; after the war, in 1947, Artie was signed up by Joe Craig for the Norton works team.

The Ideal Motorcycle

During the war years both Bell and McCandless were engaged in aircraft work at the local Short Brothers factory in Belfast. There they became engaged in a heated and lengthy debate over just what was required to constitute the ideal motorcycle. Rex McCandless was of the opinion that with ever-increasing power output from the engine it was frame design that had been lagging behind. Artie Bell had to agree, pointing out that the biggest weakness of racing bikes that existed in 1939 was that the rear of the machine was apt to attempt to take over control from the rider, or; as *Motor Cycling* put it, 'the tail was prone to wag the dog.'

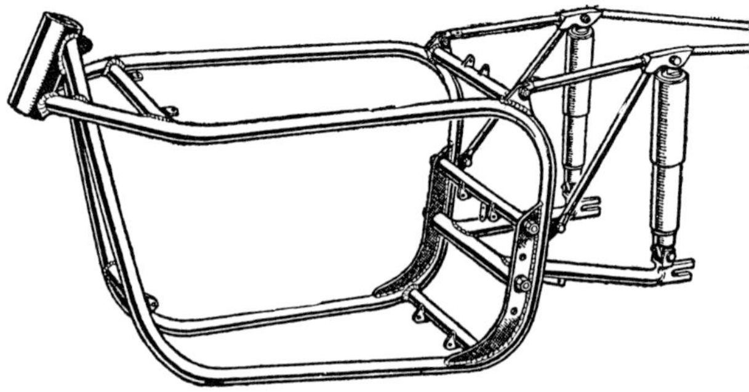

For 1951 the works Featherbed racing frame had an integral tail member, and new hydraulic rear shock absorbers.

Unlike the majority of motorcycle design engineers, Rex McCandless had a major advantage: he was also a top-class rider. When, because of the war, competition events had come to an end, he already had a lengthy list of victories and leaderboard places to his credit, both on grass and tarmac. He could lay claim to being the victor of the very last pre-war road race staged in the British Isles, the 1940 Dublin 100, and he was the leader of the 100 miles Championship of Ireland, together with the 500cc Hill Climb Championship. It was experience in events such as these that provided the germ of an idea that was to see him create his own racer, incorporating certain features that he realized were lacking in conventional motorcycle design.

One of the major problems with the average motorcycle of the immediate pre-war era was over-hard or non-existent rear suspension, which meant that the machine and rider were subjected to an appalling pounding while the road holding and handling were affected, particularly on uneven surfaces. McCandless reasoned that if he could smooth out the undulations and therefore obtain improved road holding, he would be able to make far greater use of the additional power he had managed to extract from his self-tuned Triumph Tiger 100 engine.

The Featherbed's creator, Rex McCandless, was also a rider of considerable ability. Here he is seen at the Norton West 200 meeting in May 1953 aboard a 500cc Norton; directly behind McCandless in the centre of the picture is his friend and associate, Artie Bell, whose racing career came to an end following a serious accident in the 1950 Belgian GP.

'Spring Heel'

So he set about designing what *Motor Cycling* referred to as a 'spring heel'. This proved so successful that he decided to add to it an equally special frame. Perhaps this latter component was the most vital development of all, for certainly it established the name of Rex McCandless as not only a successful rider but an influential designer.

McCandless was strongly of the opinion that frame design had not kept pace with power output. Although there had been spring frames before, to obtain the best results he believed that the main-frame and rear-wheel springing had to be designed as a whole. After much consideration he conceived an idea to achieve the correct combination. He then laid this out on paper, and for some twelve weeks the concept was 'drafted, modified, studied and amended', until finally he was satisfied that it was ready to proceed to the workshop. By 1942 McCandless had produced the first suspension units (from a Citroën car fitted with Salter springs, which at the time was the only ready source of telescopic struts), and had actually built and tried them on his Triumph twin (nicknamed 'Benniel') before the visit of the Belfast *Motor Cycling* correspondent that year. He was therefore able to demonstrate how 'the dog was showing distinct signs of exercising more control over the tail.' The Triumph engine was not only highly tuned but also inclined in the frame at an angle of 45 degrees.

During the war years there was very little in the way of technical advancement in the British motorcycle industry, apart from Rex McCandless's achievements. By the cessation of hostilities he had all but perfected his theories, and during the immediate postwar years various riders were to chalk up impressive results thanks to his pioneering work.

Bill Nicholson

One competitor who definitely benefited from McCandless's work was fellow Ulsterman Bill Nicholson (later destined to win fame as a BSA works trials and scrambles rider). *The Motor Cycle* of 4 July 1946 carried the following:

> Riding with brilliant consistency, W. Nicholson from Belfast comfortably won the 350cc and

> Unlimited events in last Saturday's open Cotswold Scramble organised by the Stroud Valley MC … In consummate style Nicholson vanquished some of the finest scramble exponents of today, and at the same time showed the advantages of rear wheel springing over rough terrain.
>
> His BSA three-fifty was equipped with McCandless rear suspension, which worked to perfection on a course distinctly tough on men and machines.

The Motor Cycle has this to say in their issue of 18 July:

> Telescopic forks have now been almost universally adopted for scramble work and many a well-known rider has been heard to say he wouldn't dream of using girder forks again, so distinct are the advantages of telescopics. Will the same situation arise over rear-wheel springing? Without disparaging in the least Nicholson's magnificent riding in the Cotswold Scramble, it is fair to say that he appeared to have a considerable advantage over other competitors – his McCandless rear suspension worked beautifully, and he obviously got better rear-wheel traction and had a less fatiguing ride than anyone else.

A little known fact is that Nicholson was at that time an employee of McCandless and Bell, who had entered into a business partnership, back home in Belfast.

Racing Resumes

A month later, on Saturday 17 August 1946, the first major postwar road-racing event was held in Ireland. The Ulster Road Race, which took the place that year instead of the Ulster Grand Prix, was staged over a course that included part of the former pre-war GP course. The 'new' circuit was some 16.5 miles (26.5km) in length, 4 miles (6.4km) shorter than the Grand Prix circuit. The entry included Artie Bell and Rex McCandless, who were by then busy supplying McCandless rear-springing conversion kits to local riders, as well as to competition riders from the mainland, for it was a feature of the suspension system that it could be incorporated in practically any make of motorcycle.

The 132-mile (212km) 500cc class of the Ulster Road Race was notable for only one thing: all but one of the entries, including Bell and McCandless, failed to reach the finishing flag! However, Bell had the satisfaction of setting the fastest lap at almost 89mph (143km/h). Artie Bell did manage to achieve some excellent results at other venues that year, so much so that 1947 saw him invited to join the Norton works racing team. This was ultimately to lead to much greater things for both himself and Rex McCandless.

Public Demonstrations

Following public demonstrations on both sides of the Irish Sea of the McCandless springing in action, many riders, both competition and touring, had noted its seemingly effortless performance and began to put aside prejudices generated by years in the saddle. During the latter part of 1946 and early 1947 enquiries by the score were forwarded to the Bell-McCandless establishment. Those satisfied with the relatively simple and inexpensive conversion generated even more customers, and of course the previously rigid-framed machines attracted attention, including that of certain 'trade' gentlemen. One of the latter was James R. Ferriday, Chairman and Managing Director of Feridax Ltd, the Birmingham wholesalers. Mr Ferriday dispatched his Ariel Square Four to Belfast and, when it returned with its new rear springing, proceeded to test it personally around England, often at high speed. Among these activities were a number of fast laps of the recently opened Oliver's Mount racing circuit, Scarborough, this time in the hands of the travelling marshal, Arnold

Moore. Moore was so impressed that he attempted to purchase the McCandless-Ariel, but James Ferriday simply laughed and said 'no'. Ferriday subsequently visited Rex McCandless in Belfast, the result being the formation of Feridax-McCandless Ltd.

The Feridax-McCandless company, which was launched in July 1947, carried out the McCandless spring-frame conversion for £25 from a small factory in Albion Street, Cheltenham. Involved in the enterprise was Fred Anning, a former West Country trials specialist. The Feridax operation was divorced from Rex McCandless himself, who had sold the manufacturing rights of the conversion to the Midland businessman.

Another Goal

Meanwhile, Rex McCandless had set himself another goal and kept it a well-guarded secret: applying his technology to the Norton racing motorcycle. But in truth, this proved neither easy nor straightforward. McCandless produced ideas aplenty, Bell tried them out and, often enough, convinced his friend that a little more work was needed.

McCandless, however, was not one to give up easily and each new experiment produced better results. But of course none of this hard work would have been of any use if the management at Norton had not taken notice. Credit must be given to Norton's Bill Mansell,

Some important Norton figures, circa *1951. Left to right: Crommie McCandless, Geoff Duke, Dickie Dale and race supremo Joe Craig.*

A January 1952 advertisement promoting 'The Unapproachable Norton Upholder of British Motor Cycle Supremacy throughout the World.' No idle boast at the time.

who invited McCandless to work 'freelance' for the Birmingham company. Mansell was not only interested in the Belfast project but also gave active assistance and support, so that McCandless was able to undertake a period of long, exhaustive tests of a suitable chassis to house the double-overhead camshaft, Norton single-cylinder racing engine.

McCandless's first job for Norton, however, was actually designing the 500T trial bike. Like all his practical work for Norton, the bike was built in Belfast. But obviously it was the racing side that most interested McCandless. It was in the latter area that Rex McCandless came into contact, and sometimes conflict, with race supremo Joe Craig. Both were Ulstermen and both were strong personalities, so perhaps this was inevitable.

Even though relations did not always run smoothly with Joe Craig, Rex McCandless was still kept on the payroll and kept up to date with the development of the latest racing engines, with their output, dimensions, weight and other relevant factors all taken into account.

A Superior Frame

Following a truly awful year of results, which had seen Norton soundly out-paced by the likes of AJS, Gilera and Velocette, Rex McCandless told Norton he could produce a much superior frame to replace the overweight, breakage-prone 'Garden Gate' plunger component that Norton had employed for many years.

After an intensive development programme, which commenced in the autumn of 1949, Bell and McCandless brought the completed prototype to Birmingham in early 1950. Under a veil of total secrecy, the new racer was subjected to another period of rigorous testing. This included being taken to the Isle of Man in January, before being thrashed round Montlhéry (just south of Paris) at high speed over some 400 miles (644km) and then at MIRA (Motor Industry Research Association), near Nuneaton, Warwickshire, and finally around the Silverstone circuit.

It has to be emphasized that Joe Craig was a hard man to win over to the new development, but even he realized just what an improvement it was. It was also at Silverstone that works rider Harold Daniell commented that he felt it was like riding a 'featherbed', and so the name stuck.

The Featherbed Works Racers

After the successful completion of the test programme, a full complement of McCandless 'Featherbed'-framed works racers was assembled by the Norton race shop during April and May 1952, but only after the frames themselves were built by Rex McCandless and his employee, Oliver Nelson. An interesting fact is that the 1950 factory race bikes used by the works team incorporated surprisingly few changes from the original prototype.

The Featherbed's baptism of fire came at Blandford Camp, at the first postwar international road race staged on the British mainland, on Saturday 29 April 1950. What a debut it proved! In front of an estimated crowd of 40,000 spectators, Geoff Duke, riding the new Featherbed-framed machine (the only one at the meeting), slaughtered the star-studded opposition, including the 1950 AJS Porcupine twin (which had won the 1949

After Geoff Duke quit Norton for Gilera in spring 1953, Ray Amm became the factory's number one rider. Ray is seen here with his wife Jill.

World Championship) in the 500cc race. (Duke was mounted on a 'Garden Gate' in the 350cc event.) The race was a thorough test for the Featherbed, since in spite of high winds Duke lapped at an average speed of 88.88mph (143km/h), which was not only easily the highest speed of the day but a record for the Dorset circuit. Geoff Duke then expressed his complete satisfaction with his new mount.

The 4 May 1950 issue of *The Motor Cycle* commented:

> At last the news has broken! For many months rumours have been circulating of an entirely new Norton frame and a modified power unit. At Blandford the cat metaphorically jumped out of the bag when Joe Craig lifted the all-enveloping cloth cover from Geoff Duke's 500cc model. There, most definitely, stood a new frame and one, moreover, devoid of lugs and equipped with swinging arm rear suspension!

Of full duplex construction, the main frame consisted of two continuous lengths of tubing. SIF-bronzed (SIF standing for Suffolk Iron Foundry) to the base of the large-diameter steering head, each curved outward and then ran horizontally to the saddle peak, dropped vertically, ran forward to form the cradle for engine and gearbox, then tapered upward, passing between the top rails to be SIF-bronzed to the top of the steering head. The frame was braced at strategic points by SIF-bronzed cross tubes, and a large gusset on each side provided support for the rear engine plates, footrests, gearchange, brake pedals (the rear brake was cable-operated) and the swinging arm. A pair of adjustable oil-damped coil spring units provided the rear suspension. These, like the vast majority of earlier McCandless rear units, were mounted vertically, not slightly angled, as on later models; the swinging arm was supported by Silentbloc bushes. Norton Roadholder forks with the upper shrouds removed completed the frame assembly and the separate clip-on handlebars were of the 'swan neck' variety. The front wheel was equipped with a 3.00 × 20 tyre, with the rear being a wider 3.25 section, but of smaller 19in diameter. Both were of Dunlop manufacture, and the tyres were soon to show up as one of the new machine's few really serious failings. Rex McCandless had been involved in a bitter struggle (with Craig) to get these smaller wheel sizes accepted, as previously Norton had employed a 21in front and 21in rear tyre, which were obviously outdated by the new frame technology.

The massive 4gal (18ltr) capacity aluminium alloy fuel tank, with its recesses for the rider's arms and knees, was held in position by a broad, longitudinal steel strap running the full length of the tank. The matching oil tank was housed neatly between the rear frame tubes, and the saddle nose was cut away to provide access to the filler cap. A small platform at the front of the tank carried a rubber mounting for the remote float chamber feeding the downdraught Amal racing carburettor.

A new-style gearbox – in essence the type that was to be used on the early Dominator twins – was attached to the engine by light-alloy plates, and the complete assembly was

From the 1951 model year Norton produced Featherbed-framed Manx 'customer' racers. Here Tony McAlpine is shown in action at the Dutch Zandvoort circuit in May 1953.

A February 1955 advertisement showing Ray Amm, the Featherbed frame and the 88 Dominator de Luxe model. There was always the suggested link of a race-bred design with Norton during the 1950s.

bolted to the frame at three points, one at the front and two at the rear.

Although still featuring four ratios, the 'new' gearbox technically was the old one tidied up. It was to be referred to in future as the 'laid-down' type. A major difference between the two was that the original version had the selection mechanism in a separate chamber above that housing the gears and shafts, whereas in the new one all components were housed in an elongated body.

Frame Construction

Not only had McCandless used SIF-bronzed welding, which made it possible to join tubes together without lugs, but the Featherbed frame was much easier to manufacture than the plunger type.

The older design needed ninety-six separate machining operations per frame. SIF-bronze welding had been developed during the war

Besides the Dominator 88, Norton also fitted their overhead cam International singles (in both 350 and 500cc guises) with the Featherbed frame from the 1953 model year.

years, using an alloy that melted at a lower temperature than steel. Unlike brass, which was previously used on motorcycle frames, SIF-bronze could be built up into fillets.

Rex McCandless had constructed the original prototype frame assisted by his right-hand man and chief welder, Oliver Nelson; but it was not just the bare frame, as was often believed, but a complete machine that was delivered to the Norton factory in early 1950. The basic layout was to remain virtually unchanged throughout the life of the Featherbed, at least in the race bike.

On the series production roadsters, however, there were two distinct types of Featherbed frame, the original 'Wideline' and, from the 1960 model year, the 'Slimline'. The purpose of the latter was to decrease the width between the rider's legs and thus provide a more comfortable riding stance.

Although tyre troubles limited Norton's success in the 1950 World Championship series, in 1951 Geoff Duke scored a famous double, taking both the 350 and 500cc titles. He also retained the 350cc crown in 1952. Subsequently Duke left to join the Italian Gilera marque.

The First Production Featherbeds

The first production Featherbed frames arrived on the over-the-counter Manx dohc single cylinder racers for the 1951 season. Its SIF-bronze frame was almost, but not quite, a replica of the 1950 works Featherbed design, slight changes being needed to make it suitable for series production, rather than a no-expense-spared one-off.

The swinging arm was controlled by a pair of spring-loaded hydraulic shock absorbers. Although based on the type used on the 1950 works machine, these were cleaner externally since the damping oil was now contained within the spring boxes. Another change was that the streamlined tail section, as employed on the original works Featherbed, had been deleted.

Following these successes, it was hardly surprising that the public was soon clamouring for the new frame to be fitted to at least some of the touring models – with the twin being seen as a prime candidate. As the following chapter reveals, this is exactly what transpired, with Norton's production roadsters about to enter a new era.

Finally, from the 1959 model year the ohv singles in 350 (Model 50) and 500cc (ES2) gained the Featherbed frame; a Model 50 is shown here from that year. A year later the new 'Slimline' Featherbed frame was introduced on the roadster range of heavyweight twins and singles.

4 88

As revealed in the previous chapter, the famous 'Featherbed' duplex cradle frame was not actually a Norton creation at all: instead this significant design was the work of Rex McCandless. It was also initially developed for racing, making its debut in the hands of Geoff Duke at Blandford in April 1950.

Soon the question on many enthusiasts' lips was 'What about a road-going version?' Norton did put the Featherbed-framed Manx production racer on sale for the 1951 season, but it was obvious that a roadster, at least with the Manx engine, was not practical. Even the long-running overhead cam International was only ever seen as a limited production model that with its high costs and exposed valve gear was never really going to be a serious mass-production option.

This made the new twin-cylinder engine, which had debuted on the Model 7 in late 1948 (*see* Chapter 2), seem the obvious answer.

The original McCandless Featherbed Dominator 88 prototype, built in late 1950 using a combination of double cradle (front) and stressed skin (rear) construction. It was deemed too radical by the Norton management.

Rex McCandless's own idea of how the Featherbed Norton twin should be is now displayed in the Sammy Miller Museum, New Milton, Hampshire. Completed during the second half of 1950, this was a pretty radical approach, with a standard twin-tube front section of the frame, but using a faired-in rear section of stressed steel construction. This original prototype was, like the other pre-production examples, constructed by Rex McCandless and his welding wizard, Oliver Nelson. But the Norton board did not like so radical an approach, and so the roadster twin employed a frame similar to the racers.

As Derek McGrath says in his *Norton – The Complete Story* (Crowood, 1991): 'When Norton wanted the frame produced in large numbers they approached Reynolds who were leaders in welded assemblies and tube technology. At the time all-welded frames were an advanced idea, one which even twenty years later had not been adopted by all manufacturers.' Actually, at this time all this was secret, the general public thinking that Norton made the frames themselves!

One of the pre-production prototypes of the Dominator 88 de Luxe (not to be confused with the later faired-in 1960 model) was seen in the paddock at the Dutch TT and French GP, a photograph appearing in the 19 July 1951 issue of *The Motor Cycle*. It is worth noting that this prototype employed a genuine racing frame, made of Reynold 531 aircraft-quality tubing, whereas the actual production 88 models that were to follow were built from mild-steel tubing.

The Dominator 88 Makes its Official Entry

A few months later, at the beginning of November 1951, *The Motor Cycle* reported 'Featherbed Dominator Makes Its Bow', and continued 'Norton Eve-of-Show Surprise: The Dominator 497cc Parallel-twin Engine in the "Featherbed" Racing Frame.' One journalist described the newcomer as possessing 'a "greyhound straining at the leash" appearance – in keeping with its illustrious ancestry.'

According to *The Motor Cycle*'s show report:

> For more reasons than one is the Norton Stand an immediate Mecca for many Show visitors. There is so much of interest to see that enthusiasts cannot seem to pause for long at any one exhibit. They dash from one model to the next – talking excitedly – unable in the excitement to spend much time on any one feature. Pride of place is shared by the new Dominator de Luxe (designated Model 88), the 500cc World's Champion (Geoff Duke's machine) and a magnificent array of silverware representing Norton successes in trials and racing throughout the year …
>
> The term race-breeding as it applies to standard machines has never been more truly exemplified than it is by the similarity between the Model 88 and the pure racing machines. Frames and forks in each case are identical to the nth degree, and indeed, according to the willing Norton staffman on the Stand, it was an actual racing frame which was used throughout the new model's testing period (as covered earlier) …
>
> In its polychromatic grey finish and with their sleek lines, the new Dominators may be said to be stealing the Show so far as the motor cycle exhibits are concerned.

Another feature in *The Motor Cycle*'s 1951 Show Issue was a feature by 'Ixion' entitled 'Round the Show'. Contained within this was the following:

> Ten minutes after the Show opened, I spotted two distinct surging crowds. That on the AJS stand was partly inspired by a desire to inspect a naked Porcupine at short range, and partly the passion for Doran's autograph [Bill Doran being a senior member of the AJS works Grand Prix team]. That on the Norton Stand was due to the debut of the standard Featherbed Dominator. I honestly suspect this very modern specification desires to rank as the best motorcycle in the world. It certainly turned all the other Norton models pea green with envy, and no wonder.

The following week's 'Blue 'Un' had an article 'Random Thoughts on a Random Tour – Earls Court Reflection', in which Dennis May and Gordon Horner considered which were the most important models. Horner concluded that: 'I finally settled on the lean-flanked Dominator with Featherbed bridgework.'

In his book *Norton* (Osprey, 1992), Mick Woollett comments: 'The snag was that it was for export only … this was a tragedy, for at last Nortons had a roadster that was in advance of anything the opposition could offer, yet the British enthusiast had to make do with the existing range.'

Inspecting the 88 in Detail

So what of the new 88 itself? As we already know, the basis of the new mount was the race-bred Featherbed frame, together with the Norton ohv twin-cylinder engine and the gearbox already used in the Model 7, plus a host of novel features.

As for production, this was 'due to start soon', but for 'export only'. *The Motor Cycle* reported that 'eventually the model will be available in quantity for the home market.'

In the most basic terms the Featherbed frame consisted of a pair of tubes bent roughly to rectangular shape and braced by cross-members. For the roadster production Featherbed frames, Dominator and soon the International, these

1952 model year Dominator 88, with bolted-up sub-frame, deeply valanced front mudguard and pear-shaped silencers.

used B (14-gauge) and A-class (16-gauge) mild steel respectively. For the Dominator 88 production frames 14-gauge tubing was specified, this being of the cold-drawn, weldless steel type.

This is how *The Motor Cycle* described the frame in its 1 November 1951 issue:

> From the rear of the bottom of the steering-head the twin tubes mentioned earlier run rearward and outward, sweeping downward at a point just to the rear of the tank, forward again just behind the gearbox, and then they return to the top of the steering head. Forming the steering head is a short length of heavy-gauge plain tube. Heavy gauge is employed so that recesses can be turned in each end to accommodate the head bearings. These are robust, angular-contact ball-journal bearings – which are capable of taking both axial and radial thrust – instead of the more usual loose ball races. Dimensions of the bearings are 25mm bore, 52mm outside diameter and 15mm deep …
>
> Arc welding is used throughout in construction of the frame since it is a better production proposition than SIF-bronze welding. Extending from roughly halfway down the vertical rear-frame members to beyond the bottom bend are two stout, mild-steel gusset plates, forming locations for a cross-tube, which carries the top-rear engine bolts, and for the pivot rod of the rear fork.

The Swinging Arm

The swinging arm (rear fork) was manufactured from parallel $1\frac{1}{4}$in × 10-gauge tube, and was bridged at its forward end by way of a $1\frac{1}{16}$in × 10-gauge cross-tube, which housed Silentbloc bushes. Each of these was 3in (84mm) in length and fitted into the pivot tube from each end, these being separated by a short length of plain tube.

Although not quite as efficient as 'solid' phosphor-bronze bushes, the advantage of the Silentbloc type (built from rubber and steel) was that no lubrication or any other form of maintenance was required. However, in service it was found that the Silentbloc bushes could be pulled sideways, so they were often swapped in favour of the Manx-type phosphor-bronze components, particularly by hard riders.

Controlling the swinging arm was a pair of near vertical shock absorbers, which provided a total of some 3in (76mm) of movement. Norton, which had applied for a provisional patent specification, claimed at the time that these units 'are the best shock absorber units that have ever appeared on a production machine.'

According to *The Motor Cycle*'s description:

> Each assembly is as follows: at the bottom there is a malleable iron end-cap incorporating the Clayflex-bushed eye for fitting to the fork-end. Copper brazed to the cap is a steel tube which forms the outer oil cylinder of the unit. Clamped to the 'floor' of the unit – in the centre of the base of the outer cylinder – there is a spring-loaded flap valve, and fitting over a spigot on the valve is another vertical tube which acts as a cylinder, or inner oil chamber.
>
> Inserted into the top of this cylinder, and attached to the lower end of a $\frac{3}{8}$in [9mm] diameter steel rod is a piston incorporating a second spring-loaded flap valve. At its top end the piston rod is anchored to the top cap of the leg which, of course, also incorporates an eye, is also fitted with a Clayflex bearing, and anchors to the sub-frame of the machine.

There was a series of valves and seals, together with bushes, and of course the main cylinder plus the two-rate springs themselves. The suspension unit also featured cylindrical covers, both top and bottom.

The oil employed was listed as Castrol Shockol, 70cc of which was inserted into the inner cylinder of each leg.

However, even though these units received considerable acclaim at the time of their launch, in service they did not perform too well, and were soon replaced by bought-in Girling assemblies.

The Front Fork

Like the frame, the front fork fitted to the new Dominator 88 de Luxe was based on, but not identical to, the racing type. Known as the Roadholder, it also differed considerably from the type fitted to the Norton ohv and side-valve singles and the Model 7 twin. At the time the press claimed it was identical to that employed on the racing models. And it is true that the 88's fork did feature positive, hydraulic control throughout the entire fork movement (unlike the other roadsters at the time). In the 'standard' fork that these latter bikes used, there was simply a solid damper peg at the lower end of the fork slider. This provided progressive downward damping by passing oil through a gradually decreasing orifice between the main stanchion and the taper damper peg.

In the racing fork and the road version fitted to the 88, a proper damper cylinder was provided instead of the basic damper peg. Working in conjunction with the cylinder was a piston-controlled valve fitted to the lower end of a piston rod passing from the top plug down the middle of the stanchion. Comprising the valve was a steel bucket-type device that was free to move slightly in a vertical direction on the rod. Its upward movement was controlled by a small cross-pin in the rod; below this was a steel star-shaped washer.

In the static position, the fork oil (Norton recommended Castrolite at the time) was contained within the fork slider. On impact, the slider member telescoped into the fixed one, generating negative pressure on the upper side of the inverted piston-valve. Oil flowed from the main chamber into an area formed between the rod and damper cylinder above the piston.

The actual damping on impact was quite small, since the restriction caused as oil flowed through the piston was equally small. On rebound, the oil trapped above the piston was forced back via the controlled clearance between the walls of the cylinder and piston, because of the pressure above the piston and the star washer.

Each fork slider was a light-alloy forging, with the top bush that it carried being of sintered-bronze and equipped with a gartered synthetic rubber oil seal (one per leg). The lower bush was manufactured from steel.

Another difference between the 88's fork and the rest of the roadster range was that, whereas the fork of the latter was fitted outside the stanchion, in the 88 the spring was fitted between the top of the damper cylinder and the top plug. Total movement was given by Norton sources as approximately 4.5–3in (115–77mm) on impact and 1.5in (38mm) on rebound.

No steering damper was fitted and indeed was not really needed, considering the excellence of the frame and suspension – and the relative lack of power (the original 88 de Luxe being quoted as 29.5bhp at 7,000rpm).

More Racing Practice

As on the pukka racing models, a strap was employed for fixing the fuel tank on the 88. The 3.5gal (17ltr) tank, which was described as 'a sleek, steel design', sat on rubber pads on the top frame rails. It was equipped with a single tap incorporating a reserve facility.

A feature of the first production 88 de Luxe models was the front mudguard design. Both it and the rear were deeply valanced, but the front was attached to the sprung section of the fork, reducing unsprung weight. On the tip of the mudguard there was a reverse lip, and there were channels on the edges, by which Norton claimed 'the water is led back to the bottom of the blade'. Again, as with the shock absorbers, Norton had a provisional patent on this design, which it should be noted was actually conceived by Rex McCandless.

As explained above, the new 88 de Luxe made use of not just the Model 7's engine, but also its transmission, including the 4-speed foot-change 'laid-down' gearbox. However, the actual ratios were changed, these now being higher: 4.64, 5.61, 8.2 and 13.8:1.

Other features of the newcomer included the use of 19in tyres (Avon being specified) at front and rear (this being something of a pioneering move at the time, copying the latest

A December 1952 advertisement showing the 1953 model year Dominator de Luxe model, now with conventional front mudguard.

racing models), a dual seat, 7in (180mm) Lucas headlamp with underslung pilot light, a console at the top of the front fork (containing the speedometer, light switch and ammeter) plus two stands (centre and side). Dry weight was given as 380lb (172kg), thus making it some 33lb (15kg) lighter than its older Model 7 brother.

Road Experience

The newcomer may have been officially 'export only', but this didn't stop Arthur Bourne being loaned one of the very first 88 de Luxe models, for what was to prove an extended period covering many months.

Prior to this, as reported in the 1 November 1951 issue of *The Motor Cycle*:

> A member of the staff ... who has had road experience with the prototype Dominator de Luxe, covered, on one occasion, 69 miles [111km] in one hour and five minutes, without having the impression that he was hurrying unduly. This exceptionally high average was achieved because of a combination of five factors: impeccable steering and roadholding – which is the equal (except for the increased top hamper) of that possessed by the works' racing machines, excellent all-round engine performance, a first class gear change, above average braking power and a riding position that was not only very comfortable, but which also furnished perfect control. Mudguarding is good enough to allow speeds of 30mph [48km/h] on wet roads without the rider's legs becoming damp from spray off the wheels of the machine.

On Top of the World

It is also worth mentioning that, in the very same issue of *The Motor Cycle*, Norton had a full-page advertisement showing a globe of the world with a Union Jack flag hoisted above the North Pole, the flag displaying Eric Oliver's World Championship winning sidecar outfit in action. The message was reinforced with the slogans 'World Champions' and 'The Unapproachable Norton – Upholder of British Motor Cycle Supremacy throughout the World'.

When one considers that the company won no fewer than three of the possible five world racing titles in 1951, this proud proclamation was no idle boast. But unfortunately this was to prove the high point of Norton postwar racing successes. Soon the glory days on the track were to be extinguished by foreign competition and financial constraints.

For this brief period, however, the Norton name basked in a blaze of acclaim from press and public acclaim alike, not just in Great Britain, but all around the world. In an article headed 'Good Looks', which appeared in the 15 November 1951 issue of *The Motor Cycle*, for example, 'Ixion' became really enthusiastic about the new Featherbed-framed Norton twin:

> I implore you to consider the photograph on the lower half of page 438 in our November 1 issue, or the broadside view on page 525 of this issue. Is the machine not easily the best looker you have seen for a long time? Now beauty, whether in girls or horses or motors, is a very composite whole. But it can never completely satisfy if it betrays a single blot ... Can you detect within ten seconds study which common flaw has been eliminated from the new 'Featherbed' Dominator? Here is my suggestion. Note the very narrow gap between the curve of the front mudguard and the front down tubes of the frame. Most rival makes, which have the mudguard moving with the wheel, have to allow a far wider clearance at this point. This prevents the fore assembly from looking like part of a balanced whole, or even suggests that the frame is cracking just aft of the steering head. Few machines look really attractive with an empty saddle, but the Dominator de Luxe scores a top in my view.

Certainly, in the author's opinion, no other series production road bike in 1951 could beat the new Norton. The only problems were that it was only available on the export market and it was around 20 per cent more expensive than a comparable BSA or Triumph: the BSA A7 Star twin cost £222 6s 8d and the Triumph Tiger 100 £223 12s 3d, but the new Norton came in at £260 13s 4d (all these figures include British purchase tax).

Willoughby's View

During September 1952 the late Vic Willoughby, a respected and able racer/journalist, was able to try the 'export only' Dominator 88 de Luxe on the evening after the conclusion of the Senior Manx Grand Prix in the Isle of Man. Actually, Norton had provided some of these bikes for travelling marshal duties during the races. Writing in the 9 October 1952 issue of *The Motor Cycle*, Vic said:

> Seldom have I been more quickly and completely enamoured of a machine's steering, road-holding and general handling qualities. In these respects the Dominator de Luxe sets a standard which will be hard to match, much less beat. I first sampled and was impressed by featherbed Norton characteristics in June, when my good friend B W T Rood [Benny Rood, later to become a founder member of Cosworth Engineering] lent me his Manx racer for the Senior TT [in which Vic had finished an impressive eleventh]. The export version Dominator seems to afford even better steering. No steering damper is fitted or remotely desired. The suspension absorbs bumps most effectively, yet without a trace of pitching. Finally, the model can literally be steered to an inch over good or bad road surfaces. Gear change and clutch operation, I felt, were also up to racing standards.

And remember that Vic Willoughby was not simply any old editorial hack, but an international class racer in his own right.

The 1953 Model Year

In announcing the 1953 Norton model range in October 1952, great emphasis was placed

The 1953 88

Engine	Air-cooled, ohv twin with vertical cylinders, cast-iron head and barrel, two main bearings, 360-degree, 3-piece crankshaft, split con-rods and shell big-end bearings, chain-driven magneto (rear) and dynamo (front), coil valve springs, vertically-split aluminium crankcases
Bore	66mm
Stroke	72.6mm
Displacement	497cc
Compression ratio	6.7:1
Lubrication	Gear pump, dry sump
Ignition	Magneto, 6-volt
Carburettor	Amal 76 1in
Primary drive	Simplex chain
Final drive	Chain
Gearbox	4-speed, positive stop, foot-change
Frame	Norton Wideline Featherbed, full cradle, twin front downtubes, bolted-up sub-frame
Front suspension	Norton Roadholders, oil-damped, telescopic
Rear suspension	Swinging arm with oil-damped twin shock absorbers
Front brake	7in single-sided drum, SLS
Rear brake	7in single-sided drum, SLS
Tyres	3.25 × 19 front (some early bikes had 3.00 section front tyres); 3.50 × 19 rear
Wheelbase	55.5in (1,410mm)
Ground clearance	6.75in (171mm)
Seat height	30in (762mm)
Fuel tank capacity	3.75gal (17ltr)
Dry weight	380lb (172kg)
Maximum power	29.5bhp @ 7,000rpm
Top speed	92mph (148km/h)

upon the Norton pedigree. According to *The Motor Cycle*:

> Race breeding is no idle term as applied to Nortons. For a quarter of a century the marque has held a leading position in road racing throughout the world, and the vast experience gained in this most searching of all fields of test has borne fruit in the production models – not only the over-the-counter Manx racers but also the normal road machines ... In the 1953 Nortons, this reputation is upheld and enhanced.

Several modifications and changes were introduced on the Dominator 88 de Luxe at this time. Some, like the modified lubrication and pear-shaped silencers, were shared with the Model 7, while others were exclusive to the Featherbed-framed model.

On both twin-cylinder machines the rocker-box lubrication had been improved. A spring-loaded ball valve had been arranged in the oil return line to ensure an adequate supply of lubricant to the rocker gear. As for the silencers, these were very similar in appearance to those fitted to the original 88 de Luxe, but the baffle design had been altered.

The front-end appearance of the de Luxe had been considerably altered by the fitment of a conventional type of front mudguard to the unsprung portion of the fork legs: the guard now moved up and down with the wheel, and the gap between tyre and guard had been eliminated.

Following service experience with the 88 de Luxe, the Norton factory also found it desirable to revert to the standard (thus Model 7) Dominator gear ratios (5, 6.05, 8.85 and 14.88:1), in order, Norton sources said, 'to provide optimum performance'.

Other changes to the de Luxe model were a rubber-mounted handlebar and the addition of thin (rubber) kneegrips to the fuel tank. One thing had not changed, though, the Dominator de Luxe was still for export only.

Improved Braking

All Nortons, including the Featherbed-framed Dominator de Luxe, benefited during the 1954 season from the introduction into production of a larger 8in (200mm) front brake. Still of single-sided layout, this had originally been developed for the Dominator twins that were raced at Daytona in early 1953. As already explained in Chapter 2 covering the Model 7, this new brake produced a far greater rise in braking efficiency than could have been expected simply by increasing the diameter by 1in (26mm). In fact a 25 per cent addition to brake lining area had been achieved: this not only greatly improved braking performance, but also reduced wear considerably.

The 1954 Dominator de Luxe, still with cast-iron head and barrel. Other features include chrome-finished tank, 'laid-down' gearbox, forward-mounted dynamo/rear-mounted magneto and thin rubber knee-grips.

A die-cast light alloy brake shoe plate was employed. The hub itself followed the traditional built-up Norton construction, comprising a cast-iron shell spigoted and riveted to a malleable cast-iron brake drum. The assembly was carried on two ball-race bearings and featured a knock-out spindle.

The basic export price of the 88 de Luxe on 17 September 1953 was £216. For those fortunate few who somehow managed to get an example on the British home market, the figure including UK purchase tax was £259 4s.

Welded-Up Sub-Frame

When the 1955 model was announced in September 1954 it was evident that the Dominator 88 had not only lost its 'de Luxe' tag, it was also undoubtedly the most altered of those models already in the range.

Advertisement of November 1954 showing the 1955 model year 88 de Luxe. Features new for that season included light-alloy cylinder head, Amal Monobloc carb, welded-up sub-frame and light alloy full-width hubs.

For starters, the frame had been further strengthened by a welded, rather than bolted-up sub-frame. This structure, which supported the dual seat, rear mudguard and the upper ends of the rear shocks, had previously been bolted to the main frame at four points. To increase the stiffness of the assembly, the sub-frame tubes were now not only welded direct to the main frame, but also of larger diameter.

Norton also claimed that weather protection had been improved by fitting a rear mudguard of the type found on the cradle frame (Model 7 and ES2) roadsters. This was wider and featured a longer tail extension with deeper side valances than the type employed previously.

But undoubtedly the most noticeable (and notable) change was to the brakes, which were now of the full-width type with aluminium hubs. Integral spokes, flanges and cooling ribs were a feature of both front and rear hubs. On the offside (right) of the rear assembly were a trio of circular access holes, which were normally filled by rubber plugs. Front and rear brake diameters remained at 8in and 7in, respectively.

Another addition, common to all Norton 1955-model pushrod engines, was the new Amal Monobloc carburettor. On the 88 this was a type 376 1in instrument with (in the UK) a 240 size main jet and 3½ slide cutaway. Also on the 88 only, there was an air cleaner of the circular pancake variety, mounted directly on the carburettor intake.

A number of smaller changes had also been introduced:

- Lower ends of the aluminium fork sliders were polished instead of enamelled.
- A new plastic tank badge, circular in shape. The motif, in the traditional Norton colours of black, red and silver, bore the name 'Norton' superimposed on a large letter 'N'.

1955 was the final year for the large pressed-steel instrument/switch console as shown. Not only did it house the speedo, ammeter and light switch, but also the clutch and front brake cable passed through the assembly.

- New boxed-in, rubber-sealed rear number plate/light holder. Mounted below the number plate was a circular red reflector, which became obligatory in the UK from 1 October 1954.

The price remained as before: £216 basic, £259 4s with UK purchase tax.

Technically, Norton's twin-cylinder engine, fitted in both the 88 and Model 7, gained light-alloy cylinder heads, as did the ES2 and Model 19 ohv singles. The actual design was almost identical to the cast-iron heads used previously. The same applied to the respective compression ratios. The main reason Norton gave for this quite major change was not about increasing performance, but further improving cooling abilities – and weight reduction.

But one has to ask, why wasn't this done from the start? The answer was twofold: cost and the original low compression ratio/fuel quality.

Early 1956 Dominator 88, still with 'laid-down' gearbox, but now without separate instrument console. This machine, owned by Geoff Scales, is pictured here at the Coupes Moto Légende, Dijon, held over the weekend of 22–23 May 2004.

The 1956 Model Year

When the 1956 Norton range was launched in mid-September 1955, it was seen that the 88 five-hundred had been joined by a new bigger brother, the 597cc 99 (*see* Chapter 6), while the 88's older brother, the Model 7, had been discontinued. It would be correct to describe the 99 as a larger-engined 88.

The several changes made in the specification of the 1956 model year 88 constituted features that it shared with the new 99, including a restyled oil tank and a matching box (on the nearside) to house the battery, both being cradled by the frame tubes. There was also a pressed-steel plate that ran transversely across the forward ends of these units. Provision had also been incorporated for a flexible rubber hose from the single Amal Monobloc carburettor air intake to pass through this steel pressing to a concealed air filter; this was now available as an optional extra. The tool kit and voltage control box were accommodated beneath the dual seat, as they had been previously.

The oil tank, with a capacity of 4½ pints (2.5ltr), employed rubber push-on connections for both the delivery and return pipes. There was also a flexible breather pipe that led from the top of the oil tank to the rear chainguard, from where it passed through a rubber grommet to supply lubricant to the chain.

To provide a slightly less stiff action for the Roadholder forks, the two-rate coil springs had been lightened to provide a softer initial movement around the static-load position.

Another change was to the headlamp, which now incorporated a 'built-in' speedometer in a close-fitting panel attached to the shell, together with lighting switch and ammeter. Previously the instruments had been carried in an entirely separate panel (console) mounted on the top of the forks. The 7in (180mm) diameter Lucas pre-focus light unit used an offset dipped beam and a pilot bulb located in the reflector, whereas previously it had been underslung, outside the lamp.

Higher Compression Ratio

With the advance and availability of premium grade fuels, the Norton engineering team had seen fit to increase the compression ratio of the 88 engine quite considerably – from 6.8 to 7.8:1. In addition, the sweep of the exhaust

From May 1956 Norton started fitting the new AMC-made gearbox as illustrated here on a Dominator 88 from later that year. Also note the last year of footrest design with elongated rubber. This machine has the sheet-steel plate to close the gap between frame and rear of gearbox (introduced for 1957 and thus retro fitted).

1956 88 engine with alloy head, single Amal Monobloc carburettor, separate dynamo and magneto; note the non-standard chrome-plated primary chain cover and aftermarket horn.

1956 full-width 8in front hub.

header pipes had been altered, a modification that the factory claimed was mainly to improve appearance. With the same objective in mind, the cover plate on the aluminium full-width brake hubs was now polished, to match the brake plate.

At the London Earls Court Show in November 1955, *The Motor Cycle* pointed out:

> If it were not for the name plates and distinguishing markings on some of the Norton exhibits, the display would provide excellent practice for amateur sleuths. Their task would be to differentiate between the reintroduced 348cc Model 50 and the 490cc ES2, and between the new 597cc vertical twin Model 99 and its forerunner, the 497cc Model 88. Both pairs of models bear a very close resemblance but are distinguishable by a slight difference in engine height … The twins in particular have a magnetic attraction for fast tourists. This can hardly be wondered at since they incorporate the twin-loop frame and springing systems which have proved so successful in road racing for many years. Appearance is enhanced by full-width composite hubs and by matching and blending of the oil tank and battery box. Another contribution to the sleek looks is made by the elongated headlamp shell in which are housed the speedometer, lighting switch and ammeter.

Hinged rear mudguard.

The 1956 88

Engine	Air-cooled, ohv twin with vertical cylinders, alloy head and cast-iron barrel, two main bearings, 360-degree, 3-piece crankshaft, split con-rods and shell big-end bearings, chain-driven magneto (rear) and dynamo (front), coil valve springs, vertically-split aluminium crankcases
Bore	66mm
Stroke	72.6mm
Displacement	497cc
Compression ratio	7.8:1
Lubrication	Gear pump; dry sump
Ignition	Magneto, 6-volt
Carburettor	Amal 376 Monobloc 1in
Primary drive	Simplex chain
Final drive	Chain
Gearbox	4-speed, positive stop, foot-change (bikes from spring 1956 were fitted with AMC gearbox)
Frame	Norton Wideline Featherbed, full cradle, twin front downtubes, welded-up sub-frame
Front suspension	Norton Roadholders, oil-damped, telescopic
Rear suspension	Swinging arm with oil-damped twin shock absorbers
Front brake	8in full-width drum, SLS
Rear brake	7in full-width drum, SLS
Tyres	3.00 × 19 front; 3.50 × 19 rear
Wheelbase	55.5in (1,410mm)
Ground clearance	5.5in (140mm)
Seat height	31in (787mm)
Fuel tank capacity	3.5gal (15.9ltr)
Dry weight	390lb (177kg)
Maximum power	30bhp @ 7,000rpm
Top speed	92mph (148km/h)

In spring 1956 the 88 (and 99) Dominator twins made the switch to a new AMC-made gearbox (*see* Chapter 6).

Original 1956 petrol filler cap: a nice detail feature.

The 1957 Range

When the 1957 Norton range was announced in September 1956, the 88 and 99 were joined by the Model 77, which was essentially a replacement for the old Model 7 but with a 597cc engine (*see* Chapter 6 for full details).

All Norton models, except the new Model 77, featured a redesigned, cast-aluminium, full-width front hub and a restyled brake shoe plate. The twins, including the 88, also now had modified cylinder head finning, although the alteration was best described as minimal.

Much more noticeable were the new 'cylindrical' silencers, which featured a single pipe passing at an angle through the expansion chamber. The pipe was blanked midway along its length, with louvres in the front section to allow exhaust gases to escape into the expansion chamber, while round holes in the rear section of the pipe re-admitted the gases. No tail section was used.

As on all other models in the 1957 range, a minor but nonetheless important departure from previous Norton practice concerned the footrests, which were now forged hangers carrying conventional, round-section rubbers; these replaced the previous, built-up assemblies comprising side plates, nuts and bolts as well as an elongated rubber foot section.

As for the revised front brake, this saw the replacement of the previous composite front

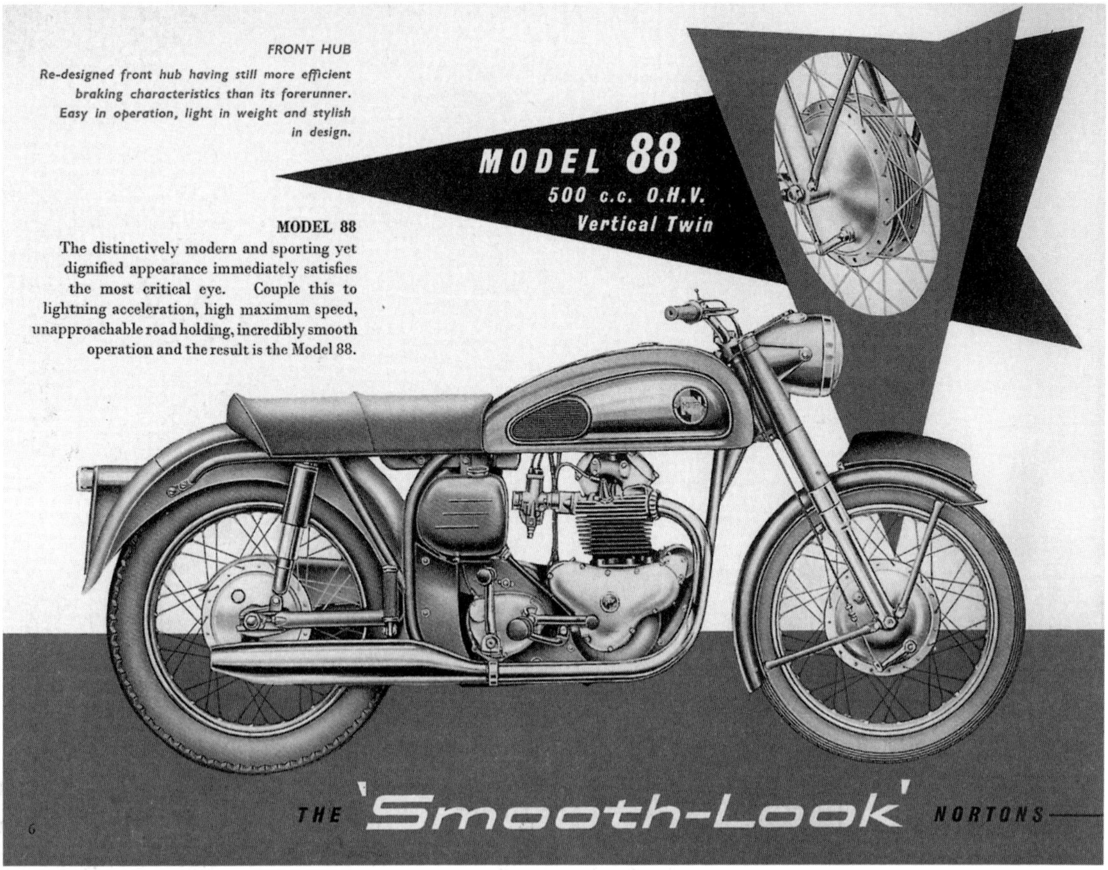

For the 1957 season Norton introduced its 'Smooth-look'. New features included cigar-shape silencers and a redesigned front hub.

hub by a new, ribbed aluminium casting that featured a cast-in iron brake liner. Though the brake shoe assembly remained unchanged, the shoe plate, as mentioned earlier, had been restyled and now fitted inside the open end of the hub. Norton claimed an appreciable saving in weight.

The layout of the rear brake control and stop-light switch had been tidied up. The outer face of the pedal pivot boss was now flush with the end of the spindle. Lateral location of the pedal was achieved by a pin that engaged with an annular groove in the spindle; this pin also served as a grease nipple. An inward extension of the pivot boss enshrouded the pedal return spring. Taking the form of a tab washer, the adjustable pedal stop was clamped between a shoulder on the spindle and the frame lug into which it was screwed.

Spring-loaded internally, the plunger of the stop-light switch protruded forward and came up against a small plate brazed on the yoke at the front end of the brake rod. Operation of the rear pedal thus permitted the plunger to move forward under spring tension and operate the switch.

Rear brake torque had previously been transferred to the pivoted fork by a bolted-on torque stay. This was now axed in favour of a brake-plate pin that engaged with a slot in the fork end. The resulting change further cleaned up the appearance, an aim helped by a more comprehensive rear chainguard.

On the offside (right) of the frame a sheet-steel fairing was bolted to the gusset plate to close the gap at the rear of the gearbox. The front edges of the fuel tank were extended further forward to conceal the frame tubes where

Another change for 1957 was that the instruments were now mounted directly in the headlamp shell.

they joined the steering head. In addition, the dual seat was blended more closely with the rear of the tank, which Norton claimed improved the riding position. Other minor 'tidying up' details concerned the Lucas dynamo, which now had a more shapely end cover, and the headlamp, in which the speedometer, ammeter and lighting switch were now mounted directly in the shell rather than, as before, in the close-fitting separate panel attached to the shell.

There were also now separate detachable chromium-plated fuel tank panels, attached by the knee-grip and motif screws, and framed in a plastic beading.

The Norton advertising department went into something approaching overdrive with the launch of the 1957 model-year machines, proclaiming 'The "Smooth Look" Nortons – Built in the light of Experience.' Rhapsodizing over the latest Model 88, they said: 'The distinct modern and sporting yet dignified appearance immediately satisfies the most critical eye. Couple this to lightning acceleration, high maximum speed, unapproachable roadholding, incredibly smooth operation and the result is the Model 88.'

Testing the 88

Because it could sell every Dominator 88 it could build, very few road tests, if any, were carried out on the model during its early life. This theme was touched on in a test that appeared in the 28 February 1957 issue of *The Motor Cycle*:

> So successful was the Norton duplex-loop frame on the factory racing machines in 1950 and subsequently, that a roadster combining a similar frame with the 497cc Dominator parallel twin engine was an obvious development … Because of its indirect racing associations, the Model 88 has always been surrounded by an aura of speed, and there was for some time a widespread misconception that the model was of the super-sports type. In point of fact it was, until late 1955, essentially a touring mount with an unpretentious camshaft and a modest compression ratio (6.8:1). From that time onward, however, pistons giving a compression ratio of 7.8 to 1 have been standardized, as has the Daytona camshaft evolved in connection with the famous American races. As a result of these modifications the Model 88 now has a speed and acceleration potential which place

> it in the super-sports bracket, while the use of a light-alloy cylinder head (introduced in 1955) makes it possible for the engine to sustain its high power output without tiring.

Although the tester appreciated 'the stylish way in which the model could be heeled through bends and corners, especially at high speeds', he considered that:

> [on] ultra low-speed corners slightly lighter steering would have been appreciated and a more generous steering lock would be an advantage when manoeuvring the model in confined spaces ... Contributing partially towards the absence of pitching was the relatively short and firm action of the front and rear springing. Roadholding at high speeds is unimpeachable although at slight expense in comfort – insulation of the rider from road shocks could be better, especially when the model is ridden without a pillion passenger.

The test also showed up a problem with the Wideline Featherbed Dominator frame of which the author is all too aware: 'Minimum width of the seat at the front (12in) is dictated by the spacing of the frame loops and is rather too great for maximum comfort for short-legged riders.' The footrests were adjustable for height and the tester found that 'the most satisfactory setting for riders of various statures was with the hangers lowered one serration from the horizontal position in which they leave the factory.'

Another moan was that: 'In relation to the seat, siting of the footrests is a shade too far forward for a high performance machine; in consequence, several consecutive hours of high speed riding produced a mild ache in the rider's thighs and forearms.'

It was also discovered that the latest version of the Model 88 'revelled' in high engine revolutions, the tester going on to say: 'Indeed the effect of the Daytona camshaft is such that the best results, both from the viewpoint of power and comparative fuel consumption, are obtained in the upper engine-speed ranges.'

Whereas the earlier 88 (and the Model 7) of the early 1950s would easily accept top gear at surprisingly low speed, this was not quite the case with the 1957 88, as the test revealed:

> When the Norton was ridden at a steady 30 mph (such as in built-up areas) the engine pulls top gear happily, but acceleration from that speed revealed a trace of hardness in the transmission and, as would be expected, sweeter as well as brisker results were obtained by using one of the lower gears for acceleration.

Despite this, the tester found things to praise:

> Probably the most endearing characteristic of the Dominator power unit was its rapid acceleration. Provided the engine was turning over moderately fast, its response to throttle opening was extremely brisk and the revs would continue to build up unhesitatingly to valve-float point or the maximum possible in the circumstances, according to which gear was engaged.

He also thought that its ease of starting deserved full marks. The test was carried out during extremely harsh winter conditions, with the air temperature often below freezing point. Yet, as the test revealed: 'provided the carburettor was liberally flooded (but not excessively so) and the air lever closed, one hearty swing on the kick-starter would always bring the engine to life from cold.' It was then necessary for the air lever to be partially opened for around a mile to ensure even firing. In warmer weather, however, or with the engine warm, this procedure could be dispensed with, as the author has discovered during several rides on a late 1950s Dominator 88 of the same type.

The brakes were yet another area where the 88 received the thumbs up: 'No matter at what speed they were applied, the brakes were always smooth, controllable and very powerful.' As were the lights: 'The headlamp furnished an intense and concentrated beam which made night riding a pleasure, while the offset of the dipped beam to the left was appreciated alike by the rider and other road users.'

Perhaps, then, the final section of the test sounded positive: 'To sum up, the latest Model 88 is a good-looking five-hundred twin with a zestful and tireless engine, remarkably powerful brakes and a well-subdued exhaust. Steering is in the best Norton tradition and will please the many enthusiasts who rightly insist on first-class high speed handling.'

Alternator for 1958

The big news concerning the 1958 Norton model range was that the 88 and its larger brother, the 99 six-hundred, were to be equipped with Lucas RM15 AC generators, as *The Motor Cycle* disclosed in its 5 September 1957 issue:

> Following standard practice, the 2¾in (70mm) diameter rotor of the RM15 alternator is pressed and keyed on to an extension of the drive-side mainshaft outboard of the engine sprocket. To ensure that the co-axial relationship between rotor and stator is maintained regardless of any flexure of the primary chaincase, the stator is mounted directly to the crankcase. A light-alloy casting fits over a spigot boss on the case and is secured to it by three screws. The outer end of the casting has a female spigot to accept the stator, three bolts hold the stator to the casting.

As for the primary chaincase itself, this was similar to the one used previously, being of pressed steel and sealed by a taper-section band of synthetic rubber clamped between the two halves of the case by the tightening action of a single nut on the footrest hanger-bar tube. However, to ensure clearance for the stator, the nose radius of the new case had what Norton called 'a more pronounced dome'.

At the forward end of the inner section was a circular cut-out of slightly larger diameter than the stator holder; this hole fitted over a shallow secondary spigot on the crankcase, the pressing being secured by a trio of countersunk screws.

In place of the previous chain-driven magneto, which had been flange-mounted in the timing case behind the engine, there was now a Lucas 3812A distributor incorporating an automatic advance and retard mechanism. The two spring clips that retained the distributor cover were readily accessible, as was the contact breaker when the cover was removed.

With the axing of the separate dynamo in front of the crankcase, both the timing cover and the front engine plates had been redesigned, resulting in a much tidier appearance.

Another change had been accomplished by redesigning the pressure-relief valve of the lubrication system. Previously this had been housed in a domed compartment screwed into the rear edge of the timing case, but for 1958 this was now entirely enclosed within the case, giving a much neater appearance.

To carry the ignition coil for the new system a lug had been welded to the offside (right) top tube of the frame, just ahead of the seat nose. The rectifier was attached to the underside of the tool tray, below the seat, while the key-operated ignition switch was embodied in the light switch on the headlamp shell. There was an emergency key position in case of a flat battery.

On 5 September 1957 the Model 88 list price was £227 10s (basic), or £283 16s 2d with UK purchase tax.

Twin Carburettors

Also available for 1958 88 and 99 twins, at additional cost and to special order, were two carburettors. The inlet manifold was of the splayed type and carried a pair of Amal Monobloc Type 376 instruments, which were the same as those fitted to the single carb models: 1in (26mm) for the 88 and 1⅙in (28mm) for the 99.

It should be noted that for maximum benefit when going for the twin-carb option, due to improved breathing abilities, Norton recommended the use of high compression pistons in place of the standard components. Then, it was claimed, 'All-round improvement in performance of around 8–10 per cent can be expected.'

One man who certainly took advantage of the new twin-carb option for his 88 was former World Sidecar Champion, Eric Oliver. Now aged 47, Eric, together with Mrs Pat Wise of Louth, Lincolnshire, a housewife and former beauty queen, announced in May 1958 that they were to compete in the following month's international Sidecar TT in the Isle of Man, riding a series production Norton Dominator 88 with Watsonian Monaco single-seat sports chair.

Eric Oliver was quoted as saying that his 'intention was not serious racing … [the] object is not to race but to complete the course and if possible finish within replica time using machinery that can be bought by the general public.' Both the motorcycle and sidecar came from the stock at Eric's own London showrooms, and the twin carbs were, of course, official Norton optional extras. Since Pat Wise was to sit in the normal 'everyday position', *Motor Cycle News* pointed out that: 'This should provide a complete contrast on the course to the usual acrobatics of the other competitors.'

Not only did Eric and Pat complete the race, they came home in tenth place and certainly deflated those pundits who had forecast the pair would be 'blown off'.

One journalist who didn't fall into this trap was Mick Woollett, who excused himself from making any pre-race comments by claiming far too much respect for Eric's common sense and natural riding ability. But even he was later to admit:

> What did surprise me was not so much his lap times – amazingly fast and consistent at between ten minutes 42 seconds and ten minutes 52 seconds [the race was staged over the shorter Clypse course] except for the initial lap and refueling lap – but that the standard Norton Dominator lasted the distance and appeared to be going just as well at the end.

In order to find out just how well the machine had lasted, Mick Woollett borrowed the outfit a mere two hours after the race ended and took it up the mountain for what Mick called 'a gallop'. Even with the silencer fitted (open megaphone had been used for the race), the Dominator outfit had what he described as:

> an amazing amount of 'poke' and romped up the long climb to the Bungalow … for a hotted up 500cc production machine with a virtually standard Watsonian Monaco sidecar, it really was incredible and even more so when you remember that none other than Eric Oliver had well and truly wrung its neck for over a hundred miles to average just a shade under 60mph and win a bronze replica.

The standard Dominator 88 and Watsonian Monaco sidecar, driven to tenth place in the 1958 Sidecar TT by ex-world champion, Eric Oliver, passengered by Mrs Pat Wise – a fantastic performance.

Yes, that performance on 4 June 1958 was one that would stick in the mind of every enthusiast fortunate enough to witness it.

The 1958 88

Engine	Air-cooled ohv twin with vertical cylinders, alloy head and cast-iron barrel, two main bearings, 360-degree. 3-piece crankshaft, split con-rods and shell big-end bearings, coil valve springs, vertically-split aluminium crankcases
Bore	66mm
Stroke	72.6mm
Displacement	497cc
Compression ratio	7.8:1
Lubrication	Gear pump; dry sump
Ignition	Battery/coil, 6-volt
Carburettor	Amal 376 Monobloc 1in (twin carburettors as cost option from May 1958)
Primary drive	Simplex chain
Final drive	Chain
Gearbox	AMC 4-speed, positive stop, foot-change
Frame	Norton Wideline Featherbed, full cradle, twin front downtubes, welded-up subframe
Front suspension	Norton Roadholders, oil-damped, telescopic
Rear suspension	Swinging arm, with oil-damped twin shock absorbers
Front brake	8in full-width drum, SLS
Rear brake	7in full-width drum, SLS
Tyres	3.00 × 19 front; 3.50 × 19 rear
Wheelbase	55.5in (1,410mm)
Ground clearance	5.5in (140mm)
Seat height	31in (787mm)
Fuel tank capacity	3.5gal (15.9ltr)
Dry weight	390lb (177kg)
Maximum power	30bhp @ 7,000rpm
Top speed	92mph (148km/h)

Small but Important Changes

For the 1959 model year the 88 and 99 were reduced in price (by £3 14s 11d and £7 9s 8d, respectively) and also incorporated several small but important refinements.

The 1959 Dominator twins featured a redesigned camshaft. Reduction of mechanical noise had been a main consideration and to achieve this the cams incorporated quietening ramps, but the new profiles were claimed to provide a slight increase in power output.

In addition, the engines of the 88 and 99 twins were further improved by tipping both inlet and exhaust valves with welded-on Stellite to prolong life and thus reduce the need for valve clearance adjustment. A fully enclosed final-drive chaincase was now listed as an optional extra, costing £2 19s 3d. Also available at an additional charge were: twin carburettors, £7 12s 2d; polished ports, £1 4s 11d; larger inlet valves, £1 4s 11d; and a non-standard finish, £2 16s 2d.

The chaincase was attached to the nearside (left) arm of the pivoted rear fork at four points, and comprised top and bottom steel pressings. A slot in the upper section embraced the brake camshaft bearing boss and permitted chain adjustment. To inspect the chain a circular rubber plug was retained in the upper half of the outer case. A pipe connected to the oil tank breather tube and was led to an area above for lubrication purposes. Unfortunately, although it looked efficient, this chaincase was to gain a poor reputation with owners, who often accused it of keeping the dirt in rather than keeping the elements out!

Slimline Frame

The really big news when the 1960 Norton range was announced in September 1959 was the new Slimline version of the, by now legendary, Featherbed frame. As previously described above, a major failing for road use of the original Wideline frame was the width

For the 1960 model year Norton introduced their new Slimline Featherbed frame, and also offered de Luxe models with rear enclosure and the Standard (naked) version of both the 88 and 99 twins.

between the rider's knees, which was too wide for optimum comfort. The essence of the new Slimline design was that the area around the rear of the tank and the front of the seat had been reduced in width – hence the Slimline tag (for full details of the layout, *see* Chapter 6).

Another notable addition for the 1960 model year was the reintroduction of the 'de Luxe' label. This now had a new meaning, however, indicating a then fashionable rear enclosure manufactured from steel pressings and secured by Dzus quick release fasteners. Although much publicized at the time, the de Luxe Dominator models with rear enclosure did not prove popular; after less than three years they were dropped from the range.

Also new, on both the standard and de Luxe versions, were the fuel tanks (deeper and narrower than before), dual seat and a deeper section front mudguard. All Dominators gained new-pattern absorption silencers, for which the factory claimed a reduction in exhaust noise, combined with less back pressure.

Engine Changes

Also for the 1960 model year, there were a number of engine changes (to both the 497 and 597cc sizes) aimed at increasing performance.

First among these was the fitment of larger valves (previously available only at extra cost) with redesigned porting of the light-alloy cylinder head and, in consequence, a new inlet manifold for the single Amal Monobloc carb. There was also a reprofiled camshaft with quicker lift than previously. Both the 88 and its larger 99 brother were also given higher compression ratios, the smaller engine rising from 7.8 to 8.1:1. Norton also claimed more efficient cooling thanks to a superior flow of air around the cylinder head, achieved by providing more and deeper finning.

To make fuller use of these improvements the gear ratios had been revised, including a notably narrower gap between top and third.

Also new for 1960 were two-tone colour schemes. For the standard (unfaired) machine the normal finish was Norton grey, contrasting with dove grey for the mudguards, rear spring units and lower section of the fuel tank. At no additional charge the Norton grey could be replaced by red or black. The de Luxe models were offered in blue, red or forest green, with dove grey for the frame, front mudguard and lower parts of the tank and rear panelling.

As for prices, the standard 88 cost £223 (basic) and £268 19s 10d (with UK purchase tax); the de Luxe version £227 10s (basic) and £274 8s 5d (with UK purchase tax).

Few Changes for 1961

Compared with 1960, there were few changes for the 1961 model year. The Slimline Featherbed frame had been modified: a cross-tube at the upper rear of the frame's main loops was provided with two rearward-pointing pegs to engage with rubber-lined sockets under the seat nose. After the seat was pushed home on the pegs it was retained by a single quick-action fastener located on the rear mudguard. There was also an alternative, almost flat, handlebar available at no extra charge.

On both 88 models, the compression ratio was raised from 8.1 to 8.5:1.

The relatively wide choice of colour schemes available for 1960, however, had caused problems, including production hold-ups at the factory. So for 1961 the Dominator 88 models were standardized green and dove grey for the basic version, while the de Luxe was offered in red and grey.

As in previous years, twin carburettors could be supplied ex-factory as a cost option when ordering a new bike, together with other extras including the rear chain enclosure.

Prices had again risen, with the 88 Standard now £234 (£282 5s 3d) and the de Luxe £238 10s (£287 13s 10d).

SS – Sports Special

During early spring 1961 the Dominator 88 (and 99) SS (Sports Special) models were introduced. Essentially what Norton had done was to take the standard 88 or 99 and fit all the high-performance bits and pieces formerly listed as extras – plus a siamesed exhaust.

At 8.5:1 the compression ratio was standard on the new 88SS, but the cylinder head had polished ports, combustion chambers and was equipped with twin 1 1/16in Amal Monoblocs; the inlet ports were 1/16in larger than stock.

In addition the 88SS (and 99SS) featured sports camshafts, as fitted to the American market-only 650cc Manxman (*see* Chapter 8), together with taper-tube dural pushrods (3/8 in tapered to 9/32in), also fitted to the 650.

Outwardly the SS models didn't look very different from their single-carb 'standard' 88 and 99 brothers, but the 88SS could certainly go: *Motor Cycling* electronically timed one at 111mph (178.6km/h) at MIRA – one way.

Costing £291 5s (including £49 16s UK purchase tax), the forest green/dove grey 497cc 88SS was also very successful in long-distance production racing (*see* Chapter 9).

Available at extra cost were chromed mudguards (£4 8s 5d), rev counter (£6 6s 8d) and rear chaincase (£3 10s 4d), all including tax.

Motor Cycle News, in its 26 April 1961 issue, commented:

> To our mind these smooth-powered roadsters should rate high in the choice of anyone contemplating competition in production machine races. For such enthusiasts, rear-set footrests, brake and gear pedals are available from Norton's service department ... In their element on the M1 and other 20th-century highways, here are two powerful but gentle twins offering an all-round performance second to none.

With the SS versions Norton had created a true sporting classic road burner.

From early spring 1961 the Dominator 88 (and 99) SS (Sports Specials) were introduced. These featured many tuning parts as standard, including a twin-carb head, sports camshaft, dural pushrods, plus all the 'go faster' specials such as higher compression pistons and larger inlet valves previously listed as cost extras.

The 1962 Range

For 1962 there were no fewer than fifteen roadster Nortons on the British market, headed by the Dominator 650SS. There were also three 88 models: the standard, de Luxe and SS. The last of these had extensive improvements, many garnered directly from the new 650SS rather than the 99SS, including a new downdraught splayed-port alloy cylinder head – of the type employed on its new 647cc counterpart. The compression ratio had been stepped up to 9.5:1. Both the 88SS and 650SS were kitted out with a magneto featuring manually operated advance and retard, and an RM19 alternator of lower output than that employed on the standard and de Luxe versions. In addition an Avon Grand Prix rear tyre was fitted.

As before, the 88SS was equipped with twin Monobloc carburettors, multi-rate valve springs, hi-lift camshaft and light-alloy, taper-tube, pushrods.

Unlike the 650, the 88SS (and 99SS) gave of their best when a siamesed exhaust system was fitted and consequently they were normally supplied in this trim, though separate pipes were available as an option.

The finish of the 1962 model-year 88s continued to be green and dove grey for the standard and SS versions and red/grey for the de Luxe. As for prices, the standard cost £233 10s basic (£284 17s 5d including purchase tax), the de Luxe £238 basic (£290 7s 2d including purchase tax) and the SS £241 basic (£294 5d including purchase tax).

The 1962 88SS	
Engine	Air-cooled ohv twin with vertical cylinders, alloy downdraught head and cast-iron barrel, two main bearings, 360-degree, 3-piece crankshaft, split con-rods and shell big-end bearings
Bore	66mm
Stroke	72.6mm
Displacement	497cc
Compression ratio	8.5:1
Lubrication	Gear pump; dry sump
Ignition	Magneto, 6-volt
Carburettor	2 × Amal 376 Monobloc 1⅟₁₆in
Primary drive	Simplex chain
Final drive	Chain
Gearbox	AMC 4-speed, positive stop, foot-change
Frame	Norton Slimline Featherbed, full cradle, twin front downtubes, welded-up sub-frame
Front suspension	Norton Roadholders, oil-damped, telescopic
Rear suspension	Swinging arm, with oil-damped twin shock absorbers
Front brake	8in full-width drum, SLS
Rear brake	7in full-width drum, SLS
Tyres	3.00 × 19 front; 3.50 × 19 rear
Wheelbase	55.2in (1,402mm)
Ground clearance	5.8in (147mm)
Seat height	31in (787mm)
Fuel tank capacity	3.62gal (16.5ltr)
Dry weight	390lb (177kg)
Maximum power	36bhp @ 7,000rpm
Top speed	105mph (169km/h)

Sporting Successes Bring Record Sales

During 1962 there were record sales of the 'Sports Special' version of the Dominator twins, thanks in no small part to their sporting success in such events as the Thruxton 500 miler and Silverstone 1000 kilometre. This meant that Norton Motors had enough on their order books to keep them busy – even in the winter months. Given this situation, and an increasing export business, the marque said that it would not be launching any new models for the 1963 season. The six-hundred 99 series, however, was to be axed; it should be noted that Norton had already announced the new 745cc Atlas (*see* Chapter 12) earlier in 1962. At the same time the de Luxe versions of all models were withdrawn.

The continued success, particularly of the 650 and 750 versions, meant that by the end of 1963 the standard single-carb 88 had also been axed, leaving the 88SS as the sole remaining five-hundred Norton twin. But even this single model proved a slow seller and was eventually dropped from the range in 1966. Anyone who is lucky enough to find a late 88SS, however, not only has a fine motorcycle with a good performance and largely vibe-free powerplant, but the advantage of 12 volt electrics from 1964 onwards.

In many ways the 88SS was the finest of all the Dominator series; certainly for someone travelling solo, without a passenger. And from personal experience I can certainly vouch for its effectiveness as a true 'Super Sports' model.

And so the original Dominator, the 500, finally came to the end of the road – but what a journey it had been from the late 1940s until the end of the 1960s. During this time it had built up a strong ownership base, thanks to its combination of good performance, Norton handling abilities, reliability and, at least from the mid-1950s, strong braking.

Model Recognition

1949	Model 7	497cc (66 × 72.6mm) ohv vertical twin with iron head and barrel, built-up crankshaft, telescopic forks, plunger rear suspension, single downtube frame, 4-speed 'laid-down' Norton gearbox, oil pressure gauge in tank top, 7in brakes, magneto and dynamo electrics.
1950		Prop stand now fitted.
1951		New front brake, still 7in. Mid-year, due to nickel shortages, petrol tanks and wheel rims silver instead of chrome.
1952	88	Wideline Featherbed frame, shortened forks, valanced mudguards and pear-shaped silencers, engine specification as Model 7, but with higher gearing, initially export only.
1953	Model 7	Swinging-arm frame (still single downtube), new silencers, modified rocker lubrication, underslung pilot lamp.
	88	Unsprung front mudguard, knee grips, rocker lubrication as per Model 7, gear ratios now as Model 7.
1954		Both machines, 8in front brake (still single-sided).
1955		Both machines, light-alloy cylinder head and Amal Monobloc carburettor.
	88	Welded sub-frame, deep section rear mudguard, full-width light-alloy hubs.
1956	Model 7	Deleted from range.
	88	Restyle – battery cover and oil tank, instruments in separate panel fitted to deeper headlamp shell. Revised camshaft profile, AMC gearbox and clutch.
	99	596cc (68 × 72mm), otherwise as 88.
	77	596cc engine in Model 7 single downtube, swinging-arm frame.
1957		All models, new cylinder head, with additional fins between exhaust ports to improve cooling, 'cigar'-type silencers, aluminium pushrods.
	88 and 99	Instruments mounted directly in headlamp shell, panel deleted, new lighter cast-alloy full-width front hub with cast-in brake liner and new brake shoe plate.
1958	88 and 99	AC electrics (coil and alternator). Twin carburettor available as cost option from spring that year.
	77	Retained magneto/dynamo, production ceased later that year.
		Nomad Export model in Street Scrambler guise, with knobbly tyres, twin carburettors, siamesed exhaust, abbreviated (alloy) mudguards, small tank, 77 frame, oil tank etc., available with 500 or 600 engine.
1959		New camshaft, incorporating quietening ramps. Both exhaust and inlet valves now Stellite-tipped.
1960	88 and 99	Introduction of new Slimline Featherbed frame, revised fuel tank, revised front mudguard, engine modifications, revised finning, new silencers. De Luxe versions with rear enclosure.
1961	88 and 99	Increased compression ratio.
	650 Manxman	New model, 647cc (68 × 89mm), twin Amal Monobloc carbs, downdraught induction tracks, high-compression pistons, hi-lift cams and widely splayed exhaust ports, export only for first year. Later Standard and De Luxe (latter with rear enclosure) go on sale.
	88SS and 99SS	Sports models added to range, equipped with siamesed exhausts and twin carburettors
1962	650SS	Sports model added to range with magneto ignition. Latest 88SS now has magneto, but 99SS continued with coil. All SS models with chrome-plated mudguards.
	750 Atlas	745cc (73 × 89mm) single Amal Monobloc carburettor, revised breather, extra plate for clutch, otherwise spec very much as 650SS.
	All 600s, Plus De Luxe (enclosed) models dropped at end of year.	
1963	Atlas Scrambler	750 engine in AMC frame, AMC aluminium primary chaincase, Norton hubs.
	88 and 650 Standard models	These models axed from range.
1964	All models	12-volt electrics, with two 6-volt batteries in series.
	G11	750 engine, in Matchless G85CS frame, AMC competition hubs, desert racing and enduro mount.
1965	G15 and G15 CSR	Atlas engine in AMC frame with Norton forks and wheels, sold under Matchless brand name. Also some machines sold as AJS (Models 33 and 33CSR).
1966	88SS	Dropped from range.
	650SS and Atlas	From engine number 116372, six-start worm-drive oil pump, small engine mods including enlarged oilways, plain rocker spindles, Wellworthy 'Duaflex' oil control piston rings.
1968	All models	Capacitor ignition. 650SS becomes the Mercury. All hybrids and Atlas models axed from range. From engine number 125871 pushrods shortened by 1in and valve stems lengthened by same amount.
1970	Mercury	Chromed mudguards and rev counter as standard.

5 Off-Road

During the immediate postwar period Norton ran an official trials team, mainly using the specialist 500T and 350T ohv singles. Soon after the introduction of the Model 7 in 1948, therefore, Norton started on experiments to prepare it for trials work.

For the 1950 International Six Days' Trial (ISDT), held on home ground, with headquarters in Llandrindod Wells, Norton built a small batch of special Dominator twins. As *The Motor Cycle* reported in its 17 August issue, those machines sported 'a number of interesting features. These had been a works headache at Bracebridge Street. Some castings for the special, quickly detachable wheels had not arrived. Parts had to be machined from solid.' This caused the Norton squad something of a panic during the official team selection exercises.

This is how *The Motor Cycle* described these hand-built bikes:

> Apart from light-alloy cylinder heads [the production Model 7 having cast-iron heads at the time], the Norton Dominator engines are standard. The frame is also standard except that the bridge at the front of the chain-stays is moved forward one inch to allow for a 4in rear tyre. A Manx-type [conical] front brake is fitted. Both exhaust pipes are led into one [siamesed] on the offside. In place of a normal saddle is a special seat which is hinged at the rear and spring-clipped to the frame at the front. It takes no more than a second to pull up the seat at the front and swing it right back over the mudguard. This gives access to two spare inner tubes in a neat container underneath. Removable in 13 seconds, the petrol tank pushes on to studs at the front and has a through bolt at the rear provided with an integral tommy bar at one end and a wing nut at the other.

The four Norton riders who took part were A.J. Blackwell, R.B. Young, R. Clayton and R.J. Woolaway, with Blackwell being selected to represent the British Vase 'B' team.

The new works Dominators were only slightly heavier than the ohc International singles Norton had entered the previous year. When the trial got underway in mid-September, it was seen that Clayton had replaced Blackwell as the official member of the Vase 'B' squad.

On the second day Woolaway went into retirement. However, worse was to come on the fourth day, as *The Motor Cycle* Trial Report of 28 September 1950 so vividly recalls:

> Between Hirnant and the lunch check at Llys, near Denbigh, far to the north, R Clayton (497 Norton) of the British Vase 'B' Team, was attacked by the Fates. Sweeping round a fast corner, and about to overtake a Swedish rider, he encountered an unexpected and quite deep watersplash. Both riders braked heavily. Then Clayton opened up to go through, but the Swede swerved. Clayton shut off just as he entered the splash. Too late – water was drawn up into the cylinders and that was that. The cylinder head gasket had blown.

Then, on the fifth day, J.R. Blackwell retired. Nevertheless, the only Dominator left in the event won a gold medal, ridden by R.B. Young in an excellent performance. Most of the trial had been run in awfully wet conditions – a severe test for man and machine alike.

So how did Norton's entry into the 1950 ISDT with the twin come about? The 490cc ohc International had been the previous factory choice for the event, but it was now considered that the twin was a better bet for a long and gruelling slog.

Before building the Featherbed-framed machines that actually took part, Bob Collier, who was employed as a fabricator in the Experiment department at the Norton works, had constructed a Dominator-powered 500T (Norton's ohv single-cylinder one-day trials bike). This combination should never have worked, but when Bob was told the twin wouldn't fit on the 500T frame, it was just something that had to be tried. He simply took his welding torch to the front downtube and bent it sufficiently to make room for the twin-cylinder engine to slot into place! Even so, after testing the 'Collier Special' the factory chose the spring-frame, which had made its debut with the works race team only that year, since it was considered a superior choice for the rigours of six gruelling days of cross-country riding against a tight time schedule. But as is related later, this wasn't to be the end of the Collier twin.

The 1951 ISDT

The 1951 ISDT event was staged in northern Italy, based around the town of Varese, around 30 miles (50km) north of Milan. After his 'gold' in 1950, perhaps it was to be expected that Rex Young should be promoted to the 'B' Vase Team squad, but this was not to be the case. Once again, the team selection exercises had been held in Wales, with headquarters at Llandrindod Wells.

The Motor Cycle, in its 16 August 1951 issue, reported:

> For sheer unorthodoxy, however, the chain oiler on Clayton's Norton must be awarded full marks, since the container is, in fact, one leg of the rear fork … Racing enthusiasts will have noted a similar arrangement on the works 500cc racing Nortons in the past few classic road races … Clayton was delighted with his mount and spoke of it with genuine enthusiasm.

Norton's famous 500T trials bike. The first Dominator-powered prototype machine of early 1950 was built by Bob Collier, who simply heated up the front downtube with a welding torch to allow the large twin-cylinder engine to be fitted!

The Motor Cycle also included some interesting details of his machine:

> Wheels were of 18in diameter and the front wheel had a Manx-type brake with conical hub. Apart from the features mentioned [Dominator engine in a racing-type frame], the fitting of tommy-bar nuts to the rocker covers and the provision of an air-bottle and tyre levers under the tank, the Norton looked remarkably 'un-International'. The sprung, valanced front mudguard, incidentally, was very efficient. The fuel tank is of the light-alloy racing pattern.

Detail Differences

A month later, with the trial about to start, it emerged that there were differences in detail when compared to the Norton twins, which were to be ridden by Clayton, plus Rex Young and Jack Breffitt. These now featured primary and rear chain oilers fed directly from the oil tank, necessary since there was no oil carried in the primary chaincase because the clutch was of the racing type and had to run dry. The bikes were also equipped with small (but effective) silencers. An air bottle (for tyre inflation) was now carried on top of the primary-chaincase and in the toolbox under the seat was a small battery, which could be connected up instantaneously to a spare rear light – of which there were no fewer than three!

And what a success the 1951 ISDT was for Norton. All three of its riders won gold medals: the trio were one of seven manufacturers' teams who qualified for Gold Medal Diploma awards by finishing the trial without loss of marks.

Of the 220 starters, there were 146 finishers, of whom 89 were awarded 'golds', 26 'silvers' and 17 'bronze' medals. Another Norton twin (one of the 1950 models) also gained a gold, ridden by a certain 17-year-old J.V. Smith, Jnr – later famous as BSA works rider Jeff Smith, who was double 500cc Moto Cross Champion in 1964 and 1965.

The 1952 ISDT

Only two riders were officially backed on the twins the following year: Rex Young and the up-and-coming youngster, Jeff Smith. Norton was suffering something of a cash crisis and this explains why they used the previous year's mounts, although at the time the official explanation was 'total satisfaction with last year's mounts.' Young was a member of the British Vase 'B' team.

The 1952 ISDT was held in Austria, with its headquarters some 45 road miles (72km) east of Salzburg at Bad Aussee, about 5,500ft (1,700m) above sea level. As things turned out, Jeff Smith was unable to take part following a mishap prior to the weighing-in ceremony, when he badly gashed his leg in collision with an Austrian rider. Since this wound required stitching, he was announced as a non-starter. H.L. Williams took over Jeff's machine and, together with Jack Breffitt, went on to gain gold medals in the trial.

But this was to mark the end of Norton's participation in the ISDT, as the following year the firm was acquired by the London-based AMC group (*see* Chapter 13) and the factory trials operations (both one-day and six-day) were axed.

The Rigid-Framed Collier Twin

Bob Collier put in a lot of hard work behind the scenes at Nortons. He was also a special builder of considerable repute and a fair competition rider. Working in the Experimental department at the Bracebridge Street factory, he had been responsible for building a Dominator-engined machine by modifying a 500T trials chassis (*see* above).

This interesting bike stood idle for many months until Collier himself decided to turn it into a sidecar trials outfit. Bob made his debut during August 1953 in the Clayton Trophy Trial, held in the peaks and dales of north-west Derbyshire. The Collier twin appeared with trade plates fitted, which was all very well until Norton's managing director, Gilbert Smith, heard about the exercise. Collier was subsequently carpeted over the affair, not least because the company's trade-plate insurance did not cover sporting events!

Actually Collier had done rather well, since *The Motor Cycle* report of the event stated: 'R.G. Collier on his Norton twin outfit made a spirited charge and with the aid of some energetic footwork the outfit went up the hill non-stop.' He also finished runner-up in the sidecar class and was thus able to argue successfully that his performance had brought Norton some valuable publicity. So Gilbert Smith relented and the machine was officially registered. Proof that this was the right decision came with class victories in the Red Rose (Lancashire) and Cotswold Cup trials, both events of national status attracting trade support.

Conventional wisdom at the time insisted that a big single-cylinder machine, able to grip on muddy sections, was essential for sidecar trials, but Collier's own view of his twin's abilities was quite simple: 'Start three fields back and let rip!'

Les Archer

As well as in one-day and six-day trials, the Dominator twin was also used, albeit briefly, in the world of international motocross. This came via the great Les Archer, who went on to become the 1956 European champion riding a Manx-engined Norton special.

The saga of Archer and his Norton dirt racers really began back in 1952, when the factory built four scramblers using a combination of racing and trials components. The chassis used was from the 500T ohv trials bike of the era, but with the swinging-arm rear suspension grafted on. Both 350 and 500cc ohc single-cylinder engines were used. Various riders tried them including Geoff Duke and John Draper. But they didn't handle very well: after testing them against his own Manx-engined machine, developed at the same time, Les Archer decided to stick with his own machinery.

In November 1952, however, Norton announced that they would be supporting Les Archer and Eric Cheney, both of whom were associated with the Aldershot Archer family dealership. Apart from the occasional scramble at home, the pair would compete in international motocross events in Continental Europe. Les Archer got off to a flying start when he won the prestigious Moto Cross de Marseille on 8 February 1953. This was followed by a succession of wins and places all over Europe that summer. But what many people have forgotten is that many of these were achieved aboard an experimental Norton twin. The engine was essentially a 497cc Dominator with cast-iron head and barrel, single Amal carb and 4-speed Norton 'laid-down' gearbox. Eventually, with the work carried out by mechanic Ron Hankins, the ohc Manx single was chosen ahead of the pushrod twin, but not before the twin had shown itself to be fast, competitive and reliable. In fact, because of its enclosed valve gear it was in some ways superior to the single. But in the end the single won – and was developed into a championship winner at the very highest level.

The twin was never raced by Les in the UK. And when interviewed by *Motor Cycle News* in 1957, he said:

> Our main reason for attempting to use the 'twin' was really the problem of air filtration is so much more easily overcome and on the Continent this is of major importance, because the dry, dusty courses ruin an engine in no time at all. The machine was, in many ways, very satisfactory, but I did not consider the type of power it produced to be as suitable for scrambling as the 'single', and so, after using it on and off throughout the season, it was eventually dismantled, but not before we had proved our point concerning air filtration because the engine had never been disturbed.

The Nomad Scrambler

Norton's next involvement with the dirt bike scene, at least as far as its twins were concerned, came in March 1958 with the announcement of the new Nomad Scrambler. This was not a scrambler in the European sense, however, but an enduro bike evolved for Desert Racing in the western states of North America.

As one period commentator put it: 'Competition riders in the United States are tough hombres. They have to be for their cross-country enduros (or point-to-point scrambles) may embrace as much as 200 miles [320km] of forest and scrub.' Any bike to be campaigned had to be both fast and rugged.

Designated the Nomad, the model had been conceived for just the above purpose. It was in fact a much modified 597cc Model 77 (*see* Chapter 6).

Based on the existing roadster (the same engine also powering the Model 99 Dominator), it featured a light-alloy head and cast-iron cylinder block. The compression ratio had been increased to 9:1. There were now twin, stub-fitting Amal Type 276 carburettors (1 1/16in) with separate float chambers, these being handed left and right. Rubber inlet pipes led from a pair of what Norton described as 'oil-wetted, metal-and-fabric' air filters located at the rear of the frame's saddle-tube and sandwiched between the oil tank and toolbox assemblies.

Built especially for the American market, the Nomad used the engine from the six-hundred 99. It was what Stateside riders referred to as a 'Street Scrambler', but could also take part in many sporting events including desert racing, enduros and even scrambling.

Norton sources claimed higher than average torque figures at low engine revolutions for the Nomad – 21.9bhp at 3,500rpm, with maximum power being quoted at 36bhp at 6,000rpm. The gearbox was the standard 4-speed AMC unit, providing ratios of 5, 6.64, 8.84 and 13.35:1.

The newcomer was equipped with a full lighting set. A 6-volt, 12 amp hour battery was fed, via a metal rectifier, by a crankshaft-mounted Lucas alternator. Ignition was taken care of by a Lucas K2F competition rotating magnet magneto with manual control.

To lower weight, and to provide optimum performance for the purpose required, there was a siamesed exhaust pipe layout, with a small, upswept silencer on the offside (right). The nearside (left) exhaust header pipe passed through the engine's triangular forward mounting plates and was thus located between the front downtube and the crankcase.

Frame Changes

The frame was of the brazed-lug variety found on the roadster Model 77, but suitably modified. The changes made, Norton said, were to permit the use of appropriate mountings for the special scrambles footrests and the use of a heavy gauge support tubing, which was protected, together with the underside of the crankcase, by a sheet-steel bash plate. Also the swinging arm had been widened to accept a bigger section scrambles-pattern rear tyre. Controlling this rear fork were a pair of Girling spring-and-hydraulic shock absorbers featuring three-position adjustment.

Both centre and side stands were of the quickly detachable type; when removed this provided a ground clearance of no less than 8in (200mm).

The 1958 Nomad

Engine	Air-cooled, ohv twin with vertical cylinders, alloy head and cast-iron barrel, two main bearings, 360-degree, 3-piece crankshaft, split conrods and shell big-end bearings, coil valve springs
Bore	68mm
Stroke	82mm
Displacement	597cc
Compression ratio	9:1
Lubrication	Gear pump; dry sump
Ignition	Magneto, 6-volt
Carburettor	2 × Amal 276 1$\frac{1}{16}$in
Primary drive	Simplex chain
Final drive	Chain
Gearbox	AMC 4-speed, positive stop, foot-change
Frame	Cradle, single front downtube
Front suspension	Oil-damped, telescopic
Rear suspension	Swinging arm
Front brake	8in full-width drum, SLS
Rear brake	7in full-width drum, SLS
Tyres	3.00 × 21 front; 4.00 × 19 rear
Wheelbase	56.5in (1,435mm)
Ground clearance	6.5in (165mm)
Seat height	32in (813mm)
Fuel tank capacity	2.5gal (11.4ltr)
Dry weight	385lb (175kg)
Maximum power	36bhp @ 6,000rpm
Top speed	100mph (162km/h)

Nomad fitted with alternator

The front fork, a modified version of the Roadholder assembly fitted to the Model 99, incorporated two-way hydraulic damping. Besides featuring stronger springs, both the main tubes and rods had been lengthened. A steering damper was fitted as original equipment.

Tyres were Avon Gripsters – a 3.00 × 21 at the front and a 4.0 × 19 rear. Both wheels employed the full-width Norton light-alloy hubs, with an 8in at the front and the QD rear wheel of 7in diameter at the rear.

Several other components were aluminium, including the narrow-section mudguards and two-piece AMC-type primary chain case.

As for the colour scheme, the frame was enamelled black. Upper and lower parts of the front fork and headlamp brackets were of polished light-alloy, while the middle section of each fork leg was enamelled black. The fuel tank, rear chainguard and rear brake shoe plate were finished in red. A distinctive feature was the dual seat, which had black sides with a white top section.

The Nomad was to remain an export-only model for its entire production life, although by the end of 1959 it was possible to order the bike with a choice of either 497cc or 597cc engine sizes.

The Desert Racer Concept

The Desert Racer Concept inspired by the Nomad was, as related in Chapters 10 and 12, to lead to the Atlas Scrambler (also known as the Ranger) and more specialized P11 models. Both of these were powered by the 745cc (73 × 89mm) engine. All were clearly aimed at the American market, rather than the British or European ones. Years later, very similar bikes, at least in engine type and purpose, were to be built by Japanese, Italian and German manufacturers. This made Norton pioneers in the development of the large displacement twin-cylinder enduro-type mount.

6 99 and 77

In response to the arrival of a new 597cc twin and a 348cc single to be included in the company's 1956 programme, the headline in the 15 September 1955 issue of *The Motor Cycle* read 'Stimulating Nortons'.

The new, larger twin was based on the existing and popular Dominator 88 de Luxe five-hundred (*see* Chapter 4). Like the 88 de Luxe, the Model 99, as the newcomer was designated, was equipped with the famous Featherbed frame, Roadholder forks and swinging-arm rear suspension, together with full-width, cast-aluminium front and rear brake hubs.

Externally similar in appearance to the Dominator 88 engine, the new six-hundred twin-cylinder unit had bore and stroke dimensions of 68 × 82mm respectively (the five-hundred's being 66 × 72.6mm), so the new engine had a considerably longer stroke.

An aluminium-alloy cylinder head was specified, the compression ratio being 7.4:1. The bottom half of the 99's engine was essentially the same as the five-hundred, with a 3-piece built-up crankshaft featuring forged-steel crank cheeks and a cast-iron flywheel in the middle. The main shafts were supported in a large diameter roller bearing on the drive side, with a ball bearing on the timing side. Connecting rods were forgings in RR56 light alloy and featured steel-backed shell (plain) big-end bearings.

A notable variation of the design concerned the pistons. On the six-hundred engine these were of the flat-top, wire-wound aluminium-alloy variety, designed, said Norton, to run with closer tolerances resulting in quieter operation, especially when the engine was cold.

Valve operation, as on the five-hundred, was by means of a single chain-driven camshaft mounted at the front of the engine and operating pushrods contained within two tunnels, the latter being cast integrally with the one-piece cast-iron cylinder barrel. A new style of timing cover, which bore a miniature replica of the Norton tank badge, was fitted.

Comparing the new six-hundred with the existing five-hundred twin, *The Motor Cycle* had this to say in the same issue:

> Some months ago a member of the staff covered about 80 miles [130km] on a prototype six-hundred twin. Compared with its 497cc counterpart (itself a lively performer) the newcomer gave a main impression of superb acceleration from a standing start up to about 80mph [130km/h]. It was particularly satisfying to note the increased power output derived from the larger-capacity engine had not been employed purely in the interest of a higher maximum speed. Rather was it evident in the way the machine could sustain high cruising speeds. Indeed, at speeds between 75 and 85mph [120–138km/h] the engine produced its power in smooth and tireless fashion. As anticipated, steering, roadholding and braking were excellent. Even when the road surface was of a bumpy nature the model could be heeled over with confidence into fast bends, neither front nor rear wheel showed the slightest tendency to deviate from the line chosen by the rider.

As already detailed in Chapter 4, several changes in the specification of the Dominator 88 constituted features that were also common

October 1956 advertisement for the 1957 'Smooth-Look' Norton range with John Hartle's works development Manx racer (top) and the latest six-hundred 99 twin (bottom).

to the new Model 99.These included a restyled oil tank and matching battery box, the action of the two-rate coil springs of the Roadholder front forks had been lightened and there was a new headlamp incorporating a plate to carry the speedometer, lighting switch and ammeter (previously these instruments had been carried in a fork top mounted panel).The 7in (180mm) diameter Lucas headlamp now carried a pilot bulb located in the reflector (previously this was in an underslung compartment).

The 99's price, on 15 September 1955, was £216 (basic) or £259 4s (including UK purchase tax).

During the spring of 1956 two important things happened at Norton: Bert Hopwood rejoined the company in April as chief designer, then the new AMC manufactured gearbox was introduced for the 99 (and other heavyweight models).

The 1956 Model 77	
Engine	Air-cooled, ohv twin with vertical cylinders, alloy head and cast-iron barrel, two main bearings, 360-degree, 3-piece crankshaft, split con-rods and shell big-end bearings, chain-driven magneto (rear) and dynamo (front), coil valve springs, vertically-split aluminium crankcases
Bore	68mm
Stroke	82mm
Displacement	597cc
Compression ratio	7.4:1
Lubrication	Gear pump; dry sump
Ignition	Magneto, 6-volt
Carburettor	Amal 376 Monobloc 1¹⁄₁₆in
Primary drive	Simplex chain
Final drive	Chain
Gearbox	4-speed, positive stop, foot-change
Frame	Cradle, single front downtube
Front suspension	Oil-damped, telescopic
Rear suspension	Swinging arm
Front brake	8in full-width drum, SLS
Rear brake	7in full-width drum, SLS
Tyres	3.25 × 19 front; 3.50 × 19 rear
Wheelbase	56in (1,422mm)
Ground clearance	5.5in (140mm)
Seat height	31.5in (800mm)
Fuel tank capacity	3gal (13.6ltr)
Dry weight	402lb (182kg)
Maximum power	31bhp @ 5,750rpm
Top speed	96mph (154.5km/h)

A Twin for Sidecar Duties

In September 1956, when introducing its 1957 model range, Norton sprang something of a surprise by launching the Model 77, an additional six-hundred twin intended 'primarily for sidecar duties'. Finished in polychromatic grey, *The Motor Cycle* commented:

> To readers who are familiar with the Norton range up to 1955, the Model 77 is probably best described as a 597cc version of the Model 7 Dominator [*see* Chapter 2] twin which was discontinued after that year. In other words the new twin has a similar power unit to the Model 99 and a brazed-lug frame incorporating a malleable-iron engine cradle … Although … the new model is intended primarily for use with a sidecar (the frame incorporates the necessary attachment lugs and a steering damper is standardized), it is equally suitable for solo use because the steering geometry is a compromise between the two extremes.

The 597cc (68 × 82mm) Dominator 99 and Model 77 engine with single carb and alloy head – clearly based on the existing and successful five-hundred 88 series.

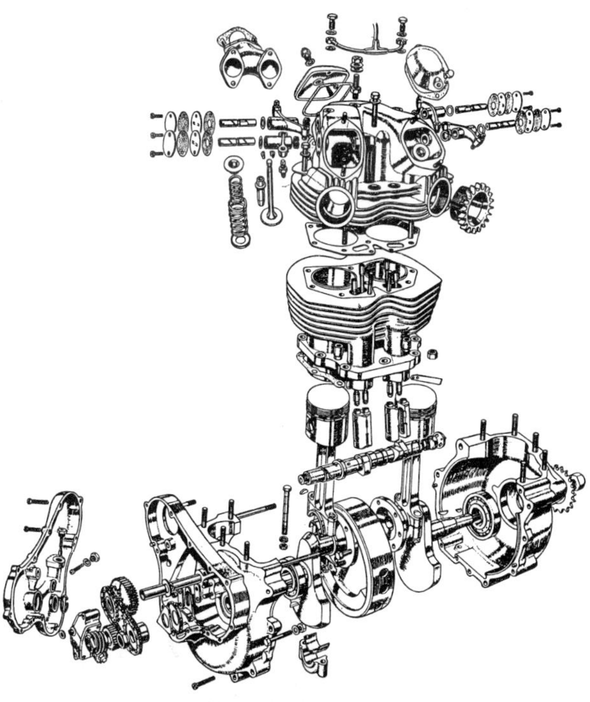

It has to be said that the 99 and 77 engines of the era were to all intents and purposes identical, using the same 7.4:1 compression ratio and single Amal Type 376 Monobloc carburettor. Also the 99 and 77 (and also the 88) shared the new cylindrical silencers that were introduced for the 1957 season.

Overall gear ratios for sidecar use were: 1st, 13.35:1; 2nd, 8.85:1; 3rd, 6.65:1; and top, 5:1. When the 77 was supplied for solo use, the corresponding ratios were: 12.1, 8.02, 6.02 and 4.53:1.

Although the Model 77 only had the single downtube cradle frame, the suspension followed the latest Norton practice with hydraulically damped, telescopic front fork and a pivoted rear fork controlled by proprietary shock absorbers.

The quickly detachable wheels were shod with 19in tyres, while full-width hubs were featured on both wheels, the front hub being of composite construction and the rear an aluminium casting. Both the 8in (200mm) diameter front brake and 7in (180mm) rear brake had 1¼in (32mm) brake shoes.

As on the latest (1957 model year) 88 and 99 models, the fuel tank, although of different style, featured separate chrome-plated side panels, the 77's tank capacity being 3gal (13.6ltr). As on the other models in the range, a minor but notable departure from previous Norton practice concerned the footrests: these were now forged hangers carrying conventional, round-section rubbers instead of the previous, built-up assemblies comprising side plates, nuts and bolts as well as rubber foot pieces. The oil tank, with a capacity of 4 pints, was shaped to blend with the lines of the offside (right) frame tube. On the other side of the frame was a matching box that housed the battery, tools and voltage regulator.

Ignition and lighting were taken care of by separate magneto (rear) and generator (front), using, as with all Nortons of the period, 6-volt electrics. The price of the new 77, on 20 September 1956, was £210 (basic) and £260 8s (with UK purchase tax).

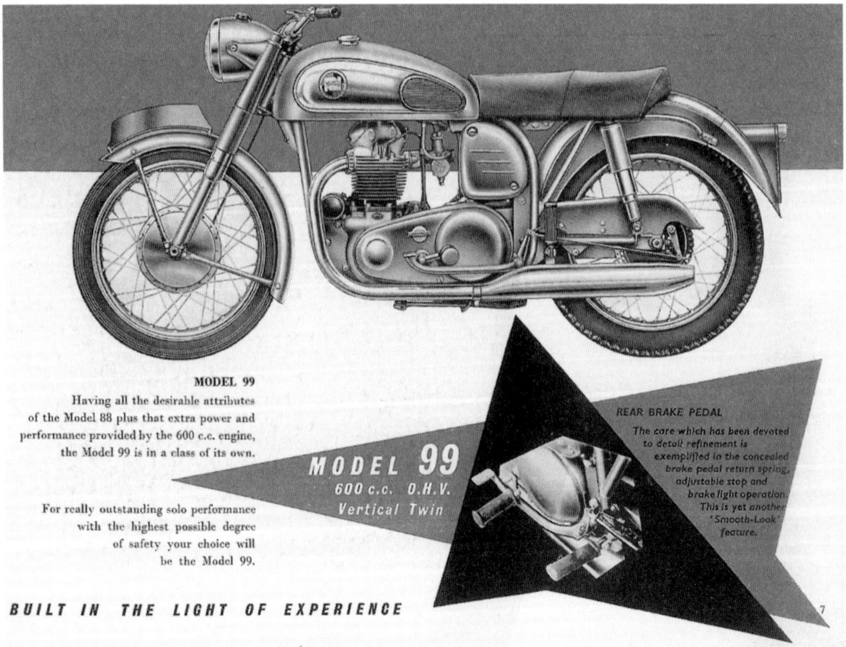

The Model 99 as shown in the 1957 Norton range brochure.

A 1957 Model 77 six-hundred twin with Busmar Double Adult sidecar.

Fitting a Third Wheel

As the Model 77 had been introduced mainly for sidecar work, it was perhaps fitting that almost the first test published was with a third wheel attached. This appeared in the 24 January 1957 issue of *The Motor Cycle* and was headed 'A Zestful and Elegant Sidecar Outfit for the Owner Requiring Super-sports Performance and First-class Handling'. And the 'chair'? This was a Swallow Jet 80 single seater.

According to the tester:

> It is scarcely a utilitarian outfit (though the engine is certainly tractable enough for traffic work) but as a provider of fun on the road it would be hard to beat … Surging acceleration, superb steering and powerful braking are the outfit's chief attractions and it seems almost to beg to be driven in an exhilarating manner. It is no exaggeration to say that every journey undertaken during the test brought a thrill whether the sidecar was laden or empty, though in the wintry weather prevailing, a certain degree of hardihood was required in a passenger if he or she was to share the driver's enjoyment to the full.

There was certainly no denying the attractive good looks of the Model 77-Swallow outfit, the ensemble being finished in silver and grey, while the sleek lines of the sidecar body, streamlined wheel arch and chassis loop blended well with the motorcycle itself.

The Motor Cycle tester noticed that:

> There is little that is entirely novel about the newcomer. The engine is identical with that of the Model 99 and has the high-performance Daytona camshaft and light-alloy cylinder head. A 1957 modification is the use of light-alloy for the pushrods. Of single-loop pattern and incorporating sidecar lugs, the frame is well-established on the single-cylinder models and was used on the obsolete Model 7 497cc twin. The AMC four speed gearbox and clutch were standardized throughout the Norton range early in 1956 but the eyeable silencers and plastic-framed, chromium-plated tank panels, now featured on all the roadsters, were not introduced until the new model made its debut.

The Model 77 engine (the same as the 99) but with a single tube frame from the outgoing Model 7 five-hundred.

As for the Swallow sidecar:

> Though the Jet 80 is an old-established favourite with sporting drivers, the most up-to-date construction is now used, for the body is a one-piece plastic moulding incorporating the windscreen frame. Appearance is unquestionably enhanced but the stark simplicity of appointment remains. Essentially the Jet 80 is an uncompromising sports model – light, low, open, beautiful in an ascetic sort of way and devoid of frills.

Although a maximum speed of 73mph (117km/h) was the best recorded in the official test session, *The Motor Cycle* gave this proviso regarding the figures:

A 1957 Model 77 owned by Kevin Feltoe, seen at Snetterton, Norfolk, September 2004. Note the siamesed exhaust, which probably means this bike was originally used for sidecar work.

> They cannot be said to do full justice to the outfit. The day on which the data was obtained was one of very stiff wind. Moreover, because of the extremely low temperatures both driver and passenger were very bulkily clad and their weights totalled about 26 stones. In the circumstances the outfit was noticeably overgeared and proved to be as fast downwind in third gear as in top.

Conversely, the tester considered that: 'the outfit's overgearing was anything but a drawback for ordinary hard driving – even with the load mentioned – for the engine has an admirably wide spread of torque which enables it to pull with lusty power from quite low speeds.'

The combined price of the Model 99 and Swallow 80 when tested was a shade under £360 (including the dreaded UK purchase tax).

AC Generator for the 99

The 11 September 1957 issue of *Motor Cycle News* carried the following leader concerning the announcement of the 1958 Norton model range:

> Believing that there is no point, as a long term policy, in making drastic styling or design changes simply for the sake of change, Norton are making no major modifications to their range for the coming year, but instead are continuing all existing models as before with the exception that two improvements are made to the 'featherbed'-framed Dominator twins – the Models 88 and 99.

The most noteworthy of these improvements was the adoption of an AC generating system with coil ignition in place of the former separate magneto and dynamo. The new generator was a Lucas RM15, mounted on the nearside (left) of the engine with its rotor fitted at the end of the driveside mainshaft. An unusual feature was that the stator (the non-rotating section of the generator on which the coils were carried) was attached to the crankcase proper instead of the more usual inside of the primary chaincase.

The object of this layout was twofold: to ensure that the position of the stator assembly could not change relative to the rotor (even a minute movement here could have affected generator output) and to enable the existing basic chaincase design to be retained, thus keeping down costs.

The ignition was by 6-volt Lucas fluid-filled coil, mounted beneath the fuel tank, and normally current for this coil came from the battery. In the event of the battery becoming flat, however, current from the generator could be switched direct to the coil so that a spark could still be obtained. Otherwise current (alternating) from the generator went to a selenium-type rectifier mounted below the tool tray (where it then became direct current) and from there transferred to the battery.

A chain-driven Lucas distributor replaced the magneto formerly fitted. An orthodox centrifugal advance and retard mechanism was incorporated in the distributor.

Norton

1958 RANGE & PRICE LIST

1st Sept., 1957, UNTIL FURTHER NOTICE

	RETAIL PRICE	PURCHASE TAX
Model No. 50	£189 10 0	£46 18 0
Model E.S.2	£194 10 0	£48 2 9
Model No. 19S	£204 0 0	£50 9 10
Model No. 77	£221 10 0	£54 16 5
Model No. 88	£227 10 0	£56 6 2
Model No. 99	£235 0 0	£58 3 3
Model No. 30 Int.	£243 0 0	£60 2 10
Model No. 40 Int.	£237 0 0	£58 13 2
Model No. 30 & 40M	£398 0 0	£98 10 1

Prices are subject to alteration without notice.

NORTON MOTORS LTD., BRACEBRIDGE ST., BIRMINGHAM, 6.

Norton 1958 Range & Price list published on 1 September 1957, listing both the 77 and 99 six-hundred twins.

Immaculate Dominator twin owned by Philippe Niels of Brussels, Belgium; photograph taken in September 1997.

The headlamp on the Model 99 (and 88) remained as the previous year, except for the provision of a larger switch.

The other, and more minor, change was that the pressure relief valve from the crankcase had been redesigned. While working on the same principle as the old assembly, the new one was smaller and thus improved the lines of the engine.

It should be noted that the Model 77 retained the magneto and separate generator instead of the AC equipment described above.

The prices that came into effect on 5 September 1957 had risen to: 77, £221 10s (basic) and £276 6s 5d (including purchase tax); 99, £227 10s (basic) and £283 16s 2d (including purchase tax).

The 1958 99

Engine	Air-cooled ohv twin with vertical cylinders, alloy head and cast-iron barrel, two main bearings, 360-degree, 3-piece crankshaft, split con-rods and shell big-end bearings, coil valve springs, vertically-split aluminium crankcases
Bore	68mm
Stroke	82mm
Displacement	597cc
Compression ratio	7.4:1
Lubrication	Gear pump; dry sump
Ignition	Battery/coil, 6-volt
Carburettor	Amal 376 Monobloc 1$\frac{1}{16}$in
Primary drive	Simplex chain
Final drive	Chain
Gearbox	AMC 4-speed, positive stop, foot-change
Frame	Norton Wideline Featherbed, full cradle, twin front downtubes, welded-up sub-frame
Front suspension	Norton Roadholders, oil-damped, telescopic
Rear suspension	Swinging arm, with oil-damped, twin shock absorbers
Front brake	8in full-width drum, SLS
Rear brake	7in full-width drum, SLS
Tyres	3.00 × 19 front; 3.50 × 19 rear
Wheelbase	55.5in (1,410mm)
Ground clearance	6.75in (171mm)
Seat height	31in (787mm)
Fuel tank capacity	3.5gal (15.9ltr)
Dry weight	395lb (179kg)
Maximum power	31bhp @ 5,750rpm
Top speed	96mph (154.5km/h)

Vibration

Just over a year after it had tested the Model 77 and Swallow Jet 80 sidecar outfit, *The Motor Cycle* published a test of the Model 99 Dominator in solo guise in its 6 February 1958 issue, beginning:

> There has never been any doubt as to the role of the 597cc Norton Model 99 twin: it is a high-performance roadster intended primarily for solo use. The wide popularity of the vertical-twin five-hundreds shortly after the war soon led to the introduction of models of similar layout but larger capacity. Most of the newcomers were dual-purpose machines, equally suitable for fast solo touring or hauling a sidecar. But the Model 99, first marketed in 1956, is not intended to woo the sidecarrist. Its duplex-loop frame has no sidecar lugs and is of the type made famous first on the factory racing models (in 1950) and subsequently on the Manx production racers and the Model 88, forerunner and smaller brother of the 99.

Although the tester said the 'engine was utterly tireless', he also went on to say: 'the only considerations which dictated the speed to be sustained on long journeys were a vibration period and the riding position.' The former was: 'Felt through the handlebar and tank, the tremor became noticeable just before 65mph [104km/h] was reached [in top gear], peaked at about 70mph [113km/h] and faded out at

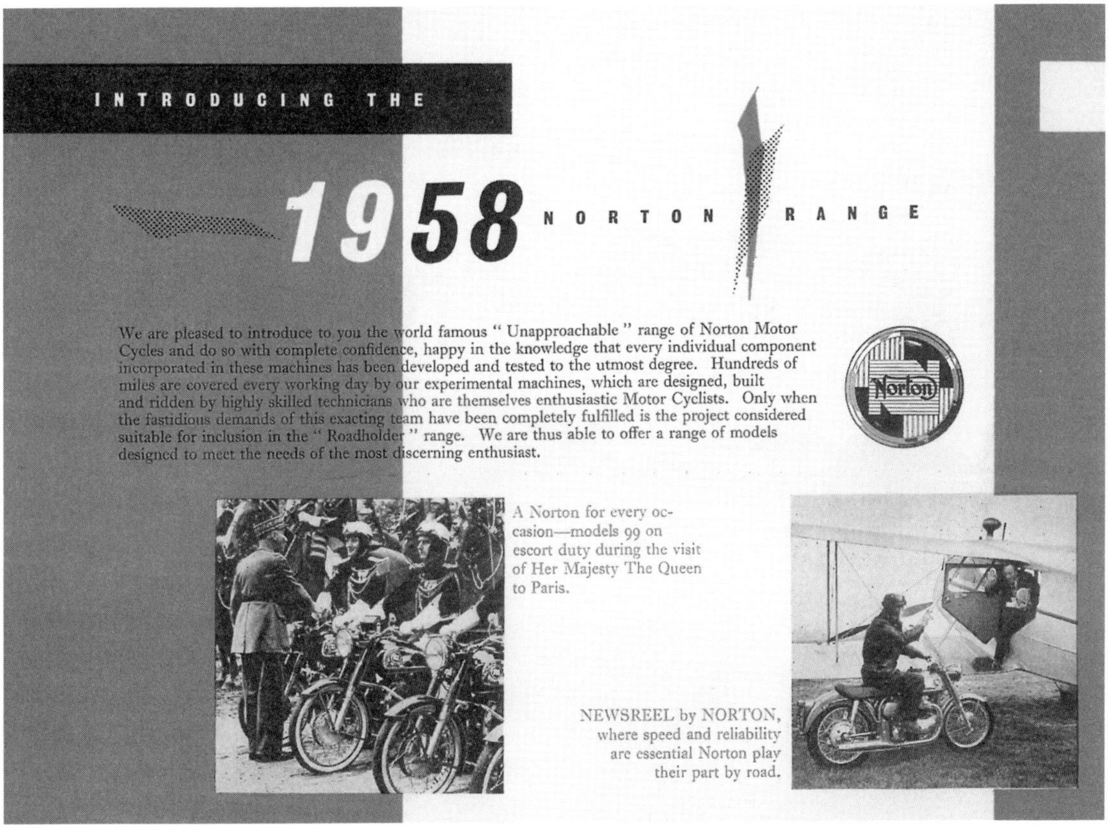
INTRODUCING THE

1958 NORTON RANGE

We are pleased to introduce to you the world famous " Unapproachable " range of Norton Motor Cycles and do so with complete confidence, happy in the knowledge that every individual component incorporated in these machines has been developed and tested to the utmost degree. Hundreds of miles are covered every working day by our experimental machines, which are designed, built and ridden by highly skilled technicians who are themselves enthusiastic Motor Cyclists. Only when the fastidious demands of this exacting team have been completely fulfilled is the project considered suitable for inclusion in the " Roadholder " range. We are thus able to offer a range of models designed to meet the needs of the most discerning enthusiast.

A Norton for every occasion—models 99 on escort duty during the visit of Her Majesty The Queen to Paris.

NEWSREEL by NORTON, where speed and reliability are essential Norton play their part by road.

An extract from the 1958 Norton catalogue, showing Model 99s during the visit of Her Majesty the Queen to Paris (left) and delivering newsreel (right).

75mph [121km/h].' As for the riding position, this was 'beyond reasonable criticism for low and medium speeds', although 'the riding posture was rather upright owing to the upward sweep of the handlebar and the forward positioning of the footrests relative to the seat. Hence the rider had to exert an appreciable pull on the bar to counter the effect of wind pressure on the body.' As in the magazine's previous test of the 88 (*see* Chapter 4), it was noted that: 'Width of tank and seat between the rider's thighs is above average', making it 'slightly awkward for riders of average height to put their feet on the ground.' In truth this was a problem that was to remain until the introduction of the Slimline frame for the 1960 model year.

The tester noted that: 'At the expense of a hard ride on bumpy surfaces the rider has the advantage of precision handling at very high speeds.' He rated the steering as 'absolutely first rate … In all circumstances it inspired the highest confidence, indeed, it was one of the most prominent factors in the joy of riding the 99.'

Other features that won praise were braking ('more than a match for the speed of the 99') and gear changing ('a joy'), the only criticism of the box being the 'rather wide spacing of the third and fourth ratios and a slight whine when the engine was pulling in either of the intermediate gears.' The clutch was 'extremely light to withdraw', but 'took up the drive abnormally quickly in the last fraction of lever movement.'

The report said that after a test:

> comprising just under 1,000 miles [1,600km] of hard riding, the engine and gearbox retained their oil well, there being only faint smears at some of the joints at the end of the test. Slight seepage occurred from the oil-tank filler cap and chaincase inspection cover. A small pool of oil formed under the crank case breather when the model was parked at the end of a run.

Oil consumption was adjudged as rather high, while the 'rear chain ran dry and required adjusting and oiling at frequent intervals.'

Another moan concerned the adjustment of the contact-breaker points. The auto-advance and contact-breaker unit of the new coil ignition system was 'situated behind the crankcase mouth in the place previously occupied by the magneto: the adjustment is inaccessible and thereby liable to invite neglect by owners who are not fastidious.'

Even with these faults the test concluded by saying: 'In appearance the Model 99 is a winner.' And to many that's exactly how they remember the 99, which of course was the stepping stone between the five-hundred and six-fifty models in the evolution of the Dominator series.

Both the Model 88 and the Model 99 were available, to special order, with twin carburettors from the beginning of 1958 (*see* Chapter 4). When the twin carbs were specified as original equipment, the additional charge was £7 12s 2d (including £1 10s 2d purchase tax in the UK). This figure also included high compression pistons, but other tuning, such as polishing of the combustion chambers and exhaust ports, was also available at extra cost.

With coil ignition came an a.c. generator (alternator). This was rigidly attached to the crankcase as shown, rather than in the primary chaincase as on rival marques.

LEFT: *For 1958 the 99 (as here) and the 88 were given coil ignition. This meant that there was now no dynamo at the front of the crankcase and revised engine mounting plates.*

A 1958 coil-ignition Dominator in original guise, except for later Amal Concentric carburettor and rear carrier; owned by Eddie Clarke.

The Model 77 is Axed

When the 1959 Norton programme was announced at the end of September 1958, it was seen that the Model 77 twin, with its single loop cradle frame, had been axed. The reason? Well, Norton now said they considered the Featherbed models 'are suitable for sidecar work and available with appropriate steering and stiffer springs.' One has to ask whether the Model 77, which had a short life of just two seasons, was simply a way of getting rid of obsolete components?

Though reduced in price by £3 14s 11d and £7 9s 8d (both including purchase tax) respectively, the 497cc Model 88 and 597cc Model 99 twins incorporated several small but important changes for 1958. A reduction in mechanical noise had been achieved by the use of quietening ramps on the cam lobes, while the valve stems were now Stellite-tipped to improve wear.

Standard finish was polychromatic grey and chrome as before, with three options at extra cost: red, black and silver or metallescent blue. Besides the twin carbs, high compression pistons and polished ports, Norton now offered larger inlet valves (£1 extra).

A New Frame

The 1960 Norton model range was launched in September 1959, and with it came the new 'Slimline' Featherbed frame. Although the basic layout of the duplex frame for the Dominator models (for 1960 there were four – two standard and two of the new de Luxe models, described below) was much as before, the tubes had been brought closer together in the area of the rear tank and front seat positions – just the area, in fact, that had drawn criticism over the years for being too wide. In consequence a new dual seat with an appreciably narrower nose was fitted, which *The Motor*

Cycle considered: 'a feature which will be appreciated particularly by shorter-legged riders.' Replacing the previous triangular rear sub-frame there were now tubular loops, welded to which were steel pressings to form the upper mountings for the suspension units and also provide attachments for the silencers and pillion footrests.

A cross-tube at the narrowed rear of the frame main loops incorporated two rearward-facing pegs to engage with rubber-lined sockets at the base of the dual-seat nose. At the rear, spring clips were provided on the seat base, these snapped into place over short transverse tubes welded to the sub-frame loops. On the two de Luxe models (having rear enclosure panel work), additional bracketry was provided on the frame and sub-frame providing mounting points for the previously mentioned rear enclosure panels (these being secured by Dzus fasteners).

There was also a notable revision in fuel tank design. The 1960 type for the new Slimline frame was both deeper and narrower than the old and secured underneath by a longitudinal strap. Chromium-plated, die-cast badges along the tank sides incorporated the name of

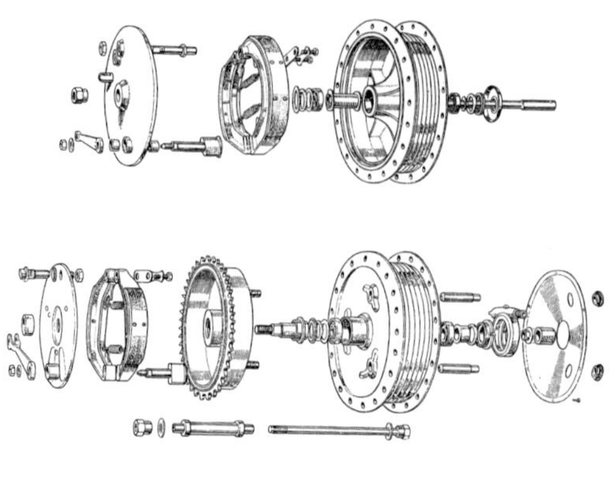

Full-width alloy hubs from 88/99 series, showing not only the hubs, but shoes, brake plates, sprocket, bearings, seals, speedo drive, spacers and spindles.

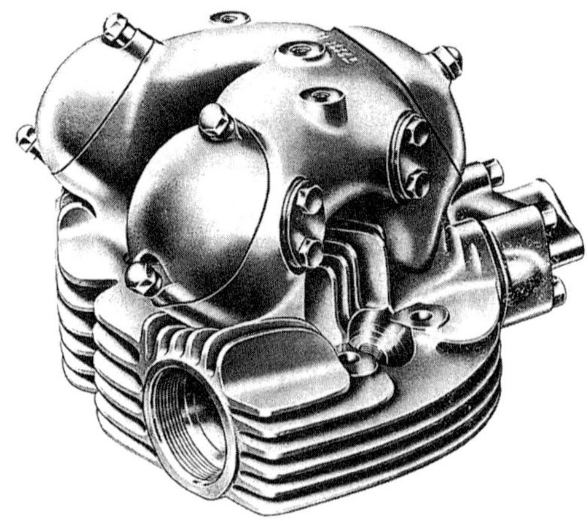

1959 alloy cylinder head, still with single carb, but increased finning compared to earlier years.

Norton and served to separate the two halves of the two-tone colour scheme. There was also a new front mudguard.

Increased Performance

Another facet of the new-for-1960 Slimline-framed Dominators was the number of improvements to both the 99 and its smaller brother, the 88. These included the fitment of larger inlet valves as standard (previously available only at extra cost), with redesigned porting of the light-alloy cylinder head and, in consequence, a new inlet manifold for the single Amal Monobloc carburettor. A further important factor was a new camshaft with fiercer lifting cam profiles than previously. There was also a rise in compression ratio in both engines: in the 99 it rose from 7.4 to 7.6:1. Norton also claimed more effective cooling from a better flow of air around the cylinder head of both engines, obtained by way of increased and deeper finning. For the larger 597cc engine only the depth of finning of the cast-iron cylinder block had been increased. To match the increased power output and provide a better on-road performance, the gear ratios had been altered. On both engine sizes this meant that the gap between third and top gears had been considerably reduced.

Finally, all the 1960 Dominator models now had new-pattern absorption silencers, which, it was claimed, offered a reduction in exhaust noise level combined with an equal reduction in back pressure.

The normal finish for the standard 99 and 88 models was Norton grey, contrasting with dove grey for the mudguards, rear suspension units and the lower section of the fuel tank. At no additional cost buyers could specify that Norton grey could be replaced by red or black. The de Luxe (rear enclosure) models were offered with a choice of red, blue or forest green, with dove grey for the frame, front mudguard and lower parts of the tank and rear panelling.

It should also be mentioned that the Nomad (in effect an American-derived street scrambler; *see* Chapter 5) was now being offered on the home UK market in both 497cc and 597cc guises.

Testing the 99 de Luxe

When *The Motor Cycle* tested the recently released 99 de Luxe in its 23 June 1960 issue, the test began: 'Latest Model 99 more Comfortable, Eyeable and Peppy than Ever. Magnificent Steering and Roadholding. Improved Riding Position.'

The tester, Vic Willoughby, was able to tell readers:

> I have ridden many a Dominator since 1952 and I just love the way they seem to steer themselves, anticipating my every wish and carrying it out faithfully to the nearest inch or less ... The latest in the series to come my way was a 1960 597cc Model 99 de Luxe with attractively styled partial rear enclosure and a smart two-colour finish of light blue and dove grey.

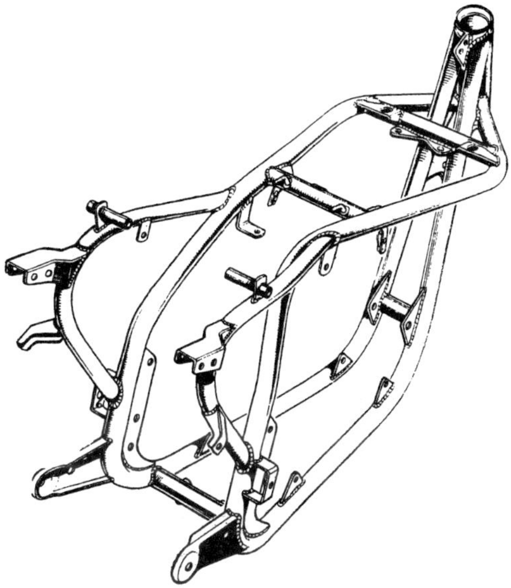

Slimline frame, new for 1960. As this drawing shows, this was narrower between the rider's knees in the area towards the rear of the tank and front of the dual seat.

So what were his opinions of the newcomer?

> It is not only in appearance that this year's de Luxe model surpasses its predecessors. One of my cribs about the earlier models was the uncomfortably wide span across the nose of the seat and rear of the fuel tank. That objection is entirely eliminated by the slimming of the frame at the rear and the use of a narrower seat.

Another unmistakable improvement over earlier models was the 'much snappier response to throttle opening at low and medium speeds ... Without hesitation the engine simply rushes up the scale as soon as the twistgrip is tested.'

The Dominator 99 also proved a:

> glutton for work ... On fast roads it revelled in being pushed up to 50 or 60mph in second gear, 70 or 80mph in third and cruising for as long as I

> wished with the speedometer needle between 85 and 90mph marks. Two or three times, by crouching low I was able to get a reading of 100 to 105mph – and once 107mph with a moderate tail wind. These are creditable figures considering I was wearing a two-piece plastic riding suit, and though it would be untrue to say there was no vibration, it was certainly not bothersome.

The 1960 99 De Luxe

Engine	Air-cooled ohv twin with vertical cylinders, alloy head and cast-iron barrel, two main bearings, 360-degree, 3-piece crankshaft, split con-rods and shell big-end bearings, coil valve springs, vertically-split aluminium crankcases
Bore	68mm
Stroke	82mm
Displacement	597cc
Compression ratio	8.25:1
Lubrication	Gear pump; dry sump
Ignition	Battery/coil, 6-volt
Carburettor	Amal 376 Monobloc 1$\frac{1}{16}$in
Primary drive	Simplex chain
Final drive	Chain
Gearbox	AMC 4-speed, positive stop, foot-change
Frame	Norton Slimline Featherbed, full cradle, twin front downtubes, welded-up sub-frame
Front suspension	Norton Roadholders, oil-damped, telescopic
Rear suspension	Swinging arm, with oil-damped, twin shock absorbers
Front brake	8in full-width drum, SLS
Rear brake	7in full-width drum, SLS
Tyres	3.00 × 19 front; 3.50 × 19 rear
Wheelbase	55.5in (1,410mm)
Ground clearance	6.75in (171mm)
Seat height	31in (787mm)
Fuel tank capacity	3.5gal (15.9ltr)
Dry weight	398lb (180.5kg)
Maximum power	32bhp @ 6,000rpm
Top speed	98mph (157.7km/h)

Note: De Luxe models had rear enclosure

Although he felt that the gearbox action was stiffer than on many similar gearboxes he had tried, the exhaust (well muted), clutch operation (both light and sweet) and starting (dependable and required little effort) all garnered praise. As to the braking: 'From almost every point of view the front brake was a honey – smooth, progressive, light and powerful,' with only the fact that it was 'prone to squeal when used lightly' counting against it. The rear brake, however, was adjudged 'distinctly below par and awkward to adjust because the silencer fouls the brake rod nut when the machine is on the centre stand.'

Willoughby 'liked the large headlamp switch which is easy to flick from one position to another with gloved fingers, and being on the left side of the lamp shell, it enables beams to be changed without taking the right hand from the twistgrip.' But against this, 'the fixed horn button was rather too low on the handlebar.'

Not Finished Yet

Even though the 99 had been improved, yet more punch was to be added for the 1961 model year. The big news when details of the Norton range were published in mid-September 1960 was, as *The Motor Cycle* headline read, 'Higher Compression Dominators'. On the 99 the ratio had been upped from 7.6 to 8.25:1. It was also now possible to specify chrome-plated mudguards as an optional extra, for an additional £3 18s 5d (including purchase tax), but only on the standard models, not the de Luxe.

Another change was that, to simplify production, the choice of colours had been reduced. The standard 99 was now offered only in dark and dove grey, while the de Luxe version was sold in a striking bright blue and dove grey.

As if to prove that Norton's six-hundred twin could go even better, the factory launched the 99SS (Sports Special) in early 1961, together with a similar 88SS (*see* Chapter 4). Once again Vic Willoughby managed to bag an example for a test session for the 27 April 1961 issue of *The Motor Cycle*, beginning enthusiastically:

> Whoa, there – just look at those performance figures – a mean 108mph (electronically timed) and a quarter-mile sprint from rest in 14.4 seconds with a finishing speed of 92mph in third gear. How's that for a fully equipped six-hundred roadster twin? The sprint figures, by the way, are only 0.2 seconds and 4mph down on those from the mighty 998cc Vincent Black Shadow vee-twin road tested in similar trim by The Motor Cycle in August 1949 … when to steering and roadholding that have long been widely admired and envied you add the new-found zip, you have the sort of machine many sporting enthusiasts regard as the ideal roadster.

Rivals *Motor Cycle News* also carried an extensive feature on the new Sports Special models, their story beginning:

> A white helmeted figure hurtled down the Hanger Straight. The faint drone of his siamesed exhaust reached our ears as he cogged down for Stowe and Club Corners. Then we heard the rasping song of those twin cylinders as Charlie streaked round Abbey Curve at a full 100mph. Wow! Someone said. And as he tucked himself down for the glorious blind down to Woodcote, Charlie Rous grinned at the speedo – a steady 112! You've guessed it, he was riding the new Norton Dominator 99 Sports Special round Silverstone's fast Grand Prix circuit.

MCN called the 99SS: 'one of the latest and certainly finest products of the British motorcycle industry.'

So how had this level of additional performance been achieved? To start with the newcomers, the 99SS and the 88SS had been given the special specification components previously available at extra cost, including the twin carburettors.

On both sizes of engine, carb choke diameter was 1$\frac{1}{16}$in (28mm) with the inlet ports opened out to suit. Ports and combustion

A group of motorcycles outside the Tower of London, including a 1960 Norton 99 de Luxe and a 1952 Sunbeam S7.

chambers were polished and, though standard pistons were employed, particular care had been taken in their selection, to ensure that the compression ratio matched the stipulated 8.25:1 figure.

The 1961 99SS

Engine	Air-cooled ohv twin with vertical cylinders, alloy head and cast-iron barrel, two main bearings, 360-degree, 3-piece crankshaft, split con-rods and shell big-end bearings, coil valve springs, vertically-split aluminium crankcases
Bore	68mm
Stroke	82mm
Displacement	597cc
Compression ratio	8.25:1
Lubrication	Gear pump; dry sump
Ignition	Battery/coil, 6-volt
Carburettor	2 × Amal 376 Monobloc 1$\frac{1}{16}$in
Primary drive	Simplex chain
Final drive	Chain
Gearbox	AMC 4-speed, positive stop, foot-change
Frame	Norton Slimline
Front suspension	Norton Featherbed Roadholder forks
Rear suspension	Swinging arm, with oil-damped, twin shock absorbers
Front brake	8in full-width drum, SLS
Rear brake	7in full-width drum, SLS
Tyres	3.00 × 19 front; 3.50 × 19 rear
Wheelbase	55.2in (1,402mm)
Ground clearance	5.8in (147mm)
Seat height	31in (787mm)
Fuel tank capacity	3.62gal (16.5ltr)
Dry weight	395lb (179kg)
Maximum power	44bhp @ 6,750rpm
Top speed	108mph (173.8km/h)

Borrowing Technology from the Manxman

In addition the newcomers had borrowed technology from the new Manxman 650 (*see* Chapter 8), which at that time was only built for the Stateside market. Both Sports Specials used the Manxman camshaft and the flat-base cam followers that went with it; additionally they also had the six-fifty's two-rate duplex valve springs.

To prevent flexing in racing or high speed road work imposed by the new sports cams and springs, together with the higher engine speeds, the light-alloy pushrods were hollow and barrel-shaped with a diameter of $\frac{3}{8}$in (9.5mm) at the middle and $\frac{9}{32}$in (7mm) at the ends.

Vic Willoughby considered that 'the trump card for power is the siamesed exhaust plumbing and its specially developed silencer.' Strangely, given his favourable opinion, this was an optional extra (but at no extra charge). If no preference was voiced when ordering the new machine, separate pipes and silencers were fitted ex-factory, something Willoughby could not understand: 'In view of the appreciable power difference, however, there seems no point in ordering a Sports Special with separate exhausts, especially if racing is contemplated.'

So what were the overall effects of these engine changes? According to *The Motor Cycle*:

> the power bonus on the six-hundred spans from 4,500rpm (about 75mph [120km/h] in top gear) to the peak of 7,000rpm ... Whereas on the standard Dominators the best torque [i.e. pulling power] occurs in the region of 4,000rpm (597cc) and 4,500rpm (497cc), both equivalent to a top-gear speed of 65 to 70mph, the peaks have been pushed up to 5,500rpm and 5,750rpm (90mph in both cases) on the comparable Sports Specials. At revs below 4,500 the new engines have slightly less punch than the standard versions.

Ex-racer Willoughby also pointed out that:

ABOVE: The first of the Dominator series, the Model 7, made its debut at the end of 1948. The engine displaced 497cc with bore and stroke dimensions of 66 × 72.6mm.

Cover from the 1951 Norton catalogue giving pride of place to the Model 7. The Dominator was designed by Bert Hopwood. All the early production bikes featured plunger rear suspension.

For the 1953 season the Model 7 gained a swinging-arm frame, new silencers, underslung pilot lamp and revised rocker lubrication.

At the end of 1953 the new Dominator 88 made its bow sporting the famous Featherbed frame, which had been developed on the factory's racing models, but it still retained the Model 7's cast-iron cylinder head.

LEFT: For 1955 the 88 (and Model 7) gained a new light alloy head, new dual seat and polished fork slides. The 88 also gained a welded sub-frame (previously bolted up).

Instrument console from the 1955 88 incorporating speedometer, ammeter and light switch.

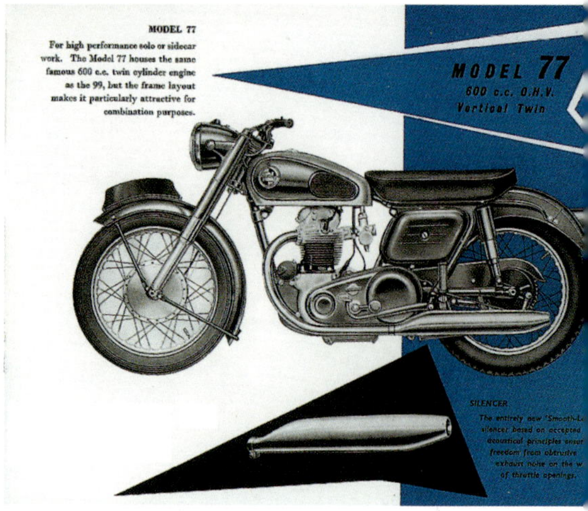

ABOVE: The Model 77 used a single downtube cradle frame (similar to the later Model 7) and was sold for both solo and sidecar work.

LEFT: For 1956 the Model 7 was dropped from the range, while the 99 (shown) and Model 77 were added; both had a larger 596cc engine.

'Dominating this jet age...' was the Norton theme for its 1958 range brochure, which was published in October 1957. Both the 99 (shown here) and the 88 now employed a.c. electrics, with the option of twin carburettors from May 1958 (at extra cost).

ABOVE: The new six-fifty Manxman arrived in 1961, initially for export only. This employed the new Slimline Featherbed frame (introduced for 1960) and a 649cc (68 × 89mm) engine producing a claimed 52bhp.

BELOW: Features of the Manxman from the original factory brochure including frame, front brake, forks, crankshaft and airflow for twin-carburettor cylinder head.

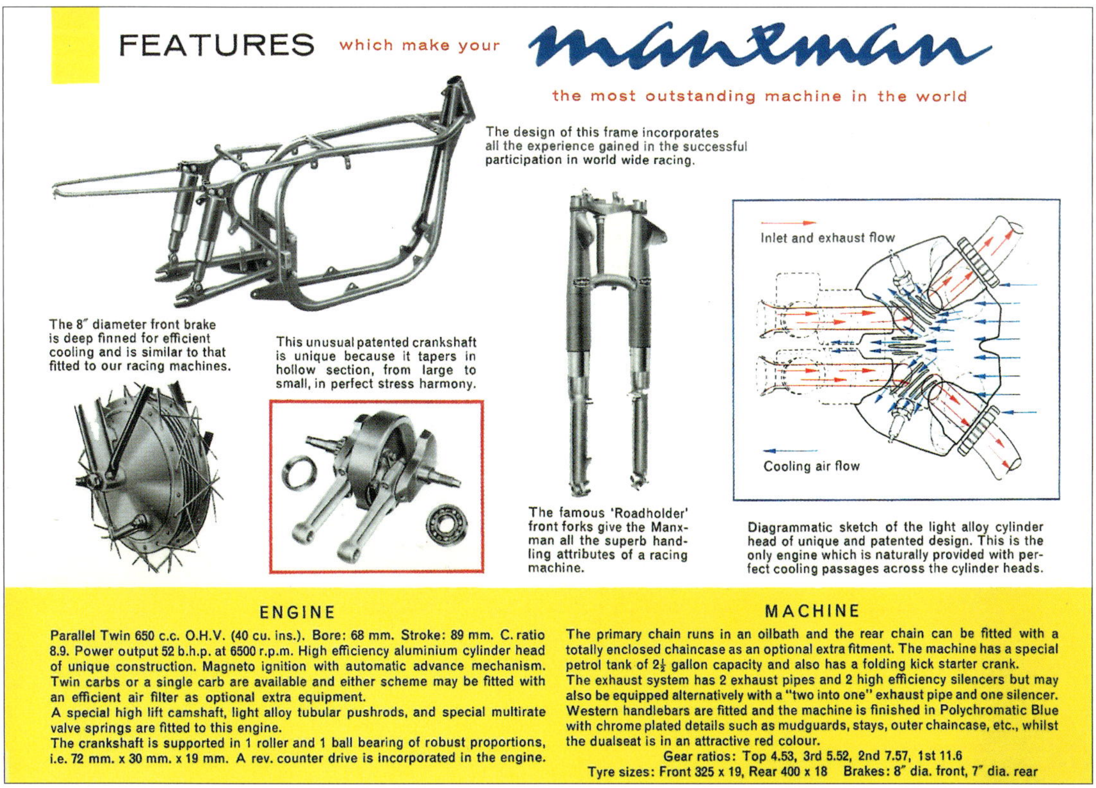

Rear enclosure had arrived for the 1960 season and was continued for 1961. Known as the De Luxe, it didn't prove popular.

The Slimline frame debuted for the 1960 model year; from the side view it can easily be identified by the curved section of the sub-frame, whereas the original Wideline frame had straight tubes.

The 650SS (Sports Special) and 88SS, as they were for the 1962 season, with silver/black finish and chrome-plated mudguards.

Dunstall 500 Domiracer at Mallory Park, September 1964.

1967 Dunstall 745cc Atlas-powered racer.

Australian racer Graeme Noonan's home-brewed 650SS Domiracer, with trophies won to 2003, including the Hartwell Club Classic Championship; 2001.

Typical Dominator Café racer (built from a Wideline 99) with racing tanks, clip-ons, rear-sets, chrome headlamp, Girling rear shocks and siamesed exhaust; Mallory Park, summer 2001.

> a test of one of the larger Sports Specials both on the open road and at the MIRA proving ground convinces me that they will take a lot of holding in marathon races ... And the more bends and corners there are on the circuit the rosier will be the chances of success. For this there is a threefold reason. First the brakes cut speed really smartly on the approach to bends (although slight front-drum ovality on the test model caused fork flutter at high speeds). Secondly the Sports Special corners so delightfully as to make it well-nigh impossible not to get the best out of the bend, especially under power. Finally, the acceleration away from corners is a match for the best.

To fit the optional rev counter, a cost option at £5 5s plus £1 1s 8d UK purchase tax, the small plate on the timing cover was removed. Ball-end clutch and brake levers complied with racing rules.

Costing £246 9s (basic) and £297 5s 7d (with purchase tax) when launched in spring 1961, the 99SS was the hottest Dominator yet.

When the 1962 Norton range arrived in September 1961, the 88SS was updated in line with the newly introduced 650SS, but the 99SS remained unchanged, as did the other two 99s, the standard and de Luxe. Prices, however, had risen: the standard cost £290 19s 5d, the de Luxe £297 1s 5d and the SS £300 2s 5d – all including UK purchase tax.

The 99 series, now effectively replaced by the new 650, didn't have much longer to run; all three versions were discontinued in August 1962. However, in many ways the 99 was an excellent bike: enough performance for most – certainly in the definitive SS guise – but largely without the dreaded vibes of many British vertical twins.

Norton 99 café racer for sale at the Bob McIntyre Memorial Meeting, East Fortune airfield, June 2005.

The AMC Gearbox

In spring 1956 the Nortons coming off the production line were equipped with a new four-speed gearbox manufactured at the AMC Woolwich plant in south-east London.

Although the basic features of the design were clearly based on the previous Norton gearbox, there were many changes, not only to its shape but to some major features, including the foot-change and clutch operation. Not only was gear changing claimed to be easier, but there was now a cam-action clutch.

The new assembly was notably more compact, but the gear clusters on the layshaft and mainshaft were very similar to the outgoing type. Engagement of all gears except first was by dogs. On the mainshaft the third gear pinion had dogs on both sides and moved on splines to engage top or second gear. The layshaft setup was much as before, but the second gear pinion incorporated dogs on one side only and pegs on the other, sliding to engage third or first gear. Block-type dogs were employed and the number in each case was three.

A fair amount of backlash was allowed between the dogs to allow gear engagement, and a 3-degree undercut had been provided on the mating faces of the dogs to ensure that the gears would not jump out under load.

The first gear layshaft pinion had been provided with four holes with which to engage the four pegs on the layshaft sliding member. This pinion, free to turn on the layshaft, was bronze-bushed, the bush being spun in for security. The other gears free to move on their shafts – second gear on the mainshaft and third gear on the layshaft – featured fully floating bronze bushes.

Ball race bearings supported the direct-drive gear, the offside (right) end of the mainshaft and the nearside (left) end of the layshaft. At the other end of the layshaft, following previous Norton tradition, ran in a bronze bush within the hollow kickstarter shaft. Steel bushes supported the kickstart shaft in the inner and outer end covers of the 'box.

The pawl on the inner end of the shaft engaged with an internal ratchet formed on the layshaft first gear pinion. A change from the previous gearbox saw the kickstart spring now being anchored in the end cover and not in the support bush.

The gears were selected by a pair of hardened steel forks, one actuating the mainshaft sliding member, and the other the one on the layshaft. These forks were carried on a spindle, which was screwed into the nearside (left) wall of the gearbox shell, and supported at the other end in the inner end cover. Following conventional practice, a peg on the body of each fork engaged in one of two profiled slots in a cam plate situated at the front of the gear assembly.

For gear indexing a spring-loaded plunger featuring a conical head engaged with a series of notches on the periphery of the cam plate. The plunger housing screwed into the base of the gearbox shell. To aid movement from one gear to the next, the cam-plate periphery was of a slightly humped pattern between the notches.

The cam plate pivoted in a bronze bush set in the front wall of the gearbox. In unit with this plate was a small pinion with which meshed a sector pivoted nearer the offside end of the casing. An extension of the sector beyond the pivot passed through a slot in the wall of the inner end cover and featured a jaw end equipped with a knuckle pin. A peg on the reverse side of the ratchet plate of the positive-stop foot-change mechanism was a sliding fit in the transverse bore of the pin.

The foot-change mechanism was of the conventional double-ratchet and double-ended-pawl pattern.

All the pinions and the shaft of the AMC gearbox were manufactured of En.34, a 2 per cent nickel-molybdenum case-hardening steel. Internal ratios of the indirect gear were: 1st 2.67:1; 2nd 1.77:1; 3rd 1.35:1. In top gear (fourth) the drive was direct.

An entirely new type of clutch operation had been developed. This mechanism embodied a cam action in conjunction with a ball and a roller, which Norton claimed provided higher efficiency with great durability.

Within the hollow mainshaft was the conventional clutch thrust rod. Seated in the inner end cover (and trapping the outer race of the mainshaft ball bearing) was a sleeve secured by a slotted locking ring. This sleeve featured two parallel extensions, one on each side of its axis; between the ends of the extensions a ¾in-diameter roller was freely mounted. A ½in ball was a running fit in the bore of the sleeve and between it and the roller, located by the extensions, 'floated' the clutch-operating lever. This lever incorporated a holder for a cable nipple and had a concave, semi-circular profile seating on the ball and an opposing cam profile that bore on the roller.

Pulling the cable caused the lever to pivot round the ball. As it did so the cam profile rode up on the roller, thereby increasing the centre distances between roller and ball. Since the roller centre was fixed, the ball was forced away from it and thus moved the clutch thrust rod. The lever had a positive off position (when the centre distance between ball and roller was minimal) and therefore adjustment was provided at the clutch pressure plate to enable the basic running clearance to be obtained. There was also the usual cable adjuster on top of the gearbox.

The clutch incorporated in its centre a rubber vane-type shock absorber (cush drive). The clutch featured five friction plates (including the sprocket plate) with Klinger insert material, which the factory claimed had a very high coefficient of friction. An innovation was adjustment for the clutch springs, making it possible to compensate for uneven spring pressure that otherwise might cause plate tilting and consequent drag.

This gearbox was to prove a great success, so much so that it was to be adopted across the board for all AMC group heavyweight singles and twins, not just in the Norton range, but also in AJS and Matchless models. A racing version was to become standard equipment on the Manx Norton, AJS 7R and Matchless G50.

7 Domiracer

The first use of the twin-cylinder Norton for road racing (and with it the birth of the 'Domiracer') was when a pair, suitably modified by their owners, took part in the 1951 Senior Manx Grand Prix. These machines (Model 7s) were remarkably standard, with little more than open exhausts and revised gear ratios. This original appearance, though, was hardly earth-shattering: Harry Bent came home fifty-fifth, while John Waite brought up the field in sixty-fourth and last place. In reality the whole event was hardly noticed at the time.

The Norton factory's own attempts to construct a racer out of the twin did not come until January 1953, when a pair of specially adapted Dominator 88 models with Featherbed frames were built at the Bracebridge Street works. Works rider Ken Kavanagh recalled that he did the actual bench-testing together with Leo Kuzmicki, a Polish engineer who worked at Norton from 1949 until late 1953. (For the subsequent history of these machines *see* Chapter 10.)

When two of the Daytona-type bikes appeared at the Manx GP that September, ridden by travelling marshal and racer George Costain, many observers wrongly thought that this would be the prelude to a Norton-type Matchless G45 (the latter based on the road-going G9 model). But in reality Norton did not follow this route for some eight years.

In between, several examples of the production Dominator 88 were campaigned in the annual Thruxton long-distance event for series production roadsters (*see* Chapter 9).

The Domiracer Arrives

In the 1 June 1961 issue of *The Motor Cycle*, Doug Hele, then Norton development engineer, commented:

> Experiments during the past four years have indicated that the Dominator would readily respond to development so that it should not be difficult to extract as much speed as from the Manx [Norton's pukka dohc single-cylinder racing motorcycle], maybe even more. Even with the engine in its present semi-standard form we start with an advantage, for it is already 28lb [12.7kg] lighter without having to resort to Elektron crankcase castings. Moreover, it is smoother, so we can get away with a much lighter frame. Finally it has a lower centre of gravity, which should ease handling problems.

Tests at MIRA (the motor industry's testing track near Nuneaton, Warwickshire) had shown that the twin possessed both speed and reliability. The track, however, could not test the high-speed handling. Only the Isle of Man could do that and fully expose any shortcomings in that respect.

Both the Roadholder forks (shorter) and Featherbed frame (lower) provided the new machine with a 2.5in (64mm) height advantage over the production Manx racer. Unlike the latter, the twin featured a neatly styled glassfibre rear mudguard, which also formed the seat pan, while between the frame loops there was a light-alloy oil tank, located at the top by a cross-bolt that passed through the tank with the base resting on a rubber-padded cross-member. The familiar Manx-type gearchange linkage was dispensed with and instead a simple pedal projected rearwards from the gearbox end cover.

The factory then took the bold move of taking the machine to race in no less an event than the Isle of Man Senior TT. Initially the Manx fairies looked with disfavour on the new Domiracer. The first attempt to practice on the evening of Monday, 5 June 1961 was forestalled by carburation gremlins. Then on Tuesday morning the fairing had to be modified before the scrutineers would approve it. Having set the sixth fastest time on his own single-cylinder Manx, Phil Read heaved the experimental twin into life on a glistening wet road. Despite fog on the mountain section of the course, Phil reached Creg-ny-Baa in, as *The Motor Cycle* described, 'a commendably short time; but here the two parted company and finished up with a generous coating of mud and grass.' Tearing off the battered fairing he completed the lap in 37 minutes 3 seconds. Tribulations apart, Phil Read was most impressed, reporting the handling as good as that of the Manx and the power equally impressive. Even so, later during the practice week the Australian Honda works star Tom Phillis took over the factory Dominator.

By then a new engine had been fitted, providing more power than the standard unit previously employed. Observers noted that Tom's standing start lap, although not timed, appeared rapid.

A 'Flyer, with Real Potential'

Then came the race, which everyone thought would be yet another MV Agusta walkover for Gary Hocking, who was piloting the sole Italian 'Fire Engine' in the race. At the end of the first lap Hocking was in front, with Mike Hailwood, Bob McIntyre and Phil Read on specially tuned Manx singles leading the British charge.

Behind them came the Domiracer, going very quickly indeed with a first lap speed of 98.93mph (159.2km/h), giving Tom Phillis fifth place, something, *The Motor Cycle* said, 'he could be proud of if he blew up on the next lap.' On the following lap Hailwood was right on Hocking's tail after the MV rider made a mistake at Ballacraine. The big news, however, was that Phillis had lapped at 100.36mph (161.5km/h). This hoisted the Australian into fourth place, only 1.4 seconds away from McIntyre, who had also moved up on Read.

Prior to the race, Norton development chief Hele had predicted that his creation was a 'flyer with real potential', but few had taken his words seriously. Now, suddenly, everyone could see his statement was entirely accurate.

The Australian Tom Phillis piloting the works Domiracer to a sensational third place in the 1961 Senior. In the process the machine became the first ohv engine and twin cylinder to lap the famous Mountain circuit at over 100mph (160km/h).

Until the end of lap 4, the leading four places remained unchanged, then race leader Hocking made a dramatic and unscheduled pit stop, and Hailwood took over at the front. Although Hocking restarted, he was destined to retire at his pit the next time around.

Norton Take the Top Three Places

At the finish, after six laps and 226.38 miles (364.31km), there was the amazing picture of three Nortons in the rostrum position in a Senior TT – the first time this had happened since the Geoff Duke Norton era of the early 1950s! But most surprising of all was the third place Domiracer. In its first race Tom Phillis had completed the longest and most gruelling of all events counting towards the World Championships. For the record this was completed in 2 hours, 17 minutes, 31.2 seconds.

Later, at the presentation at the Villa Marina in Douglas, Tom was full of praise for the experimental Norton twin. Although there had been a slight falling off in power during the last half lap (one piston crown having slightly touched the cylinder head), no other problem was obvious when the engine was later stripped for examination. Tom's verdict was that steering and acceleration were superior to those of a standard Manx model, but top speed was perhaps fractionally slower. Also the lighter weight made the front more prone to lift on full-bore bumps.

There was no doubt that the third place of the experimental Norton twin was the major talking point in the period immediately after the 1961 TT races. *The Motor Cycle* commented:

> In the technical sense, this year's TT series did not come into focus until the very end. That was when Tom Phillis's great third place in the Senior race, with a best lap of 100.36mph, demonstrated the exciting potential of the experimental Norton pushrod twin, still in the infancy of development by Doug Hele!

A Successful Twin at Last?

Before its Isle of Man performance many so-called experts had poured scorn on the likelihood of what Hele was attempting: a machine that could match the performance of the 499cc twin-cam Manx single, but could score on lower production costs and easier maintenance. The doubters pointed to the relative lack of success gained by the Triumph Grand Prix and Matchless G45, both of which had also been based on production ohv twins. By the end of the 1961 Senior TT, however, the newcomer was being viewed in a totally different light, as the prototype of a model with several clear advantages and which had considerable possibilities in both development potential and marketing costs.

Taking the latter point first, Hele estimated that the twin could be marketed at up to 20 per cent more cheaply than the Manx model (on which items such as the cam-box, bevel gears, valves, crankshaft assembly and piston were particularly expensive to manufacture), while the twin offered not only cheaper costs but easier maintenance.

Functionally, the twin's interest came from its compromise between the two extreme engineering approaches to racing motorcycle design. In the early 1960s these were represented by the sheer power of a four (or six, or eight, as had been tried by MV Agusta and Moto Guzzi respectively), with its penalty of greater weight and bulk, together with a higher centre of gravity, or the Moto Guzzi idea of emphasizing ultra-light weight, extreme slimness and the lowest centre of gravity by utilizing a horizontal single with its inevitable lower power output. Since, for a given swept volume, multiplying cylinders multiplies breathing potential, a twin comes somewhere between a single and a four on power. But when installed vertically (as with the Domiracer), the twin is (or should be) much less cumbersome than a four, and if kept slim enough it should enjoy a considerable advantage in penetration over the wider multi.

As it was lighter than the Manx, the Domiracer also had the advantage in acceleration, braking and handling. If Norton had chosen to follow Manx practice and employed a light-alloy cylinder barrel and Elektron crankcases, the difference would have been even greater. Constructed from thinner tubing than the single-cylinder Manx, the frame, as already mentioned, was also lower, thus again helping penetration. So the lower centre of gravity, combined with a shorter wheelbase, offered improved cornering abilities.

Two Engines

Two experimental engines were tried in the Isle of Man. Both used valves of standard size, so once again breathing could have been improved, and the roadster's 66 × 72.6mm bore and stroke. One differed from the Dominator 88SS only in so far as the camshaft, inlet ports and valve gear were concerned. The other engine, the one used by Tom Phillis in the race, was more extensively modified and offered, it was claimed, not only a 5 per cent power advantage, but also smoother running. The latter also had the advantage that it was not subject to the

Tom Phillis with the works development five-hundred Domiracer at Mallory Park, Race of the Year, September 1961.

same level of vibration as the stock unit. Crankshaft strength had been increased by larger dimensions and using larger main bearings: roller on the nearside (left), ballrace on the offside (right). The plain white-metal big-ends (and small ends) were also upped in diameter, while the length of the light-alloy connecting rods was reduced. With a compression ratio of 11:1, the full-skirt pistons were both shorter and lighter than the standard components, but also employed only one compression ring, this being of the Dykes L-section type. A cylinder head from the new six-fifty Manxman, later to be marketed in the UK as the 650SS, was employed because it used a steeper inlet port downdraught and wider splaying of the exhaust ports for increased cooling.

The centres of the inlet ports were further apart so that a pair of Amal 1³⁄₁₆in (30mm) carbs could be fitted. The relatively narrow angle of 58 degrees between the valve stems (the exhaust stems were inclined at 30 degrees, the inlets only 28 degrees) ensured compact combustion chambers with a low surface-to-volume ratio for good thermal efficiency and a respectably short flame trail. There was no squish band. The valves were of nimonic steel, and the clearances were adjusted by turning the eccentric rocker spindles. This design not only cut reciprocating weight by a small amount, but it also meant that the rocker ends could be ground to give line contact with the valve tips instead of employing the conventional ball-end type adjusters. The aluminium pushrods had been lengthened to reach down into the flat-base tappets, and were hollowed to reduce their weight by half. In place of the normal bronze bushes for the camshaft more efficient rollers were used, while the rocker gear was lubricated by a pressure bleed from the timing cover in place of the standard model's scavenge bleed. As used in the TT, output was limited by valve float coming in at 7,400rpm, and so Hele employed the 4.1:1 top gear ratio of the standard 499cc Manx for the Phillis machine.

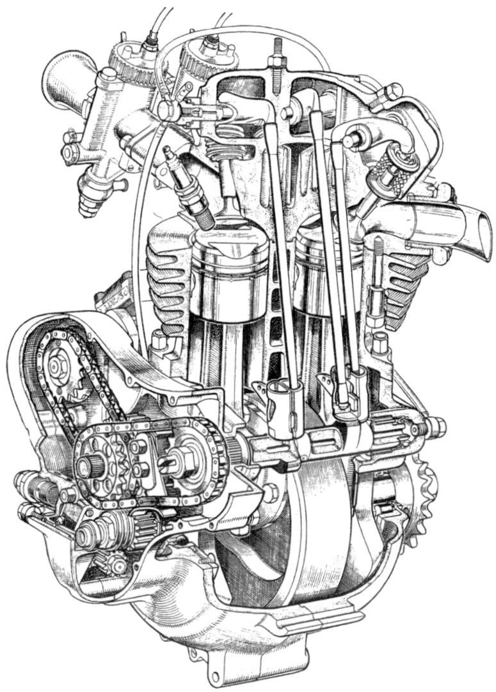

The Doug Hele-prepared Domiracer engine. Non-standard features included: needle roller bearings for camshaft; ultra-light, flat-base cam followers, pressure oil feed to the rocker spindles (eccentric for valve clearance adjustment), two-ring pistons and twin Amal GP carburettors.

A Missed Chance

An important step in the Domiracer's development would have been to make suitable changes to exploit the engine's breathing potential at higher rpm. Hele was convinced that 8,000rpm was easily within the development team's reach. Power output of the 1961 Senior TT third-place bike was around 50bhp, so it should have been possible to comfortably exceed the output of the five-hundred Manx, which was then producing a claimed 52bhp. Actually, it was later discovered the TT Domiracer produced 58bhp at 7,800rpm and was 'safe' to 9,000!

Derek Minter rode the factory machine with both 500 and 650cc engines. He is seen here with the former at Esso Bend, Oulton Park, on Easter Monday, 22 April 1962.

Following the TT, in which the Domiracer made history by becoming the first twin or pushrod engine to lap the Mountain circuit at over 100mph, Norton was to receive considerable requests to build a production version. In August 1961 all they would say was: 'We will not be marketing the Domiracer next year (1962). The established Manx singles in three-fifty and five-hundred sizes are to be continued with probably a few modifications, and the production schedules have already been settled.'

In the author's opinion a great opportunity was thus squandered. As well as winning the success garnered in the TT, this had been a chance to exploit it commercially by building and selling the Domiracer. Considering how expensive the Manx engine unit was to construct, the price could have been considerably less to the customer. Not only this, but on the evidence from the TT the pushrod twin could, with further development, also have been faster to add to its already known advantages of acceleration, production costs and ease of maintenance. As it

The Norton Domiracer 88 formerly raced by Andy Molnar (now the manufacturer of the Molnar Manx), photographed by the author at Donington Park, September 2005.

was, for the remainder of 1961 very little was seen or heard of the Domiracer.

Stagnation

In January 1962 Doug Hele was reported by *The Motor Cycle* as saying: 'Watch out for quite a number of factory Norton twins, and in several forms.' However, even though the 650SS went on sale in the UK that year, gaining much success in production events (*see* Chapter 8), the Domiracer project stagnated. Derek Minter had the occasional short circuit race and practised on the ex-Phillis machine for the 1962 Senior TT, but for the race he decided to stick with his own single. The same rider did, however, race a larger 650 version, winning in the process his first-ever outing on the larger-engined bike at Brands Hatch in the Unlimited class. But with Norton in the process of moving from Bracebridge Street to the AMC works in south London, together with the decline in AMC's financial fortunes, the entire Domiracer project was shelved, with the existing bikes and spares being sold off to Reg Dearden and Paul Dunstall later that year.

Dunstall gained considerable success with the Domiracer in subsequent years (*see* Chapter 14), but this, of course, was without the

Australian Norton enthusiast, Graeme Noonan, with his 1962 Domiracer (formerly a 650SS) and 1953 ex-Bernie Allen Cooper Manx Mark 7 Formula 3 racing car; November 2002.

advantage of continuing factory engineering development. Meanwhile, Reg Dearden did very little with his Domiracer haul, concentrating instead upon his existing single-cylinder Manx business.

A few privateers built their own Domiracers. Probably the most successful of these was the Austrian star Rudi Thalhammer, who raced his model at Grand Prix level and top international events during the period 1963–64.

The Domiracer could and should have brought a new era in Norton racing at factory level. Instead, with its fortunes controlled by the crumbling AMC empire, the once great marque was destined to slip into a downward spiral.

In the final analysis, the Domiracer was the ideal replacement for the long-running Manx single, but it was a chance passed by, a truly sad fate for a concept that had promised so much during its 1961 Senior TT debut. But finally, instead of being developed to its full potential, it simply slipped quietly away.

Doug Hele

Doug Hele will forever be remembered for his association with the successes gained by the Triumph and BSA triples during the early days of 750 Formula 1 (the forerunner of today's Super Bike racing). But there was much, much more to Doug Hele's engineering achievements than this. In fact he was very much involved with both the Manx Norton and its twin-cylinder brother, the Domiracer. He was even responsible for supervising the development of the series production Dominator roadster models.

As a young man, Doug had entered the engineering world via the Austin car company at Longbridge towards the end of the Second World War. He then transferred to the Bristol-based Douglas marque in 1945, and two years later he joined Joe Craig's racing department at Norton as a draughtsman. In 1949 he moved again, this time to BSA, where he stayed for another seven years before returning to Bracebridge Street in 1956 as chief development engineer.

Working under such luminaries as Bert Hopwood and Joe Craig had both positive and negative aspects. Under the former (at BSA) Hele was largely responsible for the potentially exciting MC1 250cc dohc Grand Prix racing project. However, when BSA's managing director, James Leek, asked Hopwood to guarantee that the newcomer could win its debut race, Hopwood backed down. Hele was always bitter about this incident, as it was this that caused the entire project to be abandoned. Shortly before his death in November 2001, Hele said: 'In my opinion, he (Hopwood) was a weak man unwilling to stand up to the pressure which was brought on him.'

Equally, working with Craig was sometimes problematic. The Ulsterman was not keen on entirely new designs, preferring instead steady development of the existing dohc single-cylinder design. Since Craig's salary and job centred around winning races year after year, it is perhaps easier to appreciate his unwillingness to explore new and untried designs. But, of course, this meant that Hele was restricted in what he could achieve during his first period at Norton. When he returned in 1956 Craig was no longer there, but Norton's independence had also gone: instead it had become part of the AMC Group, whose purse-strings were controlled by London-based accountants.

However, Doug Hele still achieved considerable advances during the late 1950s. He improved the Manx series of production racers and designed the desmodromic cylinder head (used on a works development Manx experimentally). Of more relevance to this book, of course, he also worked on the Domiracer, plus the 88, 99 and 650 SS series, and finally, the Atlas.

AMC's decision to close the Bracebridge Street works sealed Doug's fate at Norton and he quit a few days later to take up a new post at the BSA Group, where he came under the autocratic Edward Turner. But at least it led Hele into jointly designing the Triumph Trident/BSA Rocket 3, which in turn led to the hugely successful 3-cylinder racers that dominated F1 racing during the early 1970s.

8 650

The first concrete evidence that Norton had upped the displacement of their ohv vertical twin Dominator series engine to a full '650' was published in early November 1960. If British enthusiasts got excited, however, it was to prove somewhat premature because the first production version, the Manxman, was for the American market only (*see* Chapter 10).

The first six-fifty, the Manxman, was an American export-only model and arrived at the beginning of 1961. The definitive version, the 650SS (Sports Special) went on sale in the UK during early 1962.

The new model had had the stroke of the existing 597cc Dominator 99 engine lengthened from 82 to 89mm, giving a capacity of 647cc; the bore size remained unchanged at 68mm. It also had two Amal Monobloc 376 1⅙in (26mm) carburettors, downdraught induction tracts, high compression pistons, hi-lift cams and widely splayed exhaust ports.

American features abounded with high, wide and typically Stateside handlebars, acres of chrome plate and a colourful metallic blue paint job (frame, fuel and oil tanks, battery box, headlamp shell and upper fork components – plus a snazzy red covered dual seat). Tyre sizes were 3.25 × 19 front and 4.00 × 18 rear. A rev counter was part of the standard equipment – as was all the chrome plating. It was also possible to order specially, and at additional cost, the Dominator de Luxe panelling, a siamesed exhaust and an air filter.

A UK Debut

Motor Cycle News revealed in its 20 September 1961 issue that British customers would at last be able to buy the new six-fifty, saying:

> High performance is the keynote of the Norton range for 1962. New to the range are three versions of the Dominator '650', based on the powerful Manxman twin sold in the USA. All have a new cylinder head, similar to that used in the experimental racing 'twin' which made such an impressive debut in the Senior TT. [*See* Chapter 7.]

The Motor Cycle covered the same story with the headline: 'Searing six-fifty Twin in Triplicate.' The article continued: 'The existence of a bigger-capacity Norton was, of course, no secret. Indeed, as the Manxman, a six-fifty model has been exported in considerable quantities for almost a year. But that doesn't lessen its impact on the home market one whit.'

The New Engine

Although the engine displacement at 647cc was only 50cc more than the existing Dominator 99, there were far more differences than the casual observer might have realized.

The increased capacity and stroke of the new engine (*see* above) required a stiffer crankshaft, which, although based on the

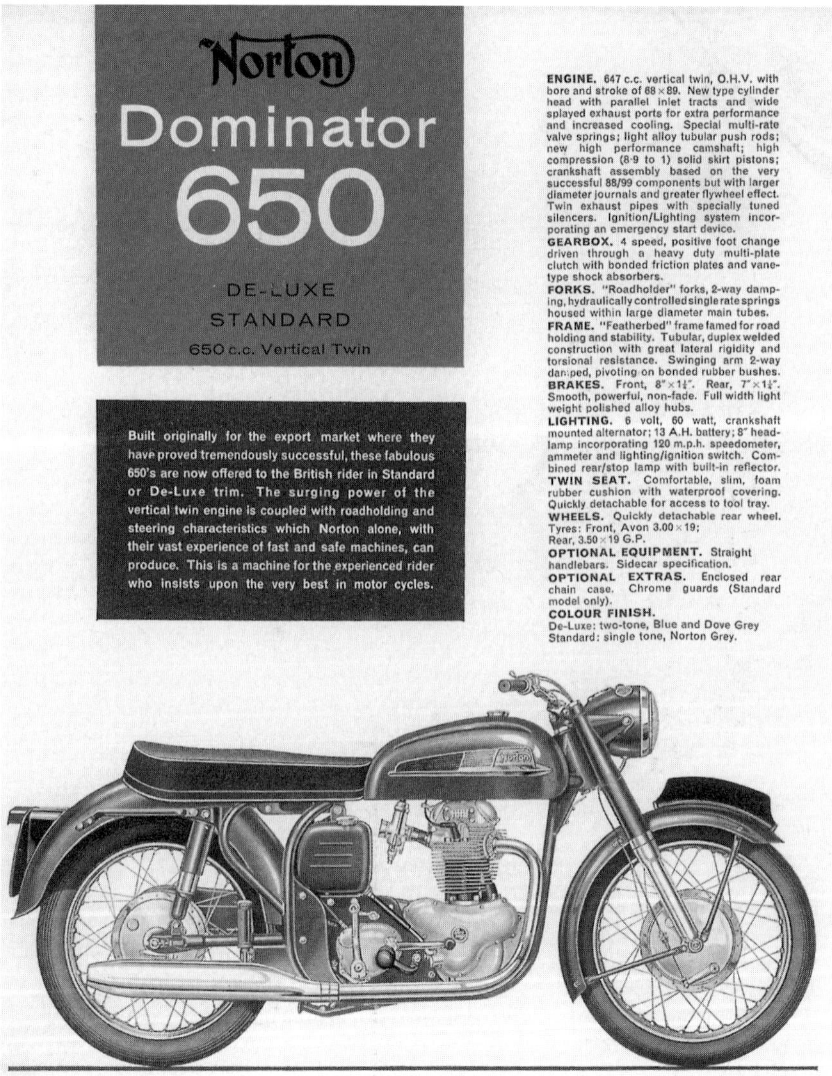

Besides the two-carb sports model, British buyers were also offered the single-carb de Luxe (with rear enclosure) and the naked Standard versions.

Dominator 88/99, featured a wider flywheel. At the same time the big-end journals were enlarged to 1¾in (44mm) to cope with the additional power output.

Derived directly from that of the works Domiracer, the new light-alloy cylinder head featured widely splayed cxhaust ports and parallel inlet tracts. On the standard and de Luxe versions a bifurcated inlet manifold and a single Amal Monobloc type 389 carburettor – of 1⅛in (33mm) – was employed, whereas the third member of the new trio had twin Monobloc Type 376 instruments of $1\frac{1}{16}$in (27mm).

Valve springs were of the multi-rate type, while the solid skirt piston had a compression ratio of 8.9:1 on all three versions.

Light alloy, taper-section tubular pushrods (operated by a sports-type camshaft) showed that the Norton development team had given the new, larger engine a more sporting flavour than earlier Dominators, except the limited production 88 and 99 Sports Special (*see* Chapters 4 and 6).

The gearbox, as on the 99, was of the normal 4-speed Norton-AMC pattern. This provided overall ratios of 4.53, 5.52, 7.52 and 11.6:1. The clutch had been given an additional (fifth) plate to cope with the increased power and torque the larger engine generated. There were also stronger clutch springs (making for a heavier clutch action than before.

Avon Grand Prix Rear Tyre

The running gear, including the frame, forks, brakes and other components, was identical to that of the smaller Dominators, but a notable change was the fitment, as standard, of the Avon Grand Prix race-derived rear tyre. This had been specially developed by Norton in conjunction with the Avon tyre company, based in Melksham, Wiltshire. This programme had included many high-speed miles on such diverse roads as the M1 motorway, the MIRA test centre, near Nuneaton, and the Isle of Man TT course. As *The Motor Cycle* said at the time of the launch: 'the tyre is virtually a racing design adapted for sustained high-average road work and is therefore safer for that purpose

The 1961 650 Standard

Engine	Air-cooled ohv twin with vertical cylinders, alloy head and cast-iron barrel, two main bearings, 360-degree, 3-piece crankshaft, split con-rods and shell big-end bearings, coil valve springs, vertically-split aluminium crankcases
Bore	68mm
Stroke	89mm
Displacement	646cc
Compression ratio	8.3:1
Lubrication	Gear pump; dry sump
Ignition	Magneto (battery/coil from 1962; alternator used with both systems), 6-volt
Carburettor	Amal 389 Monobloc 1⅛in
Primary drive	Simplex chain
Final drive	Chain
Gearbox	AMC 4-speed, positive stop, foot-change
Frame	Norton Slimline Featherbed, full cradle
Front suspension	Norton Roadholders, oil-damped, telescopic
Rear suspension	Swinging arm, with oil-damped, twin shock absorbers
Front brake	8in full-width drum, SLS
Rear brake	7in full-width drum, SLS
Tyres	3.25 × 19 front (3.00 × 19 for 1962); 4.00 × 19 rear (3.50 × 19 for 1962)
Wheelbase	55.5in (1,410mm)
Ground clearance	5.5in (140mm)
Seat height	31in (787mm)
Fuel tank capacity	3.62gal (16.5ltr)
Dry weight	398lb (180.5kg)
Maximum power	42bhp @ 6,750rpm
Top speed	110mph (177km/h)

than would be a standard-pattern tyre.' It is also worth pointing out that, in producing the Grand Prix, Avon were the first company to embrace the idea of producing a specialized high-speed tyre for road use. Later, Dunlop produced its now famous TT 100 tyre. Since the 1980s, of course, almost every tyre manufacturer has offered its own race-type rubber, but Avon – and Norton – were there first.

The 650SS

The top-of-the-range Dominator 650 Super Sports (more commonly known simply as the 650SS) combined, Norton claimed, 'Ultra-high performance allied to the highest degree of rider safety.' It was, at the time, the most powerful Norton roadster ever put on the market. This bike differed from the standard and de Luxe versions by employing, as well as twin carbs, a balance pipe between the inlet tracts to promote smooth running at low engine speeds. Another difference was that it (and the latest 88SS) used magneto ignition, with automatic advance. The lesser models retained coil ignition, with a Lucas RM19 alternator supplying sufficient current for lighting purposes.

Standard equipment on the latest SS model included a flat-type handlebar and racing-type, ball-end control levers; optional extras were a folding kickstart lever, rev counter, fully enclosed rear chaincase and chromium-plated mudguards.

It was also notable that for all three of the new six-fifties the factory recommended that separate exhaust pipes of small inside diameter be used, as these had been found to give the best results on test. However, siamesed pipes were available without extra cost if required, with Norton saying: 'maximum speed is not affected by their use, but there is a slight falling-off in acceleration.' The advice that the separate exhausts worked better than the siamesed system was in direct contrast to that given for the 99SS (*see* Chapter 6). The reason for this differing advice could be found in the use of the new downdraught-induction cylinder head.

Early 1962 650SS engine, but fitted with later, non-standard Amal concentric carbs.

The prices of the 1962 model year 650 Nortons were as follows: standard £240 10s (basic), £293 8s 2d (including UK tax); de Luxe £245 10s (basic), £299 10s 2d (including UK tax); 650SS £255 (basic) and £311 2s (including UK tax).

As for colour schemes, the standard 650 was all grey, de Luxe 650 blue and grey, while the 650SS was black with a silver tank.

Test Opinions

Both *Motor Cycling* (14 February 1962) and *The Motor Cycle* (15 February) published full test reports of this, the most sporting of all Dominator models. Since the former got in a day earlier, it's only fair to give its view first. The *Motor Cycling* test began:

> Extremely high maximum speed. Abundant stamina. Pleasant manners. Traditional Norton handling. Full road-equipment. Real comfort … that sums up Bracebridge Street's new-for-1962 sporting 'Dominator 650SS'. Motor Cycling's test sample of this twin-carburettor high-compression sports roadster was supplied fully run in. It was immediately ridden from Birmingham to the nearby MIRA track at Nuneaton for the standard neck-wringing session.

Despite deteriorating weather, Bruce Main-Smith achieved a mean speed with two-way runs of 111.9mph (180km/h). The individual, electronically timed speeds were 105.2mph (169.3km/h) into the westerly wind and 119.5 mph (192.3km/h) with it. He was impressed: 'The newcomer's ability to maintain high speeds into wind and uphill proved to be one of its strongest points.'

The MIRA tests showed the new 650SS to be:

> one of the fastest vertical twins on British roads … Like all Featherbed-framed Nortons, the 650SS steered divinely … The banking at MIRA is always an exacting test and shows up dramatically the slightest tendency to wandering at high speeds. Rounding the tight western curve, revving at 6,600 and still accelerating from the previous wind, it ran absolutely true despite the fact that water was draining off the 45-degree slope from a heavy rain shower …
>
> If anything, the roadholding of the 650SS was even better than its forerunners … [This] could be attributed to the Avon racing [GP] tyre on the rear wheel. The additional weight of the 650cc engine, with its sturdier bottom half to cope with the increased power, was in no way felt to be a handicap …
>
> As road experience mounted, it was also noticed that there were two cut-ins of power. The engine was most tractable at the bottom end, had plenty of low-speed punch and, in response to a big handful, would blast away from 30mph [48km/h] in third without the slightest objection … The most marked boost in the power as induction and exhaust came into full harmony, occurred at 4,300rpm (75mph in top). From then on one took firm hold of the bars to combat the surging

A 650SS-powered racing sidecar outfit at Brands Hatch, mid-1960s. Another SS, in solo production guise, is in the background.

> mile-gobbler trying to shoot from under the tester … All in all, the power characteristics of the 650SS were excellent – a sporting top end without the bad manners sometimes associated with such urge at low speeds.

But probably most impressive of all were the following comments: 'The unit was utterly tireless and stayed completely oil tight … Nor was there vibration at any rpm to dictate the amount of throttle to be used. The motor could be felt running but it did not produce any distressing tingling vibration.'

Another View

Another view of the same bike came from *The Motor Cycle*'s Vic Willoughby, who began his 650SS test with the following headline: 'Latest and largest in famous range approaches two miles a minute yet eats out of your hand.' After the usual introduction, Vic agreed about the lack of vibes, saying: 'By parallel twin standards the engine is smoother than average. Up to the stipulated rpm limit (6,800) vibration never bothered the rider, although at peak revs it caused the petrol tap to shut off until the cork-sleeved plunger was renewed.' He considered the reason for this comparative smoothness was due to the sturdier crankshaft.

Like his *Motor Cycling* rival, Vic Willoughby found the 650SS: 'something out of the ordinary above 4,000 rpm.' He also thought that the Avon Grand Prix rear tyre improved the handling.

As for maintenance, Vic had this to say:

> Save that the chaincase outer half must be removed to get at the clutch pressure plate adjustment, no problems are posed for maintenance. A penny serves to unfasten the dual seat and so reveal the tool kit. If required, the rear wheel can be removed without disturbing the chain or brake. Incidentally, a change from a falling to a rising rear-brake cam lever means that the finger adjuster on the brake rod is no longer tucked awkwardly behind the left-hand silencer but is really easy to reach.

The Motor Cycle achieved a mean (two-way) maximum speed of 111mph (178.6km/h) and a highest one-way figure of 118mph (189.9km/h).

Vic Willoughby summed up the newcomer by calling it: 'Norton's answer to the sportsman's prayer. It is a 49bhp roadster whose quietness, smoothness and lack of fuss makes its speed deceptive; a machine with such superb handling and braking as to make nearly two miles a minute as safe as a stroll in the garden.'

Non-standard 2LS front brake conversion on a 1962 650SS.

A Third View

A third view of the 650SS came from Charlie Rous in *Motor Cycle News*:

The 1962 650SS	
Engine	Air-cooled ohv twin with vertical cylinders, alloy head and cast-iron barrel, two main bearings, 360-degree, 3-piece crankshaft, split con-rods and shell big-end bearings, coil valve springs, vertically-split aluminium crankcases
Bore	68mm
Stroke	89mm
Displacement	646cc
Compression ratio	8.9:1
Lubrication	Gear pump; dry sump
Ignition	Magneto, 6-volt
Carburettor	2 × Amal 376 Monobloc 1⅟₁₆in
Primary drive	Simplex chain
Final drive	Chain
Gearbox	AMC 4-speed, positive stop, foot-change
Frame	Norton Slimline Featherbed, full cradle, twin front downtubes, welded-up sub-frame
Front suspension	Norton Roadholders, oil-damped, telescopic
Rear suspension	Swinging arm, with oil-damped, twin shock absorbers
Front brake	8in full-width drum, SLS
Rear brake	7in full-width drum, SLS
Tyres	3.00 × 19 front; 3.50 × 19 rear
Wheelbase	55.5in (1,410mm)
Ground clearance	5.5in (140mm)
Seat height	31in (787mm)
Fuel tank capacity	3.62gal (16.5ltr)
Dry weight	398lb (180.5kg)
Maximum power	49bhp @ 6,800rpm
Top speed	116mph (186.7km/h)

> If there was ever a steel fist in a velvet glove then that's the M1 mile-eater from Norton – the 650cc Super Sports. Docile in town traffic, a mild tweak of the throttle grip transforms it into a scintillating projectile capable of packing two miles into every minute. But sheer performance is not all. Such a road burner must incorporate so much more if it's safe and pleasurable to ride. Believe me, Norton have not failed in this respect.

It is interesting to note that Charlie Rous included a few factory recommendations in his piece, which was not so much a conventional test as his views on the machine and its characteristics. As with the other two commentators, Charlie thought that roadholding was further improved by the Avon GP rear tyre, though pointing out Norton's advice that 'the tyre pressure of 26lb for each wheel should be carefully maintained.'

He also explained the cold start procedure:

> After flooding the nearside float chamber at no time was it necessary to crank the lever more than three times before the engine responded ... A factory recommendation is to allow the engine a couple of minutes to warm up, after which the motor would idle reliably at just under 1,000 rpm.

Another factory recommendation, but one he did not mention, was that the optional rev counter fitted to the *Motor Cycle News*' test bike was the fitment of a Smiths chronometric instrument. The problem with this type was the slowness of its operation, whereas the superior racing magnetic type gave an instant, accurate reading, making it absolutely essential for racing purposes.

Machine of the Year

Norton were so pleased with their 1962 range that they decided to continue manufacturing the same bikes for 1963. When the details were released in mid-September 1962 there were very few changes. The 99 and 88 de Luxe models had been axed, while the 650 standard was now to be offered in black and polychromatic blue; the 650SS (and 88SS) would continue in black and silver. It was also revealed that the 650SS was the factory's bestseller, both at home and abroad. Sales Manager Ron Weeks commented: 'We are very pleased with it and no doubt its popularity along with other models will be continued during 1963.'

In response to the overwhelming support the model had received in the popular annual poll run by *Motor Cycle News*, the headline in its 26 December 1962 issue read: 'Norton 650 Super Sports is the machine of the year'. The article continued: 'The lead was never in doubt for the sleek, 120mph Norton which won as convincingly as it did in the production races at Silverstone and Thruxton, the races that prove a bike's speed and endurance' (*see* Chapter 9). So popular was the 650SS that it polled 23.66 per cent of the total vote, which was the biggest in the competition's history so far.

The order of the top ten was as follows:

1 Norton 650 Super Sports 650cc
2 Ariel Super Sports 250cc
3 Triumph Bonneville 650cc
4 BSA Rocket Gold Star 650cc
5 Honda Dream Super Sports 250cc
6 Royal Enfield Super 5 250cc
7 Ariel Leader 250cc
8 Royal Enfield Crusader Sports 250cc
9 Ariel Arrow 250cc
10 Honda Dream 250cc

End of the Road for Bracebridge Street

In that very same issue of *Motor Cycle News*, however, came another, not so happy story. Under the headline 'The last Nortons from Birmingham', it read:

> Sad, but appropriate, is the view of some of the last Nortons to be built at Bracebridge Street, where production ends tomorrow [27 December 1962]. For *MCN*'s Peter Howdle, seen examining the bikes last week, and for Norton enthusiasts all over the world, this ordinary scene has a special significance. For among the last Birmingham-made Nortons was a batch of 85 twin cylinder 650SS models for Australia's Queensland police, the first overseas force to use these powerful models. Bracebridge Street has been the home of Norton Motors since 1916 when the firm moved there from Samson Road North. The firm was founded by 'Pa' Norton – James Lansdowne Norton – at the beginning of the century. From now, it will be Norton of England made in London.

Graeme Noonan's 1962 650SS Domiracer conversion at Phillip Island in 2001, where it won Best Presented Bike & Rider of the meeting. Features include double-sided Italian Grimeca front brake, Dunstall pattern swept-back pipes and long (24in) tapered megaphones.

There is no doubt that the three consecutive Thruxton 500-mile endurance race victories (in 1962, 1963 and 1964) did much to promote the 650SS as the ultimate sports bike of its generation (it won the *MCN* Machine of the Year again in late 1963).

With the Atlas 750 taking over as the top-of-the-range model, however, the 650SS began to stagnate. The Atlas was released onto the home market in February 1964, boasting a European style – virtually a 650SS but with the larger engine – and the same classic Norton black and silver finish. The story of this larger-engined model is related in Chapter 12, but it is worth noting that, unless you really had to have the extra cubes, the 650 was a much smoother bet and still a good performer.

A few minor changes were made over the years – standard and de Luxe models dropped (1963), wider chain, 12 volt electrics (1964) and a name change from 650SS to Mercury (1968), seat hump and reflectors (1969) – until the last faithful 650 Norton machines were produced. As Roy Bacon said in his book *Norton Twins* (Osprey, 1981):

> With it went the famed featherbed frame just 20 years after Geoff Duke had given it its premier at Blandford. For those 20 years it set the standard for roadholding which other machines tried to emulate and on the road helped countless riders round innumerable corners. It gave all who rode it confidence and helped them to ride that little bit better.

During its life the Norton twin was built under the ownership of Norton Motors, AMC and Norton Villiers, at Bracebridge Street, Birmingham, Plumstead Road, Woolwich, and the Villiers factory in Wolverhampton.

The 650 was to outlive the 750 Atlas, which was axed in favour of the new 750 Commando in September 1968. To the author, however, the Featherbed-framed machines were the best Norton twins. Somehow the Commando was never quite the real thing. It (and the Atlas) felt overstretched, in a manner from which the 500, 600 and 650 Dominators did not suffer. And so this trio get my vote as the real deal in Norton's twin-cylinder story.

Last throw of the dice: the single carb 1969 650 Mercury with optional 2LS front brake and rev counter. Production ended early the following year.

9 Production Racing at Thruxton

Thruxton airfield, near Andover, Hampshire was the scene of countless Norton twins' successes during the decade from the mid-1950s until the mid-1960s.

The inaugural event was staged one fine summer's day in June 1955 over a 2.76-mile (4.44km) circuit arranged at the airfield venue. The rules for this event stated that two riders would be allowed for each machine and the winning team was to be the pairing that had piled up the most laps by the ninth hour.

The original concept had been to run either a 12- or 24-hour race, part of which would be in darkness. However, it was eventually decided that for this first event, at any rate, nine hours would suffice.

As things turned out, for the majority of the competitors nine hours was quite long enough. Surprisingly, the real problem was not rider fatigue or mechanical retirement, but tyre wear, owing to the abrasive nature of the Thruxton tarmac. Front tyres seemed to suffer more than rear ones. This was to cause near panic, as very few teams had come prepared with spare rubber, let alone spare wheels and tyres. As the *The Motor Cycle* race report dated 30 June 1955 says: 'Many [teams] were appallingly slow. Tubes were nipped; there were furious searches for pumps; helpers fell over one another in attempts to tighten wheel nuts.'

Some, however, were far better organized. These included a team of mechanics, managed by Southampton dealer and former Norton works rider Syd Lawton, who had spare wheels with tyres fitted at the ready for the Dominator 88 ridden by Derek Powell and Brian Newman.

Syd Lawton's professionalism paid off with fourth overall, and second in the 500cc class. The results were as follows:

1. W.E. Dow/E.B. Crook 499cc BSA, 221 laps
2. K.W. James/I. Lloyd 348cc BSA, 220 laps
3. H.L. Williams/G.W. Shekell 498cc Triumph, 217 laps
4. D. Powell/B. Newman 497cc Norton, 216 laps
5. J.F. Righton/R.J. Langston 348cc BSA, 206 laps
6. G.J. Hughes/S.W. Stevens 649cc Triumph, 206 laps

The 1956 event, still called the Nine Hours, was something of a non-event for Norton – plenty of BSA Gold Stars (more than half the field) plus a sprinkling of Matchless, Royal Enfield, Triumph and Velocette – and much the same could be said for 1957.

Thruxton 500-Mile Race

In 1958 everything changed when the event became the Thruxton 500-Mile Race, bringing new levels of interest from manufacturers, press and public alike. The race was divided into three classes: Multi-Cylinder, Single-Cylinder and 350cc. There were nine Norton twins – two 88s and seven of the 99 six-hundreds. But the really big names were mounted on Triumph and Royal Enfield machinery. The best-placed Norton was the 597cc 99 ridden by H. German/C.A. Rowe, who finished sixth overall, completing 208 laps at an average speed of 62.32mph (100.29km/h), compared to the winners Mike Hailwood/Dan Shorey on a 649cc Triumph Tiger 1100, who completed 220 laps, averaging 66mph (106.21km/h). This was the first year that a multi-cylinder bike had won the event.

Four of the Norton twins suffered retirement, owing to ignition problems, a broken valve and being excluded for refuelling on the course.

The 1959 500-miler saw a BMW victory. The bid of the early leaders, Bob McIntyre and Eric Hinton, came to an end after the primary chaincase of their Royal Enfield Constellation shed its oil and the chain broke. After repairs, McIntyre's later fall at the Anchor Corner chicane put an end to dreams of victory. The lead then transferred to a Triumph Bonneville (new that year) of Tony Godfrey and Brian Holder, but a seven-minute pit stop at the halfway stage to fix a loose dynamo ultimately cost them the race. Since an NSU won the newly introduced 250cc class, this made it two German victories.

Star-Studded 500-Miler

The Motor Cycle dated 23 June 1960 carried a two-page preview of that year's event, with the headline: 'Star-studded 500-miler'. From the previous year, classes had been changed with 250cc (Lightweight), 500cc (Senior) and Multi-cylinder (unlimited). Of the fifteen 500s there was only one Norton, an 88 ridden by Dennis Greenfield and Fred Swift (who both worked at the Bracebridge Street factory); and of the thirty Multis, three were Norton entries: John Griffiths/Bruce Main-Smith, Fred Neville/Les James and R.H. King/B.H. King.

The 88, entered by Denis Parkinson from Yorkshire, won its class by a comprehensive six laps – pretty impressive considering it was the only Norton in its class! This performance was also good enough to secure fifth overall. There was only one Norton retirement, the 99 of Fred Neville and Les James went out after twenty-six laps with a broken primary chain.

Owing to Norton's success in the 1960 event, there were three 88s in the 500cc class of the 1961 event: the 1960 winning pair

The Dominator had a successful career in long-distance production racing, notably at the Thruxton circuit. In 1960 Dennis Greenfield and Fred Swift won the 500cc class and finished fifth overall. The following year was even better, another class victory and second overall. Their 88 was entered by Denis Parkinson.

Greenfield/Swift, plus Ernie Washer/George Murphy and Bruce Main-Smith/W.D. Craig (the last of whom was ex-Norton race team boss Joe Craig's son, Des).

There were also three teams in the Multi-cylinder entry list. *The Motor Cycle* preview commented that: 'Numerically weak, the Norton challenge is nonetheless potent, with Junior TT winner Phil Read partnering Brian Setchell on a Dominator. Also Dominator mounted are *The Motor Cycle* staffman Maurice Spalding and David Dixon.' The remaining Norton 99 entry was E.A. Merryweather and P. Chapman.

Against stiff opposition from Velocette and BSA, Dennis Greenfield and Fred Swift took their 88 to another 500cc class victory, but, most impressive of all, they were classified second overall behind the winners Tony Godfrey/John Holder, riding a Triumph Bonneville. In addition Ernie Washer and George Murphy brought their 88 home fifth in the 500cc ratings.

The General Classification was as follows:

1 T. Godfrey/J.R. Holder 649cc Triumph, 220 laps
2 D. Greenfield/F. Swift 497cc Norton, 219 laps
3 T. Thorp/R.S. Mayhew 499cc Velocette, 219 laps
4 P.H. Tait/R. Fay 649cc Triumph, 219 laps
5 F.A. Neville/F.A. Rutherford 646cc AJS, 219 laps
6 R. Grant/K. Payne 499cc Velocette, 216 laps

So what happened to the Read/Setchell 99 six-hundred? This was always in with a chance of overall victory, until forced out after completing 131 laps, due to a split fuel tank.

The 650SS debuted for the 1962 season and was soon the 'must have' bike for production events. Here John Griffiths is seen at Thruxton that year on his recently acquired machine.

The only other Norton retirement out of the six entered was Merryweather/Chapman on another 99, the machine suffering valve-gear failure after only twenty-three laps. Also worthy of a mention was the Bruce Main-Smith/Des Craig 88, which was one of the fastest few on the circuit in the later stages, but a 25-minute setback with a front-wheel puncture dashed their hopes.

Phil Read (partnered by Brian Setchell) with the victorious Norton 650SS, entered by Southampton dealers Lawton & Wilson, during the 1962 Thruxton 500-mile (800km) endurance race for production machines.

A Brilliant Norton 1–2

The front page headline of *Motor Cycling* in its 27 June 1962 issue shouted: 'Norton's Thruxton 500'. The report went on to explain: 'Riding Syd Lawton's 650SS Norton on which they won the Silverstone "1000" [1,000km – held at Silverstone in mid-May], Phil Read and Brian Setchell completed a long-distance double last Saturday by scoring a runaway victory in the Southampton club's international Thruxton 500-mile production race.'

There was more good news for the marque, since, seven laps behind, a Norton 88SS entered by Denis Parkinson and ridden by Roy Ingram and Fred Swift, was second, ahead of the remaining 650s and topping the 500cc class. The winner's average speed was almost 10mph (16km/h) faster than the previous year, making the race nearly an hour shorter. The chief reason for this increase was the revised 2¼ mile (3.6km) circuit, first used at Easter 1962, in which Windy Corner's slow left and right bends had been replaced by one fast right-hander.

Roy Ingram joined Fred Swift on Denis Parkinson's Dominator 88 in 1962 and in the process the machine clocked up its third class win at Thruxton. This meant Norton won both the Multi-Cylinder and 500cc classes – a fantastic performance.

But as *Motor Cycling* went on to say: 'this in no way detracts from the winners' brilliantly consistent riding or from their machine's superb reliability. During the six-and-a-half-hours it made only five pit stops, each of under a minute, for the sole purpose of refuelling and changing riders.'

General Classification was as follows:

1 P.W. Read/B.P. Setchell 647cc Norton
2 R. Ingram/F. Swift 497cc Norton
3 E.F.H. Boyce/T. Phillips 499cc Velocette
4 S.B. Manns/M. Gunyon 646cc AJS
5 R.J. Langston/B. Main-Smith 647cc Norton
6 F.A. Rutherford/J.H.L. Lewis 646cc Matchless

Testing the Lawton Bike

David Dixon of *The Motor Cycle* was able to test the Syd Lawton 650SS that had been ridden to victory by Read and Setchell. He began his report by saying:

> Any notions you may have that a standard production model will last (maybe!) for just one endurance race can be scotched right smartly. Apart from a minute checkover and replacement of tyres, chains and rear brake linings, the model finished at Thruxton in exactly the same trim as it left the factory before Silverstone [the 1,000 km race] ... A close peek at the model was most illuminating. Nowhere, absolutely nowhere, was there a trace of oil on the engine exterior ... Thanks to meticulous initial setting, the primary chain adjustment was still spot-on and, with highly efficient lubrication, the rear chain had not been adjusted during the race; afterwards it required only 3½ turns of the adjusters.
>
> [The engine was] as lively as ever, enough to take my breath away through sheer, brutal acceleration. Throttle response was fantastically rapid; 7,000rpm was reached as quick as a flash in first and second. In only a slightly longer interval those revs were there in third.

As David Dixon discovered, the Lawton 650SS could reach 102mph (165km/h) in third, revving to 7,200rpm. In top (fourth) this meant 124mph (186km/h).

Phil Read with the Lawton & Wilson 650SS. Prepared by Syd Lawton, this machine was the most successful endurance bike in British racing during 1962, 1963 and 1964.

The Fred Swift/Roy Ingram winning Dominator 88 during the 1962 Thruxton 500-mile race, making it three wins in a row.

Dixon pointed out that: 'Sheer hard work lies behind Syd Lawton's winning machine. For instance, he and his four mechanics between them put in over 300 hours on the Norton, Triumph, BSA and Honda models for Thruxton.'

This same work had ensured not only a reliable and fast bike, but a comfortable one too: 'Beautifully tailored, the riding position gave a relaxed chin-on-the-tank racing crouch and comfortable cornering position and, as might be expected, all controls were ideally placed.'

After some 1,100 miles (1,760km) of racing only three problems had appeared: the right-angle bracket supporting the front number plate had fractured; there was heavy wear on the right (offside) of the tyre treads; and a small and particularly hard lump of something had got into the front brake drum and deeply scored the drum (the linings themselves were only half worn). Even the lights and horn were still in full working order.

The Start of a Famous Combination

The 1962 results were just the beginning of a famous combination, the Lawton 650SS and the riding partnership of Read and Setchell.

When 1963 came around the season got off to something of an unexpected start, when the Tom Kirby-entered Matchless 650CSR of Paddy Driver and Joe Dunphy emerged victorious in the Silverstone '1000'. However, the Read/Setchell Lawton 650SS won for a second time over the by now crumbling Thruxton track surface.

The next year, 1964, saw the tenth Thruxton endurance race, which also happened to be the last at the famous Hampshire venue for a

Derek Woodman was drafted into the Lawton & Wilson team to replace Phil Read in 1964. He is shown here on the winning 650SS at Thruxton that year.

number of years. So perhaps it was fitting that not only should Brian Setchell (with stand-in rider Derek Woodman) win yet again, but it was achieved aboard Syd Lawton's faithful 650SS Norton.

The following year, 1965, saw the event moved from Thruxton to nearby Castle Combe. Quite simply this was necessary because the years of racing, combined with neglect, had wreaked havoc with the Thruxton surface. The 500-miler did not return to its original home for several years, being staged first at Castle Combe and then Brands Hatch. This period also coincided with Norton's fall from grace, both on and off the circuit, and it was not until the arrival of the new Commando model that the Norton twin tasted victory again in this event.

Superb action shot of Griff Jenkins (650SS) at Quarry Corner during the 1965 Castle Combe 500-mile (800km) endurance race. The event was staged at the Wiltshire circuit because the traditional Thruxton venue was closed for resurfacing work.

10 Stateside

During the immediate postwar period, the American economy was booming, whereas Great Britain was to suffer several years of austerity, including rationing and the like. In addition, during the late 1940s virtually every motorcycle produced by the British industry had to go for export.

Britain might have been on the winning side, but when the Second World War ended in 1945 the nation was at a low financial ebb. The long years of conflict had taken their toll and peace brought almost as many problems as had the fighting.

As for the country's motorcycle manufacturers, including Norton, the questions were what to produce and what markets to pursue. In Norton's case it decided to stick with the range of side- and overhead-valve singles it had produced in pre-war days, but with the introduction on some models of the recently introduced telescopic front fork. In addition, due to the success of the Triumph Speed Twin, the company, like its rivals, realized that it needed a vertical twin in a similar mould. This would eventually lead to the Hopwood-designed Model 7 (*see* Chapter 2), and thus the first of the Dominator family.

Export or Die

The stark financial fact, however, was that Great Britain Ltd was as good as bankrupt. A combination of overproduction needed to win the war and borrowing from other nations, notably the United States of America, had left Britain with a massive trade deficit. It was a case of, as the famous phrase from Sir Stafford Cripps's 1946 budget speech so bluntly put it: 'Export or Die.'

In motorcycle production terms he specifically demanded no less than a staggering 258 per cent of the 1938 export figure by 1948. The manufacturers responded and, following the series of measure outlined below, by November 1947 had achieved no less than 278 per cent!

How was this miracle achieved? For a start, virtually every new motorcycle built went overseas. Models were streamlined so as to make best use of men, materials and production. But this export drive was not without its problems. The home market had to be satisfied by a combination of well-worn pre-war models and the sale of former War Department (WD) machinery, the latter meaning many thousands of Norton's 16H side-valve war horses.

Export meant shipping and the resultant need for additional packaging material and longer transport times than if bikes had been destined for the home market. When new models or modified ones were released first to export markets, this meant any problems were experienced by customers thousands of miles away and were therefore much more difficult to resolve effectively.

Aside from metric instruments where necessary, there was a need for translation of technical and sales literature into a number of foreign languages, which created yet additional work for hard-pressed staff.

Quality control was another problem, not only because all British motorcycles of the era used a number of ancillary components from outside suppliers, of which Smiths instruments, Lucas electrical equipment and Amal carburettors were but three examples. There was also the major motorcycle manufacturers' own ruthless quest for ever more effective ways of keeping cost per unit under control.

Despite all these problems the British motorcycle industry did many things correctly and played a vital part in putting the nation's economy back on a sounder footing. Their main overseas markets were the British Commonwealth (including Canada, Australia and South Africa), Europe and, most important of all, the USA. It would be true to say that BSA, Triumph and Norton were soon to become household names in all the nations mentioned above, the British bikes proving the biggest threat to the home-produced Harley-Davidson and Indian machines in the eyes of most Stateside riders.

American Sales

During the decade spanning the 1950s, sales of Norton products, together with those of other British manufacturers including AJS, Matchless, Royal Enfield and Vincent (but not including BSA and Triumph), were all handled by the Indian company.

Indian have vied with Harley-Davidson as the most famous of all the American motorcycle marques. Founded in 1901 by George M. Hendee and Carl Oscar Hedstrom, they built up an enviable reputation in the first half of the twentieth century. Their most famous models were the Scout 600cc v-twin (1919), Chief 1000cc v-twin (1922) and Big Chief 1200cc (1923). Like Harley-Davidson, however, Indian was hard hit by the Great Depression that followed the Wall Street crash of 1929. This saw the Indian company acquired by the industrialist E.P. DuPont in 1930.

One of the specially prepared Dominator 88s Norton built for the 1953 Daytona Beach races. Imports at that time were handled by the Indian Sales Corporation.

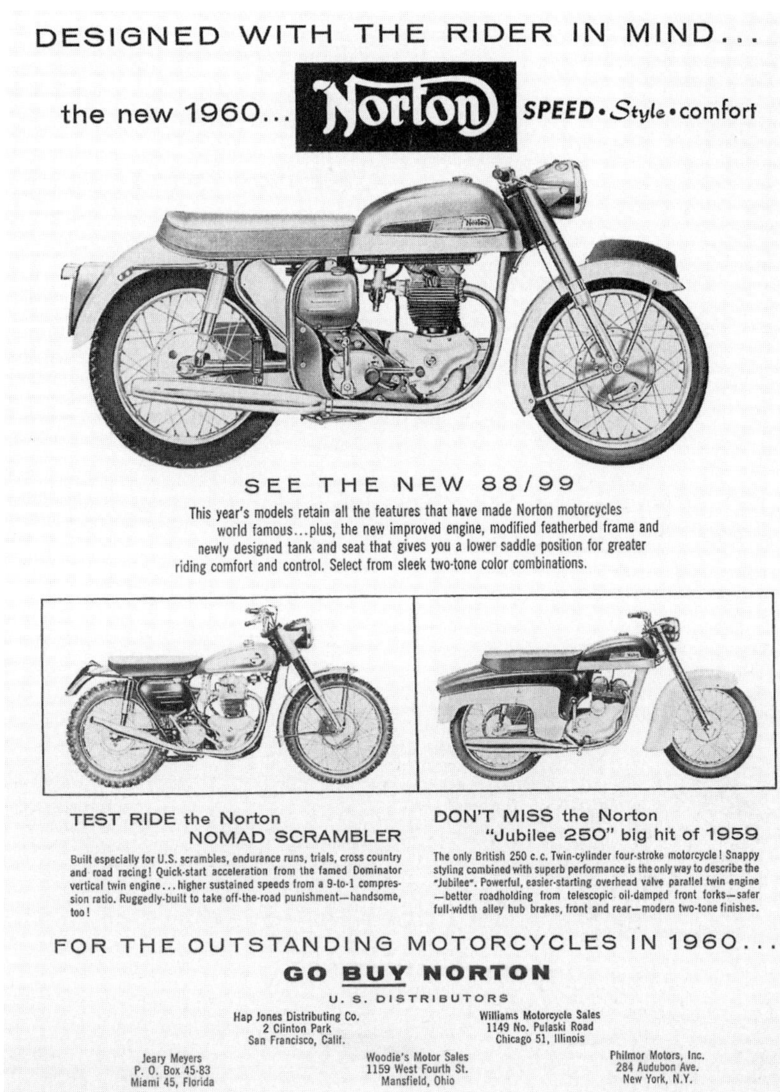

A June 1960 advertisement, just before Berliner became the exclusive American Norton distributors.

For the remainder of the 1930s Indian slugged it out with Harley-Davidson for sales on the home market. During the Second World War both firms were major suppliers to the military. Then in 1949 a cash injection was made by the British entrepreneur John Brockhouse, who soon assumed control of the firm. When this failed to generate increased sales of Indian's traditional heavy-weight v-twins, Brockhouse initiated the marketing of the British marques mentioned above, including Norton.

The Brockhouse Indian operation lasted until 1960. As far as Norton sales were concerned, relatively few machines were exported to the USA under the Brockhouse Indian arrangement, with only a small number of dealers representing this vast continent.

Racing the Dominator at Daytona

During the late 1940s and early 1950s Norton had been successful at the famous Daytona Beach races, but these victories had been garnered with the Manx ohc single, not the twin. However, for the 1953 running of the American classic, things were going to change as the Bracebridge Street factory attempted to build a racing version of its Dominator.

During January 1953 the final touches were being put to a pair of specially adapted 88 de Luxe models, with Featherbed frames. Former Norton works rider Ken Kavanagh told the author that, together with the Polish engineer Leo Kuzmicki, he did the actual bench testing: 'I worked the brake, he (Kuzmicki) read the clocks … these were put together in the Manx shop … then I did the road testing and got the carburation right at MIRA [Motor Industry Research Association].'

The AMA (American Motorcycle Association), the sport's governing body in North America, had previously vetoed the use of the new Featherbed frame in its events, after the chassis had made its debut with the works racing team in 1950 and from the 1951 season on the Manx production racers. However, because of this ruling all the Norton victories at Daytona had been achieved using the obsolete 'Garden Gate' plunger frame.

The arrival of the new 88 Dominator de Luxe in early 1952, however, and its subsequent sales in the States, had forced the American officials to accept the new twin, subject to the terms of the official AMA rulebook, which stated: 'Before a particular machine is eligible at least 30 of the type must be in use [in the USA].'

Norton themselves referred to the racing version as the Manx Twin (not the Dominator, or Domiracer). The famous Daytona races, including the 100-mile amateur and experts' 200-miler were to be staged over 13, 14 and 15 March 1953. That year the main 200-mile (320km) event was still held over the old 4.2-mile (7km) Beach course and Milt Lassiter brought his Norton twin home in an excellent third place (with Bill Truman fourth), while in the 100-miler 22-year-old John Miller won on another Norton, but this time one of the old plunger-framed Manx singles.

Later that year, in June, both Norton twins were raced at Laconia, and then a month later in the 200-mile national Speedway championship. At the latter event one of the Dominator-engined bikes put in another excellent performance to repeat the Daytona result.

Although AMA rules called for the bike to be 'production based', the 1953 Daytona specification racers were equipped with twin Amal racing carburettors with a single remote float chamber, an 8in front brake, racing handlebars (swan-neck clip-ons), rearset foot controls and short, dumpy megaphones. The racing specification also included a single bum-stop Manx pattern seat, abbreviated mudguarding and racing number plates; steel wheel rims (as on the roadster) were fitted.

The Berliner Corporation

All this was set to change with the involvement later that year of the Berliner Corporation. Bert Hopwood described the first approaches in his 1981 memoirs: 'I was fortunate enough to be alerted by a friend that Joe Berliner, the Ducati distributor for the USA, might be my man. After much thought I decided that he was and I hunted him to ground in a Frankfurt hotel and offered him the Norton distributorship.'

The Berliner Corporation was based in Hasbrouck Heights, New Jersey. The name of the company came from two brothers, Mike and Joe Berliner, the latter of whom held the post of President.

Originally the Berliners had entered the motorcycle industry with the German marque Zündapp during the early 1950s; they added Ducati to its portfolio at the end of 1958. The organization was also responsible for the now long-forgotten J-Be (Joseph Berliner) 200 Buccaneer, which was a mixture of German Metzeler tyres and Sachs engine and Italian frame, wheels and suspension.

By the time Norton joined the family the Berliner Corporation had a ready-made – and successful – dealer network throughout the States, as Bert Hopwood recalled: 'I was pleased when Joe and I finally reached agreement and we were under contract. In a few months our machines were being sold in the USA and under a joint advertising promotion for the introduction of the 650cc Manxman model' (*see* Chapter 8).

When it was launched on the American market in spring 1961, the Manxman was described by the advertising men as 'the most outstanding machine in the world', with the slogan 'Made by Norton, the most famous name in motor cycling'.

I have taken the liberty of reproducing in full the words of the original (and now very rare) Manxman brochure:

> Norton know about fast motor cycles. Norton, and Norton alone, have the unique and enviable record of success in international racing which provides the knowledge, the skill and the craftsmanship to produce the big fast machine. Brakes, frame, gearbox, every feature of a Norton is a direct

A 1962 Berliner advertisement promoting victories gained by Norton's 500 ohv Dominator twin that year, in both the States and Canada.

> development of Grand Prix racing and it is this know-how, gained from winning races all over the world during the last fifty years, including 32 TT Races, which gives a Norton the race-bred performance which is second to none. The Manxman is built on this experience of successful racing. It's a winner all the way. Turn on the gas and feel the tremendous surge of power from the 650cc vertical twin engine. Marvel at the roadholding characteristics of the race-bred 'Featherbed' frame, unequalled in any other machine. Sense the superb handling and hair-line steering of the world-famous 'Roadholder' front forks. Revel in the racing reliability of this outstanding machine. Get out in front, stay out in front, on the Manxman.

It is worth relating that the name 'Manxman' was the ideal of Joe Berliner – not anyone at Norton.

Not long after the Manxman went on sale in the States, however, Norton's managing director, Bert Hopwood, resigned; in May 1961 he became a member of the Parent Board of the BSA company, where he remained for the rest of his career. (For the reasons why Hopwood quit Norton for a second time, *see* Chapter 13.)

Ever Bigger

As we have seen, the Berliners had been responsible for stretching the six-hundred twin to a six-fifty. Not long afterwards the Norton engine size was increased again, this time to a seven-fifty (actually 745cc – 73 × 89mm). When originally conceived by development engineer Doug Hele, the Atlas engine ran on the relatively low 7.6:1 compression ratio, with mild camshaft lift and a single Amal Monobloc carburettor. However, even though Hele strongly advised against it, the American importers demanded (and were given) ever higher compression ratios and fiercer cam lifts, plus twin carbs. All this, of course, gave greater performance and acceleration, but at the cost of increased vibration levels and mechanical stress.

In mid-1963 there appeared the first of several hybrid Norton twins, all of which used the 745cc Atlas engine housed in an AMC duplex frame. Again this came as the result of requests made by the American importers, who by now were also importing AJS and Matchless bikes. The first such effort was the 750cc Scrambler (also sometimes called the Ranger), built for trail and enduro use. The motor was equipped with a sports camshaft and twin carburettors, but retained the lower 7.6:1 compression ratio. The standard AMC 4-speed gearbox and Atlas ratios were used, but the sprockets were changed to provide lower gearing. The primary chaincase was of the AMC cast alloy two-piece type held together by a series of screws and featuring a large circular plug that could be removed to assist clutch adjustment. Although an AMC frame was used, the forks, wheels and brakes were Norton components, while many of the smaller parts came from the AMC parts bin. Other details of the specification included knobbly tyres, braced scramblers' gearbox and low-level twin exhaust header pipes and AMC silencers (or straight-thru continuation pipes), the latter offering not very much in the way of silencing!

The P11 Desert Scrambler was developed from the 750 Scrambler. This was a much more serious off-roader and used the chassis from the Matchless G85CS 500cc scrambler, with a tuned Atlas engine. It dominated Stateside desert racing during the late 1960s.

The 750 Scrambler (sometimes referred to as the Ranger) debuted in 1963. This was the first of several hybrid Norton twins and used a 745cc Atlas engine in an AMC duplex frame.

From the Scrambler was developed a more serious off-roader, the P11. This was a serious desert racer that went on to win many sporting events. The basis of the bike was a twin-carb Atlas engine mounted in the Matchless G85CS scrambler chassis. Thanks to what was already a lighter set of cycle parts and the wide use of aluminium, the weight was reduced by well over 40lb (18.1kg) compared with the Scrambler. The P11 also sported twin hi-level exhausts, with small, lightweight mufflers. Although not fully appreciated at the time, this and the Scrambler trail bike represented an early attempt to offer a powerful, large capacity, twin-cylinder, on-off-road design, something that the modern industry was to embrace from the mid- to late 1980s onwards.

One must give credit to Joe Berliner for coming up with the concept. Of course he knew the American market. In many fields the United States has been responsible for setting new trends, as it was in this case, but it took the rest of the motorcycle industry no less than two decades to take up the big twin on-off-road machine. Berliner and Norton can well claim to have been the true pioneers of what is today a popular niche market – on both sides of the Atlantic.

The P11

Norton's P11 has been described by Andrew Kemp as:'One of the British industry's inspired compromises ... Something of a "parts-bin special", it was a mix-and-match combination of parts from Norton and parent company AMC, designed to suit the American market and for export only.' Yet it was such a successful marriage that eventually even home-market customers were offered the model from March 1967, following the Norton Villiers takeover.

Nicknamed the 'desert sled', the P11 was itself a more serious attempt to create a bike that was both powerful and better able to tackle off-road terrain than the Atlas Scrambler of similar concept, which was more of a street scrambler.

As outlined in this chapter, by the early 1960s America had become a vitally important market for Nortons. Stateside, the leisure sector of motorcycling was then far more popular than it was back home, with off-road sport being particularly big. AMC's US importers, the Berliner Corporation of New Jersey, knew their market, and it was Joe Berliner who suggested the marriage of the Matchless G85CS 500cc single-cylinder frame to the powerful and torquey 745cc Norton Atlas engine. And so the P11 was born. This bike was built to take part in the hugely popular West Coast desert races.

Starting out with the relatively lightweight G85CS frame, keeping down the weight was a priority that required as many components as possible to be constructed in aluminium. These included the fuel tank, which was kept as small as possible, mudguards, engine plates and many others. The result (complete with lighting equipment) weighed in at 368lb (166.9kg) dry, compared with the road-going standard Atlas at 410lb (186kg).

The result was a competitive desert racer, the P11, which reigned supreme in events such as the Mojave Desert classic during the mid- to late 1960s, although as Andrew Kemp has explained: 'That same power could get out of hand on the road, where with off-road tyres and short wheelbase, its handling was not always as sure as expected. Any criticism of its road performance missed the point, for no scrambler was equipped to deal with a performance of well over 100mph (160km/h) on the tarmac.' With its specialized frame, wheel hubs and aluminium components, this lean and purposeful-looking machine was costly – and difficult to build.

This latter statement concerns the fact that the Norton engine was a tight fit in a frame originally designed to house a much smaller 500cc single-cylinder engine.

The P11 (and its near identical Matchless brother, the N15CS) was a pioneer in its field, a full two decades in advance of the modern powerful, off-road twins that began in the mid- to late 1980s with such machines as the Cagiva Elephant, BMW GS and Honda Africa.

A 1968 Matchless G15, one of several AMC models to use the Norton engine for its motive power.

After AMC folded in mid-1966, Berliner continued for a few months to be the US importer. Eventually, however, the new Norton Villiers organization set up its own American distribution network (by this time largely for the new Commando, rather than the Dominator and Atlas). So, effectively our Stateside review ended with the Berliner Corporation. Just to complete the story, however, the New Jersey-based organization continued with Ducati until 1983; they also, from the late 1960s, became the US distributors for Moto Guzzi as a direct replacement for the former AMC/Norton line, via a satellite company, Cosmopolitan Motors.

11 Lightweights

Bert Hopwood's hand has been associated with some of the most memorable British bikes, classics such as the BSA Golden Flash, Triumph Trident and, of course, the Norton Dominator. Another design series for which he was responsible, although not often viewed in the same light, was the trio of Norton lightweight twins, the Jubilee, Navigator and Electra.

The first Norton two-fifty had been a single, but this promising design never made it past the prototype stage and was axed in 1953, a victim of the AMC takeover.

A brand new design, a two-fifty twin, was planned to mark the diamond anniversary of James L. Norton's founding of the Norton Manufacturing Company in August 1898. This new quarter-litre machine was intended to be very different from other British motorcycles of the period. At one time no fewer than three designs were placed before the Norton board, of which Bert Hopwood was now a member and also managing director.

Hopwood favoured an engine with a one-piece head and barrel with markedly over-square bore and stroke dimensions to facilitate access to the combustion chamber. The parent company AMC, however, frowned on this concept and so an alternative 'compromise' with separate heads and barrels was drawn up, with the help of Doug Hele and William Pitcher.

The Jubilee

Although it was not Hopwood's first choice, he still threw himself wholeheartedly behind the project (now named the Jubilee for obvious reasons), later calling the engine 'modern in design and attractive in appearance'. It also had the advantage of being suitable for expansion to 350cc (and as future events showed, 400cc) at a later date.

The Jubilee was to be the only twin-cylinder four-stroke British roadster of its era, enabling Norton to ask a premium price compared to rivals who could only offer either singles or two-stroke twins.

Much of the balance of the finished machine bore a strong family resemblance to the Francis-Barnett models so that, as Hopwood said: 'by this means we managed to minimize tooling and production costs which helped to shorten development time factors.'

The most striking aspect of the new Norton two-fifty twin-cylinder power unit was its squat proportions, resulting from the

Launched at the end of 1958 to celebrate the diamond jubilee of the Norton company, the aptly named Jubilee was a high-cam twin designed by Bert Hopwood, with unit construction and ultra-short stroke bore and stroke measurements.

A 1959 advertisement for the new Jubilee two-fifty twin.

unusually high bore/stroke ratio of 60mm × 44mm, respectively. The cam followers and pushrods, housed in tunnels cast in the cylinder barrels and heads, were disposed at the extreme front and rear of the unit so that the valves were operated by the inner ends of the overhead rockers.

The crankshaft was of cast iron with an integral flywheel in the centre. In addition to conventional bob-weights outboard of the crankpin journals, there were matching bob-weights formed in the flanks of the flywheel.

To minimize out-of-balance weight, the throw of the crankshaft was hollow, with the cavity being cylindrical at the crankpin journals and swelling to a larger diameter in the flywheel. Since the cavity contained the lubricating oil, which was fed under pressure to the big-ends, the middle portion served as a sludge trap. The dimensions of these big-ends was actually identical with those of the existing 88 and 99 Dominator twins (1½in journal diameter, ⅞in shell width) and so were the sizes of the crankshaft main bearings. These were a roller bearing on the drive side of the shaft and a ball race on the timing side; in both cases dimensions were: bore (i.e. shaft diameter) 30mm, outside diameter 72mm, width 19mm.

The connecting rods were in high-duty light alloy and featured thin-wall, steel-backed big-end bearings, the small-end eye being unbushed.

Cast-Iron Barrels, Light-Alloy Heads

The cylinder barrels were separate iron castings sunk for half their length inside the crankcase with five large cooling fins on their upper half. The heads were also separate castings, but of light alloy. Each barrel and head was clamped to the crankcase by six long studs and nuts. As for the pistons, these were of orthodox British layout with the skirts split and the crowns flat with cutaways for valve clearance; there were two compression rings and a single slotted oil scraper; circlips retained fully floating gudgeon pins. Compression ratio was 8.75:1.

Combustion chambers were shallow and part-spherical, while the valve seats were manufactured from iron and cast in the heads giving an included angle between the valve stems of an uncommonly narrow 42 degrees. A similar material was used for the valve guides, which were retained by circlips. Each valve employed two coil springs. Valve clearances were adjusted by rotating eccentric rocker spindles with a screwdriver after slackening a locking nut.

Unlike the Dominator engine, the Jubilee had two camshafts, these being located high in the crankcase and driven by gears. Keyed on the offside (right) end of the crankshaft and secured by the oil pump driving worm, the small timing pinion meshed with a bronze bushed intermediate gear mounted above it on a fixed spindle; this gear drove those keyed to the end of the camshafts.

Only 3in (76mm) long, each light-alloy pushrod was equipped with a hardened steel ball pressed on the lower end and a cup at the top. The unbushed rockers were one-piece steel stampings, including the ball end that mated with the pushrod cup.

The lubrication system was pretty conventional, with a duplex gear pump in the timing chest drawing oil from the dry-sump oil tank and feeding it to a chamber in the timing cover, into which the offside (right) end of the crankshaft protruded through an oil seal; lubricant was forced through this shaft to the big-end

A feature of the Jubilee engine was its separate alloy heads and cast-iron barrels. The exhaust header pipes were a push-in fit and there were four separate, detachable aluminium rocker covers.

bearings, from which it went on to lubricate the pistons, cylinders and camshaft by splash. Pressure was limited by a relief valve in the timing cover.

The contact breaker was driven by the offside end of the inlet camshaft. In later years a much more accurate and reliable method of ignition was possible with a modern electronic system. There was also a Wipac G1540 6-volt 50-watt alternator, which was carried on the nearside (left) of the engine unit.

Primary transmission was by a ⅜in (9mm) pitch duplex chain running on fixed centres. Beneath the lower run was a hardened pressed-steel, slipper-type tensioner, which could be adjusted by a slotted mounting after slackening two nuts. Apart from what were described as minor exceptions, the gearchange, gearbox, clutch and kickstart mechanisms were the same as those employed on the AJS Model 14 and Matchless G2 two-fifty singles.

Much of the Jubilee's running gear was derived from the Francis-Barnett parts stock. There were slight differences, but these were mainly to enable the Norton engine to be fitted, rather than major alterations. It is worth mentioning that the Jubilee was the first Norton to use 18in tyre sizes.

Priced at £173 (£215 16s 4d including UK purchase tax), the Jubilee was launched just in time for the London Earls Court Show in November 1958. The newcomer was one of the stars of the show, described by *The Motor Cycle* in its 20 November issue:

> The appearance of the Jubilee 250 is nothing if not distinctive. There is a stylish rear fairing consisting of two quickly detachable side panels (each held by three Dzus fasteners) and a rear portion embracing the number plate and lamp. At the front there is a deeply valanced, flowing mudguard with guttered edge. And amidships there is an entirely new and robust-looking engine-gear unit.
>
> There was even a gold-plated Jubilee machine to emphasize the company's sixty years celebration.

Prototype Testing

The Jubilee underwent an extensive test programme, involving what Bert Hopwood described as 'some of the most rigorous testing I had known a motorcycle to be given'. This included taking the first three production models to Wales and thrashing them over a 'very varied course of rough and smooth, slow and fast, and flat and hilly'. During this extended test period, many thousand miles of mixed riding were covered and very little went wrong. It should be understood, however, that these three bikes were essentially specially built, rather than in quantity.

When series production began problems started to emerge. One centred around the cast-iron crankshaft, which Hopwood said was

From the 1961 model year Norton offered the option of Standard (naked) or de Luxe (rear enclosure) versions of the Jubilee. The unit construction engine was a particularly clean design, especially when viewed from the nearside.

bedevilled with broken assemblies, although a material change cured this problem once and for all.

Having ridden a 1959 Jubilee myself, I found the bike well mannered with good handling and braking and a willing, if buzzy, engine that was remarkably frugal. Also vibration was less than I had expected, and top speed just under 75mph (120km/h).

In 1960, the final year in which the Scottish Six Days' Trial included a sidecar class, Bob Collier, with Gordon Wilde as passenger, entered the event with a Jubilee hitched to a Watsonian Bambini fibreglass scooter sidecar. Against all expectations the combination completed the 753-mile (1,211km) course, one of the most gruelling sporting events in the calendar. The Jubilee and chair even claimed a first class award!

The 1959 250 Jubilee

Engine	Air-cooled ohv twin with slightly inclined vertical cylinders, individual cast-iron barrels and alloy heads, cast-iron 360-degree crankshaft, alloy con-rods, plain bearing big-ends, aluminium vertically-split crankcases, unit construction of engine and gearbox
Bore	60mm
Stroke	44mm
Displacement	249cc
Compression ratio	8.75:1
Lubrication	Duplex gear pump; dry sump
Ignition	6-volt battery/coil; Wipac 50-watt alternator
Carburettor	Amal Monobloc 375 $^{25}/_{32}$in
Primary drive	Duplex chain
Final drive	Chain
Gearbox	4-speed, foot-change
Frame	Tubular and pressed-steel cradle
Front suspension	AMC Lightweight telescopic type
Rear suspension	Swinging arm, Girling shock absorbers
Front brake	6in full-width iron drum, SLS
Rear brake	6in full-width iron drum, SLS
Tyres	3.25 × 18 front; 3.25 × 18 rear
Wheelbase	53.5in (1,359mm)
Ground clearance	5.5in (140mm)
Seat height	29in (737mm)
Fuel tank capacity	3gal (13.6ltr)
Dry weight	330lb (150kg)
Maximum power	16bhp @ 7,750rpm
Top Speed	74mph (119km/h)

The Navigator

In late 1960 Norton announced the new Navigator. Essentially a beefed-up Jubilee, this machine had been given an extended development. A forged steel crankshaft and a monobloc (single) cylinder barrel casting were included to provide additional strength to the design.

Based on the Jubilee engine, the Navigator displaced 349cc with bore and stroke dimensions of 62 × 56mm (compared to the Jubilee's 60 × 44mm), requiring far less radical measurements.

Another major change was to the cycle parts, which saw a strengthened frame and the addition of two-way damped Roadholder front forks as used on the Dominator models, though with shorter springs. With the forks went the front wheel, which incorporated the 8in (200mm) front brake also found on the Dominator; the front tyre size was 3.00 × 19. The rear wheel used the Jubilee's 6in (152mm) diameter brake and 3.25 × 18 tyre. Also, owing to the different fork geometry, the wheelbase at 51.5in (1,310mm) was 1in (26mm) shorter than before.

As with the latest version of the Jubilee, each set of points could be moved independently on the base plate so that the ignition timing could be set with greater accuracy for each cylinder (a problem on the early Jubilee models).

The 349cc Navigator arrived for the 1961 model year and was a much better machine than its smaller brother. It featured a forged, instead of cast, crankshaft, one-piece cylinder barrel, strengthened frame and the front end from the bigger twins, which meant the excellent Roadholder forks and 8in full-width alloy front hub assembly.

The Navigator's price in November 1960 was: standard £190 10s (basic), £229 15s 10d (with UK purchase tax); de Luxe £197 (basic), £237 12s 7d (with UK purchase tax).

A standard version of the Jubilee had been introduced a couple of weeks previously, in addition to the rear wheel enclosure of the original design, so now there were both naked (standard) and enclosed (de Luxe) versions of Norton's 250 twin.

The Two Trials Test

The 8 March 1961 issue of *Motor Cycle News* carried a story by Peter Howdle headlined: 'Anglo-Belgian weekend try-out for an all-weather Norton Navigator'. Peter went on to explain:

> What a weekend! Maybe I didn't get a fat lot of sleep but I saw two very good trials, one in England, the other in Belgium, and clocked 764 miles (1,229km) towards running in of a fascinating Norton. And, to add to the interest of getting more closely acquainted with the new 350cc Navigator, the twin was fitted with the first of a new range of glass-fibre accessories now listed by the Bracebridge Street factory.

The extras included leg shields, handlebar fairing and streamlined panniers. Fitted to a de Luxe version, and colour-coded, the end result was really attractive. Incidentally, the two trials taken in by Peter Howdle were the Cotswold Cup and the Lamborelle.

Britain's first full test report of the Navigator (the same bike Howdle had used for his

A March 1961 advertisement for the new three-fifty Navigator high camshaft twin. As usual the Norton PR department pushed the firm's racing pedigree.

Anglo-Belgian trip) appeared in *Motor Cycle News* on 22 March 1961. The Jubilee never really made its mark with the motorcycle press testers, but the reverse could be said of the larger mount. *MCN* had three testers, all of whom gave the Navigator almost unstinting praise.

Here is how all three summed up the bike:

> The Navigator literally steers itself. Speedy swervery was so stable one could be forgiven for imagining an automatic pilot had been discreetly built into a comprehensive touring specification. The anchors, especially that at the front, are superb. Fairly low gearing gives excellent acceleration and road manners are as gentle as a kitten's. (Peter Howdle)

The final version of the Norton lightweight twin-cylinder family was the 400 Electra (actually 383cc). Originally built for the US importers Berliner, the model went on sale in the UK in mid-1963 listed as the ES400. Besides its push-button starting and bar-end indicators, the Electra also gained the full-width 7in rear hub from the Dominator series.

> No wonder the Navigator is in short supply! Superlatives are ten a penny in road test reports so in the case of the Navigator I'll go a bit further and say that it's the best machine I've ridden in the past 12 months. The small, overall dimensions gave me a feeling of complete mastery which were backed up by the delightfully powerful front brake. (Mick Woollett)
>
> This bike is certainly a lively contender for the 'Machine of the Year' title. I cannot remember riding any model which had so many really outstanding features. Extravagant praise? – not a bit. This bike cannot fail to sell in huge numbers. It's the surest winner in a long time. (Rick Fountain)

Sadly, this last prediction was way off the mark, since the UK government had just introduced a 250cc ceiling for novice riders. If Norton had launched the Navigator first, before the Jubilee and before the new law was mooted, it probably would have sold much better. As it was the 350cc class was to take a nosedive in popularity – and with it any chance of the Navigator proving a showroom hit.

MCN achieved an electronically timed maximum speed of 84mph (135km/h) with the rider prone. Top gear proved practical down to around 25mph (40km/h). Official Norton figures said the engine produced 23 bhp at 7,000rpm.

Since the Navigator produced 7bhp more than the Jubilee, had more torque, an extra 10mph (16km/h) and was only 5lb (2.25kg) heavier, as well as having such advantages as a stronger frame, superior front end (forks and brake) and a stronger engine (one-piece barrel and forged crankshaft), it was a far better machine than its older, smaller brother.

The Electra

The Electra (or ES400) came about following a request by the American Norton importers, the Berliner Corporation, for a bike to compete with the Honda twin-cylinder models, which featured push-button starting. At the same time could not the engine be enlarged to a four-hundred? (Something the Japanese did not have in 1962.) So the Norton engineers increased the displacement to 383cc by the simple expedient of boring the cylinders out by 3mm, giving a new bore size of 66mm, the stroke remaining unchanged at 56mm.

The machine was essentially a Navigator with the additional bore size and a Lucas starter motor. There were also a number of improvements including an uprated electrical system (now 12 volts) including a 90-watt alternator and a sturdier gearbox. In addition the rear wheel from the heavyweight range was fitted, so front and rear brakes were now both full-width polished aluminium assemblies. Like BMWs of the era, the Electra was also equipped with bar-end direction indicators.

However, the very component that made the Electra potentially popular – its electric start – was also its weakness. According to Derek Magrath: 'When the engine was cold the starter motor was not always up to its job, although it was adequate when the engine was warm. A common fault was failure of the reduction gearing, which would render the starter useless.'

The Electra first went on sale in the USA in January 1963 and in the UK during July 1963 (as the ES400), but was not much of a success in either market.

My own advice, if you are thinking of buying one of the Norton lightweight twins, is to go for the Navigator. It's the best of the trio. The Jubilee is not a bad bike, providing you find a good one and fit an aftermarket electronic ignition system, but the Navigator just does everything that much better. Owing to its electric start gremlins, the Electra is simply not as good as its 350 brother.

Both the Navigator and Electra ceased production in the summer of 1965, and the Jubilee followed a year later. Today all three are a relatively rare sight. Another potential problem is spare parts, which are much more difficult to source than those for the bigger twins.

The attraction of the Electra was supposed to be its improved electrics – a Lucas starter motor, upgraded 90-watt (50-watt on Jubilee/Navigator) alternator and 12-volt system. However, the starter system proved weak and unreliable, thus limiting the machine's appeal – as did its high price when compared to similar Japanese machines.

The 1961 350 Navigator [1963 Electra]

Engine	Air-cooled ohv twin with slightly inclined vertical cylinders, one-piece cast-iron barrel and individual alloy heads, forged 360-degree crankshaft, alloy con-rods, plain bearing big-ends, aluminium vertically-split crankcases, unit construction of engine and gearbox
Bore	63mm [66mm]
Stroke	56mm
Displacement	349cc [383cc]
Compression ratio	8.75:1 [7.9:1]
Lubrication	Duplex gear pump; dry sump
Ignition	Navigator: 6-volt battery/coil, 50-watt alternator [Electra: 12-volt battery/coil, Lucas electric starter motor, 90-watt alternator]
Carburettor	Amal Monobloc 375⅞in
Primary drive	Duplex chain
Final drive	Chain
Gearbox	4-speed, foot-change
Frame	Tubular and pressed-steel cradle
Front suspension	Norton 2-way damped Roadholder telescopic
Rear suspension	Swinging arm, Girling shock absorber
Front brake	8in full-width alloy drum, SLS
Rear brake	6in full-width iron drum, SLS (7in alloy)
Tyres	3.00 × 19 front; 3.25 × 18 rear
Wheelbase	51.5in (1,308mm)
Ground clearance	5.5in (140mm)
Seat height	29in (737mm)
Fuel tank capacity	3gal (13.6ltr)
Dry weight	Navigator: 335lb (151.9kg) [Electra: 338lb (153.3kg)]
Maximum power	23bhp @ 7,000rpm (24bhp @ 7,000rpm)
Top speed	84mph (135km/h)

12 Atlas

The seven-fifty Atlas bears the distinction of being the final development of the Featherbed-framed Norton twin as a series production model.

Although *Motor Cycling* brought the first news of the 745cc Atlas on 25 January 1962, the official press launch did not take place until 6 March. *The Motor Cycle* confirmed in the 8 March issue that it was for export only: 'Tears and piteous cries will help you not one jot, you just *can't* have a seven-fifty Norton twin, and that's flat. They're earmarked for export, every gorgeous one of the batch now leaving Bracebridge Street assembly line.' The newcomer had been clearly developed from the existing six-fifty Dominator and, it was explained, 'designed to meet an exacting – if somewhat unusual – specification from America'.

For once, sheer flat-out maximum speed was not the main criterion. Instead the Yanks required a machine described by *The Motor Cycle* as a 'top-gear-only mount', a beef-cake with an engine as tractable as could be constructed. Norton built them a 'steam engine' (their own description), with a power band so wide that the urge was on tap, all the way from 10mph (16km/h) to around the 100mph (160km/h) mark. Norton claimed 49bhp at 6,800rpm.

According to *The Motor Cycle* this had been achieved 'Principally by taking the Dominator 650, keeping the stroke at 89mm, but enlarging the bore from 68 to 73mm, by choosing the relatively low compression ratio of 7.6 to 1, by fitting a single Amal Monobloc Type 376/294 carburettor.'

One journalist commented on launch day that, 'A model of this nature has a particular appeal for police and other official duties and, though America is the initial target, the makers feel it would be equally at home on the motorways of Europe.' Another saw it as a potentially wonderful machine for sidecar duties. But still British riders could only dream of the Atlas in March 1962.

The 745cc Atlas was inspired by Joe Berliner, Norton's American distributor. When first launched back in early 1962, it sported a smaller tank and high 'Western' handlebars; it was also 'export' only. But soon the Americans (and the British from the 1964 season) got what was in essence a larger-engined 650SS.

Officially announced by Norton's managing director, Alec Skinner, the seven-fifty Atlas made best use of the existing 650SS even to the point of retaining the same gear ratios, magneto ignition and Lucas alternator. The latter was housed in the primary chaincase and used solely to supply lighting current to the battery.

Problems

The engine for the Atlas had originally been developed by Doug Hele, who insisted that the bike should be equipped with only a single carb, low compression pistons and a soft cam profile. In its original guise the engine was just about able to cope regarding both smoothness and reliability.

Unfortunately, both Hele and his mentor, Bert Hopwood, were destined to leave Norton rather than make the journey south when AMC bosses chose to close the Birmingham

The 1962 750 Atlas

Engine	Air-cooled ohv twin with vertical cylinders, alloy head and cast-iron barrel, two main bearings, 360-degree, 3-piece crankshaft, split con-rods and shell big-end bearings, coil valve springs, vertically-split aluminium crankcases
Bore	73mm
Stroke	89mm
Displacement	745cc
Compression ratio	7.6:1*
Lubrication	Gear pump; dry sump
Ignition	Magneto
Carburettor	Amal 389 Monobloc 1⅛in*
Primary drive	Simplex chain
Final drive	Chain
Gearbox	AMC 4-speed, positive stop, foot-change
Frame	Norton Slimline Featherbed, full cradle
Front suspension	Norton Roadholders, oil-damped, telescopic
Rear suspension	Swinging arm, with oil-damped, twin shock absorbers
Front brake	8in full-width drum, SLS
Rear brake	7in full-width drum, SLS
Tyres	3.25 × 19 front; 4.00 × 18 rear
Wheelbase	55.5in (1,410mm)
Ground clearance	6.2in (157mm)
Seat height	31in (787mm)
Fuel tank capacity	3.62gal (16.5ltr)
Dry weight	395lb (179kg)
Maximum power	49bhp @ 6,800rpm
Top speed	110mph (177km/h)

* Many 1962 bikes, plus later models, were built with high compression pistons, sports camshaft and twin carbs; performance was then increased to over 120mph (193km/h)

A 1966 Atlas with twin carburettors and rev counter. Increased compression ratios and tuning over the years saw vibration levels increase for Norton's biggest Dominator series twin.

Bracebridge Street factory at the end of 1962. This also meant that Hele was not around to see the problems that were to come when the enlarged Norton twin-cylinder engine was hyped up with performance components such as twin carbs, higher compression ratios and racing profile camshafts in a bid to gain ever more power. These latter developments were overseen by AMC's chief designer, the former Velocette engineer Charles Udall, assisted by Wally Wyatt.

Even in Hele's reign, however, from the first 500cc Model 7 of the late 1940s until the arrival of the 750cc Atlas, the power output had jumped from 29 to 49bhp. According to Derek Magrath, 'Such increases were never contemplated in the original design, and it was beginning to show.'

Externally, the only difference between the new seven-fifty and the existing six-fifty was in the positioning of the crankcase breather outlet. The larger diameter spigot required at the crankcase mouth obviated the need for the original, rear-facing outlet; on the Atlas the take-off was now from the nearside (left) of the

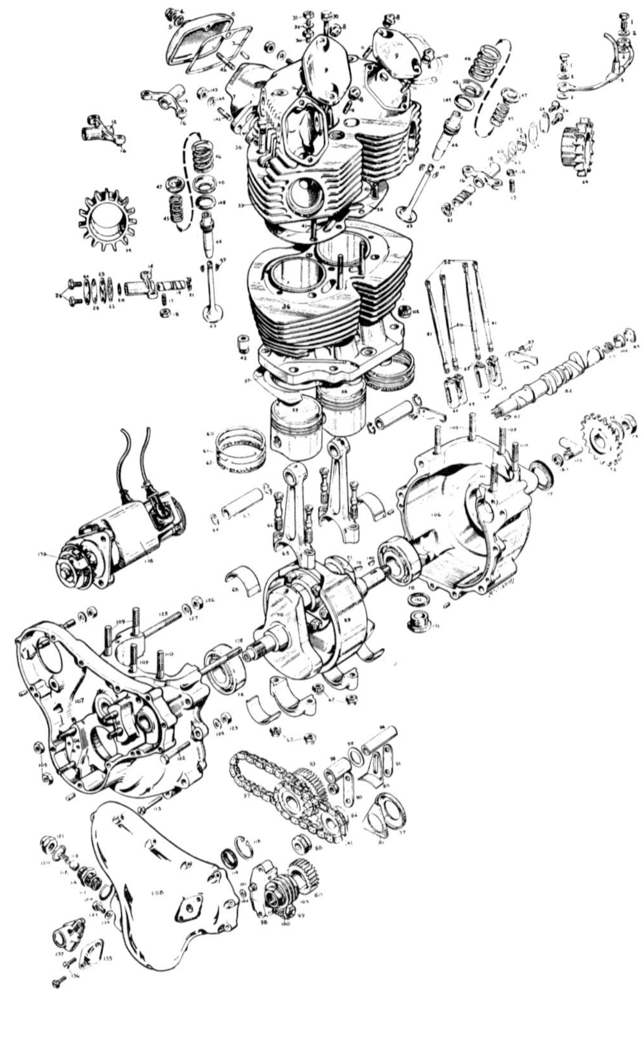

When first released the Atlas engine had low compression pistons (7.6:1), soft cam profile and a single-carb head as shown here. Development engineer Doug Hele, who left at the end of 1962, warned against any further tuning.

crankcase. As with the six-fifty, the breather discharged via a long, flexible pipe into the oil tank tower; from a higher level on the tower, a further pipe discharged to the atmosphere.

Steve Wilson pointed out that:

> On the first Atlas machine there had been a problem with the Featherbed frame; some early ones were returned to Ken Sprayton at Reynolds with the twin downtubes broken just above the motor's front mountings, by the engine's sheer grunt. Sprayston had recommended inverting the welded-on lugs so that their tails were uppermost, and this cured the problem.

Yet more troubles were experienced with early Atlas engines, including deformed cylinder barrels, broken connecting rods, pistons incorrectly machined and a clutch that could prove troublesome owing to the vast amount of torque generated by the new engine. However, well before he left Norton, Doug Hele rectified the problems, except the clutch, which was to remain something of a weakness.

Another problem suffered by the Atlas engine concerned blown cylinder-head gaskets. This was to remain a continuing glitch, even though AMC attempted a cure in the mid-1960s.

Testing the Atlas

The first test of the new Norton 750 came by way of the American magazine *Cycle World*, not long after it went on sale. Having tested the 650 Manxman roughly a year before, *Cycle World* noted:

> The Atlas is, if memory serves us correctly, a less fussy machine ... more willing to run very slowly and agreeable about starting from cold ... It seems to be utterly without temperament, and is equally willing to slog along at 1,000rpm in fourth gear, or to scream down the road making buzz-saw noises. The peak power is 6,500rpm, and the makers recommend that no more than 6,800rpm be used, but the power does not really drop away until well past the 7,000rpm level. Valve float occurs at just under 8,000rpm.

The machine tested by *Cycle World* and prepared by McLaughlin Motors of Duarte, California, had had its original high 'western' bars changed to lower, narrower ones, which the tester liked much better. Also the test bike had twin Amal Monobloc 1$\frac{5}{16}$in carbs. It appears that most of the machines sent to the States had a similar, twin carb, set-up. This meant a float chamber only in the left-hand (nearside) instrument, with a feed line transferring fuel to the narrow, floatless chamber in the right-hand carb. *Cycle World* found that this 'makes the engine idle very raggedly if the machine is leaned over on its side when standing still, but it is of no consequence when in motion, and a great deal of space is saved.' Additionally, no air filter was fitted to the test bike, although, as *Cycle World* pointed out: 'we understand that this is not true of every Atlas ... This is, in our opinion, a questionable omission, but one that the buyer can remedy at little cost in time or money.'

The *Cycle World* tester made an interesting comment about braking, which:

> is provided by the same units (8 inch drums at the front, 7 inch drums at the rear) as used on the Manxman. These brakes were entirely equal to the performance of the Manxman; they are marginal on the Atlas ... Apparently, the slight increase in performance has caught up to the braking capacity, because we noticed that when used repeatedly and hard, during a sprint through the mountains, the brakes began to show signs of distress.

One aspect of performance, however, came in for praise: 'On that same trip through the mountains, we renewed our acquaintance with the Norton's incredible roadholding. On a machine with this kind of stability and roadgrip the rider may treat a winding, secondary road as though it were a turnpike.'

On Sale in the UK – at Last

Because of relatively low production numbers (certainly if compared to Triumph or BSA) the Atlas remained for export only until the end of 1963. The first British test of the Norton seven-fifty did not come until 1964, when *Motor Cycle News* got in first, with their 11 March issue. The tester, Charlie Rous, began by saying:

> It's amazing what 100cc can do! Especially when added to what is already a big bike. Small capacity machines are wonderful but breeze along at a mile-a-minute on a breath of throttle, or to tweak it to way over the ton without having to scream the bottom out of the motor, is magnificent …
>
> The Atlas is not a new design but an enlarged version of the well established 650SS – the machine *Motor Cycle News* readers have voted 'Machine of the Year' for the past two years. The 750, in fact, was introduced nearly three years ago for the American market where it is AMC's biggest dollar earner and now, for the first time, it is being made available here in Great Britain.
>
> I didn't think there would be any first impressions when dealing with the Atlas. I imagined the reaction would be similar to the 650 which, with its higher compression ratio – 8.9 to 1 compared to 'big brother's' 7.6 to 1 is nearly as potent in developed horsepower. But there is no replacement for displacement and the kick in the pants the 750 gives from take-off is vivid, to say the least. There is far more power low down than from the 650, but the simple complete-lack-of-effort way it is delivered through similar gear ratios, is the point which is most impressive.

It is virtually impossible to tell the Atlas and the 650SS of the same era apart.

Rous found that starting couldn't have been easier, but 'a fair amount of beef is required to crank the engine over ... From cold, there did appear to be a marked degree of mechanical clatter from the works department, but this subsided as the plot warmed-up, and was not particularly offensive.'

Interestingly, the *MCN* test bike and others of the same era were fitted with twin Amal Monobloc 389 carbs of 1⅛in bore size, not the single instrument or twin 376 carbs that American bikes had (*see* above).

Vibration

Although Charlie Rous wrote the majority of the *MCN* test report, Gerard Periam and Pat Braithwaite also made their own contributions. Braithwaite, although praising performance and acceleration, was not impressed with two aspects of the machine:

> Unfortunately, it offers speed at the price of its extraordinarily heavy thirst for fuel at high speeds, and unpleasant vibration ... It was my part of the test to do the fuel consumption tests when our two-pint test tank was good for only nine miles, using all its performance ... The vibration comes mainly through the handlebar.

Like *Cycle World*, Charlie Rous was also far from happy concerning the braking performance, claiming that the standard was considerably below that usually set by Norton.

But then it was back to the plaudits:

> Steering and roadholding are truly in the Norton tradition; gear changes were silent and lightning quick; the riding position is excellent (flat, narrow 'bars were fitted) for rapid motorcycling ... In spite of the thrashing the bike took, not a smear of oil blemished its appearance ... in congested traffic conditions, it was amazing just how genteel the big Norton could be.

With its vast amount of torque and high top speed, the Atlas was able to cruise all day at 100mph (160km/h), although Rous found it tiring, with the wind buffeting his arms and chest. Even though the Atlas had the Slimline version of the Featherbed frame, high speed comfort was diminished due to the width of the rear section of the fuel tank, which Charlie Rous found to be:

> splaying my legs apart. The wind caused my knees to be constantly forced outwards resulting in unnecessary aching ... To enjoy this mile-eater to the full, a fairing is an absolute must, and one needn't be thought a cissy to think so, for this would make an already very fast machine much faster.

Because of the wind buffeting at high speed, Charlie wrote: 'The occasion I really enjoyed riding the Atlas was when I turned off the motorway and took to the roads leading across country. Riding between 60 and 70mph [96–112km/h] was a pleasure. The engine was burbling between 3,000 and 4,000rpm and, contradictory to what I have already said, the thing felt as smooth as silk.'

Sidecar Potential

The third member of the *MCN* Atlas test team was Gerard Periam. He began his piece: 'Frustrated, that's me. One brief ride on the Atlas has convinced me that here is the real shire horse pulling power combined with high performance that sidecar men have been yearning for ever since the Vincent went out of production.'

To back up its sidecar potential, Norton offered an alternative front fork crown and column to provide suitable trail for light steering with a sidecar, heavy rate fork springs, and heavy duty rear shocks, plus a smaller engine sprocket to lower the gearing. The *MCN* test bike was also equipped (as standard) with a 60-watt alternator and 12-volt electrics (two 6-volt batteries in series).

Atlas Scrambler

Another version of the Atlas, but primarily intended for Stateside sales, was the Scrambler. This had been introduced in 1963 and used the seven-fifty engine in an AMC duplex frame of the CSR type, with AMC aluminium primary chaincase, Norton hubs and forks, small 'peanut' fuel tank, extended fork length, gaiters, low level 'straight-thru' twin exhausts, braced handlebars, matching instruments, knobbly tyres and sump bash plate included in its specification.

As detailed in the accompanying specification, in October 1964 Associated Motor Cycles, Norton's owners, launched new AJS and Matchless twins powered by the twin-carb 745cc Atlas engine. These bikes used the Norton engine, the Roadholder forks and full-width Norton hubs, but fitted into the normal AMC duplex frame and with other AMC cycle parts; 4.00 × 18 tyres were fitted front and rear to 'make them specially suitable for sidecar duties', as AMC claimed. They were also equipped with magneto ignition, 12-volt electrics and AMC alloy primary chaincase.

The price for both the AJS and Matchless 750s was £355 4s 2d, compared with £358 16s 7d for the Atlas. Both prices included UK purchase tax.

At the London Earls Court Show in November 1964 the Atlas was displayed with a metallic green fuel tank and chrome-plated chaincase. There was also a sports version of the AJS/Matchless type, which took advantage of the café racer craze then at the height of fashion. This latter machine, in Matchless guise and labelled G15 CSR, was quickly given the Coffee Shop Racer tag.

Within a few short months the Atlas range had been extended from one model to a whole

From the mid-1960s AMC employed the Atlas engine in several of its own AJS and Matchless models, including this 1965 Matchless G15 CSR (nicknamed the 'Coffee Shop Racer').

family, all of which, except the Atlas and Atlas Scrambler, were AMC rather than Norton! But by way of a compliment both AJS and Matchless were now using Norton components.

As 1966 dawned, Associated Motor Cycles became the subject of increasing national press speculation concerning the group's ever-increasing financial problems (*see* Chapter 13). Here it is enough to say that, as the year progressed, things went from bad to worse and that the official receiver was appointed in August. Two months later it was announced that a new company had been formed following the purchase of AMC by the Villiers Engineering Group, whose parent company was Manganese Bronze Holdings, chaired by Denis Poore. The new company was initially called Norton-Matchless and was supposed to represent all five of the AMC marques (Norton, plus AJS, Matchless, Francis-Barnett and James).

By the time of the Earls Court Show in November the group had become Norton Villiers. As Roy Bacon commented: 'The days of the famous Featherbed were becoming numbered for just the two basic Nortons were to be seen in various guises.' These show models included a 650SS with its traditional black and silver paint job with chrome-plated mudguards, but with painted (black) primary chaincase, flat bars and small kneegrips. Meanwhile the Atlas was now finished in metallic burgundy with a black frame, side covers, headlamp and other fittings. Like the 650, the mudguards were chrome-plated. As for the previously mentioned hybrids, these continued under the three different tank badges, although they were essentially the same bike, an Atlas engine in an AMC chassis.

Later in March 1967, British customers got the chance to buy the P11 (*see* Chapter 10), an American-inspired model originally conceived for desert racing. Basically this used the Atlas engine fitted with twin carburettors and coil ignition, fitted into a Matchless G85CS scrambler frame. But unlike the roadster

Another hybrid was the Matchless G15, with AMC duplex frame and aluminium primary chaincase, Norton engine, hubs and forks.

hybrids, the P11 employed brake hubs from the Matchless competition model.

The Commando Arrives

In September 1967 an entirely new model, at least in concept, made its public bow at the Earls Court Show. The Commando was the work of three men: Dr Stefan Bauer (who had joined Norton Villiers as Director of Engineering on 1 January that year), Bernard Hooper and Bob Trigg. Although the latter two were already highly experienced motorcycle development engineers, Dr Bauer had no previous motorcycle experience and had spent the previous twelve years with Rolls-Royce. He could not even ride a motorcycle! The three men, however, came up with what was to prove a highly successful bike that achieved excellent sales and was to remain in production for a decade.

However, except for the frame, clutch, primary chaincase, bodywork and certain smaller components, the Commando was not a new motorcycle design, as it employed several major chunks of the Atlas, including the engine, AMC 4-speed gearbox, brake hubs (the front sporting 2LS as standard) and Roadholder front forks (equipped with gaiters). But it was the frame which was the clever bit, using the novel concept of employing large vibration-isolating rubber bush assemblies to support the engine.

A Clever Marketing Exercise

In the author's opinion, the Commando was actually a clever marketing exercise – and one that was received well by press and public alike. For example, the Commando won the coveted *Motor Cycle News* 'Machine of the Year' award on no fewer than five occasions. It also allowed Norton to race in both production and the new Formula 750 events until well into the 1970s. To remain competitive the Commando was ultimately given an engine size increase to 825cc (77 × 85mm), left-sided gearchange and electric start.

However, with the arrival of a new breed of sophisticated Japanese multi-cylinder machines, the Commando was ultimately seen for what it had always been, essentially an overbored and stroked vertical twin that had made its bow in the austere days of the late 1940s. The clever part was that it gave the Norton twin an extra ten years of meaningful sales.

13 Politics

An important facet in the Norton twin's story is the politics played out by the leading figures who were involved in the company. The years until the end of the Second World War (*see* Chapter 1) had been dominated at first by James L. Norton and Daniel O'Donovan, who were followed by R.T. (Bob) Shelley, Walter (Bill) Mansell and engineers including Walter Moore, Arthur Carroll, Joe Craig and Edgar Franks. In addition there were the race-track achievements by such great riders as Alec Bennett, Stanley Woods, Jimmy Guthrie, Freddie Frith and Harold Daniell.

In July 1945 it was announced that Bill Mansell was to resign as Norton's managing director, thus putting into operation a decision he had taken in 1939, but delayed owing to the war; he was, however, to remain a member of the Norton board. His replacement was Gilbert Smith, who had been largely responsible for gaining the valuable military contracts that had kept Norton busy since the spring of 1939, producing in particular the 16H five-hundred side-valve single.

At that time other notable figures included the chairman, C.A. Vandervell, and the race supremo, Joe Craig, who had rejoined Norton after spells with BSA and AMC. The engineering team included Edgar Franks and Jack Moore (no relation of the former Norton chief designer, Walter Moore).

In early January 1947 it was announced that Bill Mansell and his son Dennis, together with J. Lawrence, would shortly cease their association with Norton Motors Ltd.

A statement was issued by managing director Gilbert Smith in the first week of February to the effect that E.R. (Reg) Shelley and G.A. (Tony) Vandervell, both sons of Norton board members, had been appointed directors of the company from 1 February. In addition, Joe Craig had become 'technical director' from 1 January that year. There had been a bitter boardroom battle behind these moves that had seen the Mansell faction defeated.

Hopwood Arrives

At the end of March 1947 came news that Herbert (Bert) Hopwood would be taking up a design appointment at Norton. In his book *Whatever Happened to the British Motorcycle Industry?*, Hopwood describes his position as that of 'Chief Designer', although whether this was actually true at the time is open to question, given the subsequent actions of the Engineering Director, Joe Craig. But whatever the truth of the matter, Hopwood was an important figure in the Norton twin story, not only designing the original Model 7 (*see* Chapter 2) but also returning later to guide the company through a difficult period during the late 1950s. Another engineering figure worthy of mention here was Doug Hele, who joined Norton from the Bristol-based Douglas concern. Like Hopwood, Hele was to have two careers at Norton, the two men's time with the Bracebridge Street factory running almost in parallel.

Although Bert Hopwood, together with Jack Moore, came up with the Norton ohv twin, the company in the late 1940s was dominated very much by racing. In fact Hopwood

Bert Hopwood

Herbert (Bert) Hopwood M.I.Mech.E. was both an influential designer and a controversial man. Born in 1910, he was described in *Motor Cycle News* in 1961 as: 'Dark complexioned, greying slightly at the temples, broad shouldered and stockily built, he looks a typical senior executive ... And he possesses the shrewd down-to-earth commonsense and humour of a Midlander born and bred.'

As he was the first to admit, Bert Hopwood was the world's worst motorcyclist. Instead he was an engineer, and motorcycles just happened to be his speciality. There is no doubt that he was a designer of the top rank, having not only created the original Norton ohv parallel twin, the Model 7, but also the Navigator and Jubilee middleweight twins and the BSA A10 Golden Flash, and he was co-designer of the BSA Rocket 3/Triumph Trident.

The first engine he helped design was the Ariel Square Four back in 1930, which was when he first came into contact with the man who could be considered his mentor, Edward Turner.

Bert Hopwood was a native of Bournville, the Birmingham suburb famous for its connection with the Cadbury chocolate firm. He left school at fifteen with an aspiration to become an engineer. This led him to Birmingham's Central Technical College, where, as he was later to recall, 'I learned how to use a lathe – and make tea!'

His first job was with Components Ltd, the original owners of Ariel. Before long he was promoted to the drawing office of Val Page and then, just before his twentieth birthday, he was seconded to assist Edward Turner. When the Components group was dissolved, the Ariel firm was taken over by Jack Sangster.

In 1936 Turner was appointed general manager of Triumph at Coventry and was subsequently made managing director. Hopwood went too, as assistant on the design side. The following year brought the announcement of the then revolutionary Triumph Speed Twin, the first really successful vertical twin – and the forerunner of several future Hopwood designs.

Within two years the Second World War began. The Triumph works in Coventry was destroyed in the Blitz during late 1940. Hopwood recalled that: 'Thousands of drawings and records went up in smoke and I got the thankless task of redrawing every part from patterns!'

Having completed his dead-end job of putting Triumph's files in order, Bert quit in 1947 to join Norton. There, after designing the 'laid-down' gearbox and tidying up the engines of the 16H, Big Four and ES2, he designed the Dominator twin, which was launched at the end of 1948 (*see* Chapter 2). It was his first complete motor cycle design.

After only eighteen months, however, Bert Hopwood was on the move again, largely because he felt future progress for both himself and series production Norton was blocked by the company's engineering director, Joe Craig. Since Craig was paid according to performances gained in racing, he not surprisingly favoured a policy that meant racing came first, the production side a very poor second.

Hopwood's next stop was BSA. After his experiences at Norton he considered quitting bikes, but at the giant Small Heath works he became what he described as 'a boffin'. His first task was to design a new die-cast cylinder and head for the Gold Star single. Six weeks after joining BSA he was promoted to 'chief designer' and showed his ability by drawing out the six-fifty Golden Flash twin, also introducing a new five-hundred twin. Not all his BSA creations were so successful, however, including the 70cc Dandy and ill-fated Beeza scooter.

In spring 1956 he moved back to Norton Motors and two years later he was promoted to managing director of both Norton and R.T. Shelley. But he still found time to put pencil to paper to create models such as the Jubilee and Navigator. His time as Norton MD, however, was frustrating. He brought Norton back into profit only to see this siphoned off to prop up the failing AMC parent company. He was also faced by the downright hostility of AMC's chairman, Donald Heather, who vetoed a move to a newer, more modern factory after the conclusion of the deal and refused Norton the right to make use of the recently acquired Indian sales organization for the American market.

And so Hopwood left in spring 1961 to take up his final appointment with Triumph, where he was to remain until his retirement during the mid-1970s. As his autobiography, *Whatever Happened to the British Motorcycle Industry?* shows, Bert Hopwood was at the end an unsatisfied man. Many of his best ideas were overruled and he seems to have eventually fallen out with many, but not all, of his motorcycle industry colleagues. In truth he was frustrated by his paymasters' inability to share his forward-thinking vision.

Above all, however, he could be proud of what he did achieve, notably two of the very best of classic motorcycle designs, the Norton Dominator and BSA A10 Golden Flash.

even went as far as saying that the racing/production roadster budget was '90/10 per cent'. This situation was to cause Hopwood to quit after only eighteen months in the job, even before the Model 7 entered production.

The Four-Cylinder Racing Project

At the end of 1948, with Hopwood gone and with the backing of the board, Joe Craig set out to create a four-cylinder model for Grand Prix racing. The engine for this was to be developed in conjunction with BRM (British Racing Motors), based in Bourne, Lincolnshire, who were working on a V16-engined racing car. Norton signed a contract with BRM that would provide them with a design for their four, based on the BRM V16, and Joe Craig spent much of 1949 working with the BRM team at their headquarters. Norton's financial contribution came via its offshoot, the R.T. Shelley engineering firm.

Norton's initial contact with BRM had come via Tony Vandervell, who was also involved with that company through his London-based specialist bearing manufacturing business.

Ultimately, however, the Norton four-cylinder project was not a success, largely due to the fact that Norton's link with BRM, Peter Berthon, was somewhat ineffectual and seemed to show little enthusiasm for the project. In addition, Tony Vandervell and BRM's chief, Raymond Mays, did not get on: Vandervell thought that Mays might have known what he wanted but didn't know how to get it. So Vandervell pulled out of BRM in 1950 and went on to build his own successful Vanwall Grand Prix team, using an engine based on four 500cc Norton dohc singles formed inline.

Even so, the Norton/BRM connection continued. Eventually a 125cc single-cylinder engine, based on the four, was built for test purposes in 1953. In another move Joe Craig attempted to purchase the ready-made French Nougier 500cc four. But both the BRM-based engine project and the Nougier purchase came to nothing.

In late 1952 the Norton chairman and major shareholder, C.A. Vandervell, then aged eighty-one, decided it was time to dispose of Norton Motors Ltd and R.T. Shelley Ltd and that they should be floated on the London Stock Exchange.

An offer for a majority shareholding was subsequently made by what was described at the time as 'an anonymous bidder'. This was accepted and on 24 February 1953 it was announced that AMC (Associated Motor Cycles) were to be the new owners. It is fair to say that everyone in the motorcycle industry, not least those connected with Norton, were stunned by this news.

AMC

The company registered as Associated Motor Cycles, but more popularly known as AMC, came about as a result of various takeovers. In 1931, at the height of the Great Depression, Matchless (owned by the Collier family and based in south-east London) had acquired AJS from the Stevens brothers. Following the takeover of Sunbeam by ICI (Imperial Chemical Industries) in August 1937, Matchless subsequently acquired the Sunbeam marque from ICI. This meant that the Colliers now owned three different motorcycle brand names – Sunbeam, Matchless and AJS – all famous marques in their own right. The directors of the Matchless company decided that a more suitable name was needed to encompass all three, and so on 12 October 1937 the company was re-registered as Associated Motor Cycles Ltd.

As the 1930s came to a close, AMC could boast a level of financial stability that was the envy of the remainder of the industry. In 1940 AMC sold the rights to the Sunbeam brand name to rivals BSA: only Matchless motorcycles were built by the Group during the war

As this 1949 advertisement shows, AMC, like Norton, were encouraged to export everything they could make in the early postwar period – a national policy needed to pay off Britain's huge debts incurred during the Second World War.

years, largely the Teledraulic-equipped G3L three-fifty ohv single.

The war years also affected the future direction of the company with the deaths of young Bert Collier, who had just begun to prove himself a brilliant designer, following a motorcycle accident in 1941, and of his eldest brother Harry A. Collier, the AMC chairman, in 1944. By the end of the war only Charlie Collier remained.

In the first few years of peace every motorcycle built could be sold – most going for export. AMC also took over the Coventry-based Francis-Barnett concern in June 1947.

At the time of the takeover Charlie Collier and D.S. (Donald Spencer) Heather were joint managing directors of AMC with Samual Rollason Hogg as chairman. The other members of the board were Gordon Francis, Sir Alan Hutchings, Jack Kelleher and Arthur Sugar (it was to be Kelleher, Sugar and Donald Heather who were later to play a major role in AMC's ultimate demise).

After the acquisition of Francis-Barnett, the next marque to be swallowed up by AMC was the James concern, based in Greet, Birmingham, during November 1950.

The Birmingham-based James concern had been acquired by AMC during November 1950.

Norton Joins the Fold

But the big one came at the end of February 1953 when it was revealed at AMC's annual general meeting that a plan existed for the group to acquire the issued share capital of the famous Norton marque. It was also revealed that Norton would continue as a separate organization under the existing managing director, Gilbert Smith, and that, in the words of AMC Chairman, S.R. Hogg, 'the Norton factory team will continue to compete in major events'. In reality the trials effort was axed immediately (*see* Chapter 5), and the Grand Prix team (together with AJS) was closed at the end of the 1954 season, although production Manx models were campaigned by selected riders after this date.

In addition, the share capital and financial control had in fact been acquired by the Pearl Assurance Company, and for the first time in its history AMC had to allow outside investors to have a say.

On Monday 23 August 1954 the joint managing director of AMC, Charlie Collier, died suddenly in his office at the Plumstead factory,

AJS was also a member of the AMC group. This advertisement in January 1953 ran in the weeks leading up to the Norton takeover by the London-based group. It also shows that AMC were involved in all aspects of motorcycling.

aged sixty-nine. Not only was he the last remaining member of the Collier family, he possessed a deep knowledge of the motorcycle industry, something that with his passing would be sadly lacking in future years.

Within a few short weeks of his death the full Grand Prix effort was axed. In an interview in 1984 Wally Wyatt, a leading engineer at AMC, said: 'If anything went wrong we would soon know about it. Old Charlie Collier was a great man – he was always in the factory walking around. In fact AMC went downhill from the day he died.'

Jock West

The other personality at AMC who knew the industry inside-out was former racer, and sales boss, Jock West, who incidentally had been firmly against the purchase of Norton. One reason for this is that Jock had spent considerable time at the James factory sorting out problems and helping to improve production and sales for the Greet marque, and feared exactly the same would be asked of him with the Norton project. This, of course, is precisely what happened. Only a few months after Norton joined AMC's portfolio, Jock West was offered a vacant seat on the AMC board, provided he sorted out the Norton sales problem. Despite his earlier misgivings, Jock accepted the task (and thus the board position). The resulting improvement in Norton's fortunes was helped by the introduction of an improved 88 model, followed by the larger 99 six-hundred.

In January 1958 Gilbert Smith, then aged fifty-seven, resigned as managing director of Norton Motors and R.T. Shelley. He had joined Norton straight from school at the age of sixteen as an office boy, and had risen through the ranks to become a director in 1926 and managing director in 1945, but he had never got on with AMC. Smith, however, did remain as a member of the Norton board and as a consultant for a period after his resignation.

Jock West (pictured here during the mid-1930s) was to be one of the few senior management figures at AMC who understood the motorcycle industry after the last of the Collier brothers, Charlie, died in 1954.

At first the position of managing director of Norton/Shelley was offered to Jock West, but he turned this down, preferring instead to remain as AMC's sales director.

Bert Hopwood Rejoins Norton

Back in April 1956 Bert Hopwood had rejoined Norton Motors after being approached by Donald Heather, the chairman (appointed March 1956) and managing director of AMC:

> It was agreed that I become a Director of Norton Motors and R.T. Shelley Ltd and should be located at Bracebridge Street. Mr Heather was most anxious that I should not become too bogged down with design engineering, although this part of management should be my responsibility. The terms of reference were that I should be appointed: 'an Executive Director of our subsidiaries Norton Motors and R.T. Shelley Ltd with full executive control of the works including production, engineering and product design.'

Gilbert Smith was still the managing director, but Joe Craig had left at the end of 1955. At the time of Hopwood's return, Alec Skinner, a chartered accountant and the Norton company secretary, was promoted to the board. He was then around forty years of age and, as Hopwood recalled:

> he was able to fully understand and appreciate the more practical problems of the business and with his feet firmly on the ground, his financial control was simple and easy to understand. He and I became firm friends from the outset and we worked together with a smoothness which many regarded as quite remarkable.

In late June 1956 H.L. Hepburn resigned as Norton sales manager 'to undertake special duties' within the company. Succeeding him was W.J. (Bill) Smith, formerly a leading scrambler from north of the border and director of the Scottish Automobile Co. Ltd. Bill Smith was later one of the few Norton employees to move south following the closure of Bracebridge Street at the end of 1962 and became a senior member of the parent AMC organization. Another man to join Norton in 1956 was Doug Hele, who had already worked there several years before. Together with Hopwood, he was to be responsible for the successful evolution of the Dominator series over subsequent years.

1956 was notable at Norton for another reason – a strike lasting nearly six months that brought serious financial losses in the 1955/56 financial year. According to Hopwood's memoirs, under favourable conditions 200 motorcycles per week could be manufactured, but it was quite impossible to achieve 'anything better from this small dilapidated factory [Bracebridge Street] which was a relic of a different era and needed new machinery and, more importantly, some space and light to give the shop floor a break from the unbelievably slummy conditions.'

During the 1956/57 financial year Norton returned to profit, but it still came as a shock to Hopwood and other members of the Norton management team when Gilbert Smith announced his intention of stepping down from his post as managing director. Hopwood summed up their feelings: 'Norton Motors without Gilbert seemed unthinkable as the man was synonymous with the company with which he had grown up since his boyhood.'

The Matchless G3/LS, a typical AMC product of the 1950s. Shown here is a 1958 coil ignition version of this heavyweight ohv single.

Francis-Barnett, based in Coventry, was another motorcycle manufacturer swallowed by AMC (in June 1947). As this 1960 catalogue shows, the Cruiser 84 was closely related to Norton's Jubilee two-fifty in all except power unit.

Heather Becomes Chairman

In March 1958 S.R. Hogg resigned from the boards of Associated Motor Cycles and its subsidiaries. Donald Heather became chairman and shortly after promoted Bert Hopwood to managing director at Norton. Heather had joined the old Matchless company in 1924 and been appointed successively secretary, joint managing director and, finally, managing director following Charlie Collier's death in 1954.

On 1 September 1959 AMC acquired the Brockhouse Engineering Group, who themselves had purchased the ailing Indian Motor Cycle Co of Springfield, Massachusetts, USA, in 1951. During the 1950s the Indian sales arm had imported British bikes from various factories, including Vincent, Royal Enfield, Matchless, AJS and Norton. The main purpose of this latest acquisition was to give AMC control over the Indian import activities. Donald Heather, however, expressly forbade Bert Hopwood and Norton from making use of this service! This led Hopwood to set up an independent arrangement with the New Jersey-based Berliner Corporation.

On 31 August 1960 Donald Heather retired as managing director of AMC, although he retained his position as chairman of the group board; from this same date, Arthur Sugar and Jack Kelleher were appointed joint managing directors. Other board members at this time were Tom Cowell and Jock West, with R.S. Mays-Smith as group secretary.

A Far from Happy Ship

But things were far from happy on the good ship AMC: Hopwood quit Norton in April 1961, soon followed by Jock West. Hopwood's replacement as Norton MD was Alec Skinner.

The seeds of these two resignations could be traced back to growing discontent, which stemmed from both men's contempt for Donald Heather. Other shareholders were also becoming increasingly upset, as the Group's financial position deteriorated.

On 1 October 1961 Bill Smith, who until then had been general sales manager at Norton, took over Jock West's duties as AMC home and export manager. Then at the end of 1961 the group had to announce that the previous year's profit of £219,000 had turned into a £350,000 loss (about £3.5 million in today's money). The fallout from this was that Donald Heather was replaced by Tom Cowell in February 1962 as chairman of the AMC Group board; the latter now comprised Arthur Sugar and Jack Kelleher, with R.S. Mays-Smith as the remaining director and W.A. Hidreth the company secretary.

Early in 1962 all American sales were handed over to Berliner. Inside sources at AMC subsequently told the author that Berliner forced the group to sell many of its exports to the States at a loss, which of course made the group's financial position only worse. The loss for 1962 rose to a whopping £645,774 (around £7 million today). There was cause for deep concern about the abilities of the joint group managing directors, a former butcher (Kelleher) and 'a bureaucrat' (as Steve Wilson described Sugar).

Standardization and Declining Sales

The same year AMC introduced what it called the 'Standardization Programme'. The plan, however, could not be instigated until Matchless, AJS and Norton were on a single site. The result was that the Norton factory and the Shelley plants were closed at the end of 1962 and production moved to Plumstead. This move was announced in July that year and subsequently Alex Skinner resigned his post as managing director of both Norton Motors and R.T. Shelley. Only five of the almost 500 Norton staff moved south to AMC: Bill Smith, draughtsman Dennis Bourne, technical writer and service manager John Hudson, and two apprentices, one of whom was Dave Bean (fifteen years later he was to be the project leader of the ill-fated Hesketh 1000 V-twin of the early 1980s).

As a further part of the 'Standardization Programme', Francis-Barnett and R.T. Shelley production transferred to the James factory in Greet, Birmingham, in 1962.

Much of the Bracebridge race shop was sold off jointly to Paul Dunstall and Reg Dearden. Dunstall took most of the twin-cylinder bikes and components, while Dearden concentrated on the Manx singles.

1965 Matchless G80/85CS – last of the heavyweight 500cc four-stroke motocrossers. The cycle parts were utilized by the Norton P11 desert racer, powered by a 745cc Atlas twin-cylinder engine.

The only thing that didn't change was that the Reynolds connection remained: the Birmingham specialists were to produce all the Featherbed frames, even after Bracebridge Street itself closed.

These moves were supposed to save money. Instead they helped to destroy sales of AMC's products. Loyal customers of each of the various brand names clearly saw the whole exercise for what it was – blatant badge engineering.

By the end of 1962, with sales declining ever more quickly, AMC appointed a new chairman, Sir Norman J. Hulbert MP, who had the temerity upon taking office of proclaiming that the group was on the way to recovery – when in truth things were going from bad to worse.

The entire AMC empire seemed to be heading for the rocks by the end of 1964. According to *Motor Cycling*'s Bob Holliday:

> The range for 1965 looks as though someone had taken a collection of AMC, Jubilee and Featherbed frames, AJS, Matchless and Norton engines and, with name plates for all three marques, shaken them up with a giant hat to produce some twenty-two varieties of single and twin-cylinder ohv motorcycles.

The End for AMC

The end came in August 1966. Associated Motor Cycles had reached the point of no return: with its financial state becoming worse by the hour, the directors finally did the decent thing and quit. An official receiver was therefore appointed to take over the failed group, a move instigated by AMC's creditors, including its banks.

Berliner had shown interest in acquiring the group, but on 2 September AMC was taken over by Manganese Bronze Holdings (MBH). It was later revealed that MBH's chairman, Denis Poore, had been tracking AMC since as far back as 1962, but he simply bided his time and waited for the group to fold before dealing with the official receiver. It is generally agreed that MBH acquired the troubled group for less than £1 million.

MBH had taken over the Wolverhampton-based Villiers firm in 1965. Two years later it announced that it had also acquired the Royal Enfield share capital (although not the spares operation, service obligations or remaining factories). Apart from the BSA group and the ailing independent company Velocette, almost all the British motorcycle industry was now owned by MBH.

This state of affairs only grew worse in July 1968 when Norton-Villiers cut off the supply of Villiers engines to the remaining small producers, which included names such as Cotton, DMW and Greeves.

Originally called Matchless-Norton, then Norton-Villiers and eventually, from the early 1970s, NVT (Norton Villiers Triumph), Poore and MBH seemed destined to be the saviour of the British motorcycle. But events governed by politicians were to see this dream collapse within a decade. This left only the workers' co-operative at Meridan turning out Triumphs, which, thanks to Labour's Tony Benn, ended up costing the British taxpayer a vast sum of money before it too shut its doors in 1983.

AMC also offered other brands with the Norton Atlas engine, including this 1967 Matchless G15CS Street Scrambler. Most were exported to the USA and sold through the Berliner organization.

14 Dunstall

The general motorcycling public first heard of Paul Dunstall from a two-page feature by Mick Woollett in *Motor Cycle News*, dated 3 December 1958. This article was inspired by a letter published a few weeks earlier from a certain Mr D. Applegate of Hartley, Kent:

> Having seen P. Dunstall perform at Brands Hatch on his Norton twin, which must surely be a Dominator 99, my friends and I would like to know more of the history of this machine which can pass Manx Nortons on the straight. If there is room for an article in MCN it would be much appreciated.

Room was indeed found. Under the headline 'MCN Tries Dunstall's Dommy', the sports editor began his article: 'That letter appeared in our issue of October 15 and it certainly jogged my mind for I have a vivid memory of Paul Dunstall on this machine getting a fifth place in the 1,000cc Invitation race at Brands on August 24.'

A few days after the publication of the initial letter, Paul Dunstall contacted the newspaper saying that he would be pleased to tell them about his Dominator and offered *MCN* a test session. It was immediately agreed that both parties should meet at Brands Hatch, which they did on a morning in late October. As Mick Woollett wrote in his feature: 'The morning dawned damp, dark and uninviting as autumn mornings have a habit of doing when one intends to do a bit of riding, and I set out to Brands in my riding kit – previously packed away for the winter.'

Arriving at the Kent circuit Mick found Paul, then aged nineteen, and his father already there with the Dominator at the ready (at this time the term Domiracer had not yet been coined). After what Mick Woollett described as a quick look at the soaking track, the trio decided to discuss the machine over a cup of tea in the clubhouse – and, with luck, give the slippery surface a chance to dry.

During this enforced break, Paul quickly related the history of his bike. Ordered the previous winter from Norton with a sports kit (including twin Amal Monobloc carbs and 8:1 compression pistons), the only difference to the cycle parts was that he had specified 'Manx springing front and rear'. The bike was delivered on 4 January 1958 and cost £304, complete with all road equipment.

The Dominator 99 was run in on the public highway and the crank flywheel assembly balanced by the well-known tuner Allan Dudley-Ward. Paul also mentioned his friend Reg Curley, who at the time worked in the AMC factory at Woolwich. This was not the last time that Curley's name would appear in the Dunstall Norton story, since Reg polished and lightened various engine components, notably the rockers and valve gear.

Practice Begins

When the 99 was back in one piece Paul Dunstall began practising at Brands Hatch every week (during the Wednesday track sessions). He had his first race in a Novice event at Thruxton on Easter Monday, 1958.

This was not only the Norton twin's first race, it was also Paul's, who was then only eighteen. But considerable disappointment was to follow when the ignition system went sick as he was lying third. Not wanting a repeat of this outcome, the original coil set-up was replaced by a magneto. Further tuning saw the compression ratio raised to 9:1.

The next outing was at Paul's local circuit, Brands Hatch. With a combination of track experience gained during the practice days and the additional tuning, Paul Dunstall scored a victory in the 1,000cc Novices event.

More Modifications

In all Paul raced at some eight meetings in 1958. During the remainder of the season more modifications were made, notably raising the compression ratio again (up to 10:1) and replacing the stock 1in (26mm) Amal Monoblocs with larger 1⅟₁₆in (28mm) instruments of the same type. The engine displacement remained at the 597cc of the stock 99.

The only changes to the cycle parts during the course of the season were the fitment of a combined fuel and oil tank in glass-fibre, together with a racing dolphin fairing and hump-back racing seat of the same material. The standard Dominator brakes and steel wheel rims (still 19in) were retained, while straight-through exhausts were employed, not megaphones.

Woollett Rides the Beast

When Mick Woollett finally took to the Brands Hatch circuit he discovered that the racererised Dominator 99 presented a few problems: 'I won't pretend that I felt immediately at home on either the machine or track. Paul is quite a bit longer in the leg and also, it would seem, has double jointed ankles with which to change gear.'

After what was described as 'several ultra-slow laps', the squad readjusted the gear lever but, as Woollett complained,

> those who are familiar with this particular gearbox [the 4-speed AMC roadster unit] will know the lever is only half the battle and I continued to select neutral with nerve-wracking regularity … As the track was still awash in places and Druids was like a skating rink it was impossible to form any hard and fast impressions of the general handling but the engine was beautifully clean on acceleration and packed a real punch from almost zero revs …

Paul Dunstall had set the rev limit at 7,000rpm and there was only a slight tremor of vibration in the 6,400–6,600 region, although, unlike Eric Oliver's Dominator (the 88 and sidecar that the former World Champion raced in the 1958 TT), there was a reluctance to go over the 7,000 mark. Unlike some twins Paul had found the 99 would pull a high gear and estimated that the maximum speed on a fast circuit could be in the region of 125–130mph (201–209km/h) with the fairing.

As the day's weather didn't improve Paul then had what was described as a 'spin round, but the morning was so murky that no other motorcycles put in an appearance and at lunch time we called it a day.'

Mick Woollett ended by saying: 'It is interesting to note that the only machines that finished ahead of the Dominator during the August 24 meeting were three newish Manx Nortons ridden by Minter, Bruce Daniels and John Holder plus the rather special G45 Matchless handled by Lawrence Flury.'

Transferring from Rider to Entrant

Although Paul Dunstall was a good rider he was soon to switch from riding to entering others. Only the type of bike remained the same, the Norton twin. Although eventually he was to embrace other marques, his first loyalty was to Norton and things only began to change in the Dunstall équipe when the AMC Group got into difficulties.

Paul Dunstall working on one of his famous Domiracers in Brands Hatch paddock, circa *1967.*

The official BMCRC (British Motor Cycle Racing Club) practice day over the 1.6-mile (2.6km) Silverstone club circuit was covered the following week in the *Sports News* column of *The Motor Cycle* (9 March 1961):

> Production sports models were also being aired, in preparation for the 1,000 kilometre race on May 20 and the Thruxton 500-miler in July. Notably impressive was the standard-looking Norton Dominator 99 being whistled around by Fred Neville. It made some production racers look slow! Owned by Eltham Motorcycles and Scooters, this machine is prepared and tuned by Paul Dunstall, whose own Dominator 99 went remarkably quickly at Brands Hatch a couple of years ago.

In the Silverstone 1,000km, the Dunstall-tuned bike was ridden by Neville and Alan Rutherford. Unfortunately, first it was crashed and then went in and out of the pits until it was retired.

This 1961 99 was soon sold off, being advertised in the 2 August issue of *Motor Cycle News*:

> Specification includes full Dunstall-tuned motor, Sports magneto, rev counter, racing tyres, racing chains, racing brake linings, Manx seat, Manx suspension, reinforced petrol and oil tanks, Clubman's rear footrests, Ace bars. Intended for Thruxton but not ready in time. All original equipment included in price of £280.

A Pukka Racer

Besides the production-based bike described above, Paul Dunstall had prepared and entered a second 99-based machine in 1961. By now he was running his own motorcycle business, Eltham Motorcycles and Scooters, and had decided to quit racing himself. But Fred Neville talked him into preparing both the production bike and the pukka Manx-framed racer.

The pukka racer used the cycle parts from a 1959 Manx model (formerly raced by John Hartle) and a more highly tuned 597cc 99 engine. Aboard this bike Fred Neville scored an impressive victory at Brands Hatch in mid-August 1961, where he won the main 1000cc event at 86.59mph (139.35km/h), with a fastest lap of 88.17mph (141.89km/h), maintaining a pace that Phil Read was unable to match on his Manx Norton. Read later crashed out in spectacular fashion when hitting oil left on the track by another machine at Paddock Hill Bend. This left Tom Thorp (Manx Norton) and Mike Duff (Matchless G50) to finish way behind the flying Dominator twin in the two remaining rostrum positions.

Only a few days later Fred Neville was fatally injured while in the lead during the final lap of the Junior Manx Grand Prix on his own 7R AJS single. And so a great potential partnership of Neville and the Dunstall Dominator came to an end.

Keeping the Flag Flying

After Fred Neville was killed, Derek Minter took over for the final meeting of 1961, finishing second to Phil Read in the rain at 76.5mph (123.1km/h).

To take advantage of the extra displacement, Paul then placed an order with Norton as soon as the new six-fifty was announced for sale in the UK (rather than the early 1961 export-only model).

The new engine finally arrived in May 1962 (a twin-carb 650SS), but before it was actually raced it underwent the Dunstall treatment, being totally rebuilt and blueprinted, together with, of course, certain tuning components.

Certainly when Paul was interviewed by *MCN* towards the end of 1962, he disclosed little beyond admitting to using a special camshaft and pistons. The crankshaft, con-rods and main bearings were standard, as were the valves. Twin Monobloc carburettors had been retained (but were now of a larger bore), but with separate float chambers. A castor-base oil was used, this feeding through a larger than standard oil pump. Still wary of ignition failure, Dunstall had assured the spark department was taken care of by a Lucas racing-type rotating magnet magneto, as fitted to the works Domiracers (*see* Chapter 7).

Dave Downer

Over the winter of 1961/62 Paul Dunstall gained the services of the up-and-coming rider, Dave Downer, who was really to put the Dunstall name on the racing map.

Much development work went on with the new six-fifty engine throughout the spring and summer of 1962. But all this took time and Downer only raced the six-fifty in anger three times during that year. The first outing, strangely paralleling Paul's own first race in 1958, ended in failure when the primary chain broke.

The second meeting, however, was much more successful, bringing victory in August at Brands Hatch, where Downer won at 85.43mph (137.48km/h) ahead of Tony Godfrey with Chris Conn third (both riding Manx Nortons). A final outing at the same track in October brought runner-up spot behind the 'King of Brands', Derek Minter.

Why was everything taking place at Brands Hatch? The answer is quite simple: not only was it near Dunstall's Eltham base, but, as he recalled in December 1962, 'I built the bike for Brands.' This was why in his preparation of the six-fifty he decided 'not to concentrate on maximum speed, but to put everything into acceleration. The power from the engine is tremendous and available from very low rpm and all the way up to 7,000 and beyond.'

Motor Cycle News noted that: 'This is one of the reasons why Dunstall's machine is not fitted with megaphones. It accelerates better without them and if a mile an hour or so is lost at the top end, it doesn't matter for the thing is still very fast.'

Paul reckoned that his 1962 six-fifty racer was good for more than 140mph (225km/h).

Dave Downer was the first rider to give Paul Dunstall any major track successes. He is seen here at Snetterton on 10 April 1963 riding the 500 Domiracer. This was only a few days before his fatal accident at Brands Hatch on the final lap of what many agreed was the closest race they had ever seen at the Kent circuit, between Downer and Derek Minter.

MCN's Charlie Rous agreed, saying 'and I don't doubt this at all having seen the way it blasts normal 500cc racers from its path, and having tried it for myself I can appreciate it.' Rous, himself a competition rider (sprinting), went on to say: 'The gears are standard Manx ratios and this is one machine where more than four gears would be a waste of time – it has so much power everywhere. Another advantage for this machine is in its weight – the 650 engine is 35lb [15.9kg] lighter than a 500cc Manx.'

Another commentator at the time claimed:

> The machine now is obviously far and away ahead of a standard Dominator, but basically it remains a machine that looks much the same as money can buy. For Paul Dunstall it's an advert for success, and proof that racing with this type of machine is not such a crazy idea after all.

This was not entirely accurate, however, as by the end of 1962 there were many other features besides its Manx frame and suspension, including aluminium fuel and oil tanks (now separate assemblies), swept back exhaust header pipes and, most notably, a large diameter Italian Oldani front brake.

The Domiracer Racer Arrives

In early January 1963 Paul Dunstall revealed that he had bought the works 500 Domiracer twin from Norton and that Dave Downer would continue as rider. According to the report in the 9 January 1963 issue of *Motor Cycle News*: 'The pair, who teamed up when Dave began riding Paul's 650cc Brands Hatch Norton special last year, are planning a more ambitious racing season together. With the acquisition of the 500, plus Dave's own 350 Manx, they intend to compete at most of the home circuits.'

Actually, Paul had collected the bike from Norton's Bracebridge Street factory a couple of months earlier. When purchased it was, as he later described, 'in a semi-dismantled state', but since then he had completely rebuilt it:

> This was no small job. The Domiracers really are specials and nothing from a standard engine is interchangeable. The similarity to a standard engine is the bore and stroke of 66mm by 72.6mm ... For example, the con-rods are much shorter than standard and consequently so is the cylinder. The 10.4 to 1 pistons have much shorter skirts and the flywheel is cut away to allow piston clearance at the bottom of the stroke. The crankshaft too is 'special' but the measurements are as for the 650. The crankcase has been modified considerably and is supported on bigger main bearings. The camshaft revolves on needle roller bearings and the tappet pushrod arrangement is much different.

As Paul Dunstall continued to explain the story behind his cache, other interesting information came to light, including the true power figures of Tom Phillis's third-place 1961 TT success. The factory's brake test figures showed an output of no less than 58bhp (some 6bhp more than had generally been estimated by outsiders at the time). The same applied to the engine revolutions, Doug Hele's notes and records showing that, although maximum power was produced at 7,800rpm, the engine had been run to 9,000rpm with safety.

With his Domiracer purchase, Paul Dunstall had also acquired a couple of spare 'Lowboy' frames (*see* Chapter 7), into which he said he would be fitting his existing six-fifty engine and that from Dave Downer's own 350 Manx. These works frames were not only lower, but lighter than the standard Manx Featherbed type. He estimated that, owing to the new frame and the weight-saving exercise carried out following a rebuild of the six-fifty, the machine would be 'all of fifty pounds lighter in 1963'.

In the 6 February 1963 issue of *Motor Cycle News*, Charlie Rous wrote in his *Paddock Gossip* column:

If you would like a really close up view of Paul Dunstall's Norton twin racers, a visit to his showroom at Eltham, Kent, would fill the bill this week. Paul's 650 will be on show with his original 600 (the 1958 bike) plus his recently acquired and rebuilt 500cc Domiracer. On show too will be a display of bits and pieces to help to make them go.

Then in the 20 March 1963 issue of *MCN* it was reported:

Dave Downer had his first opportunity to try Paul Dunstall's ex-works 500cc Domiracer at Brands on Wednesday, and while he didn't have the okay from the boss to give-it-the-works (he was running in) he says he thinks it is a super machine. Dave was also out on Paul's completely rebuilt 650. The only part left from last year's mount is, in fact, the engine, for this has now been installed in a Low-Boy frame similar to the 500. Object of the plot, apart from the lower head-resistance, is to have two identical machines.

Problems

At the very next practice session at Brands the following week, however, the Dunstall team experienced what *MCN* said was a 'slight setback': Dave Downer crashed the six-fifty and the 500 Domiracer suffered what was described as a 'mild blow-up'. Dave had been 'fairly hurtling' around the Kent circuit in around 57 seconds, but then he overstepped the mark. Going into the Druid Hill Hairpin too quickly, he locked the rear wheel on braking and fell. Only his pride was hurt.

The five-hundred was in trouble with a cracked cylinder block, but, as *MCN* said, 'This has since been modified with the help of AMC's Jack Williams [Doug Hele not having moved south when Norton was transferred to AMC's base in south-east London] and the pair will be out again today [27 March] if all goes well.'

The team put these setbacks behind them when on Easter Sunday, 14 April 1963, Dave Downer took the Domiracer to an excellent third place in the International 500cc race at Snetterton in Norfolk (a race watched by the author all those years ago). With riders of the calibre of Sven Olav Gunnarsson from Sweden (the winner) and Dave Degens, Lewis Young, Paddy Driver and Mike Duff, this was an excellent result. The Domiracer and its pilot also had the added satisfaction of setting the fastest lap at 82.68mph (133.06km/h).

The following day a record 50,000 crowd at Oulton Park in Cheshire saw a Gilera 1–2 by Derek Minter and John Hartle in the main 500cc race. Even so, that man Downer impressed again, taking fourth with only the star qualities of Phil Read (Norton) between him and the factory four-cylinder Italian bikes.

The following week Downer scored third in the 500cc final at the national Wessex

Brands Hatch, 20 September 1964, Dave Degens on a Dunstall 650 (10) leads a group of riders, including Joe Dunphy (12) and Chris Conn (82).

Centre Castle Combe races. But, as the *Motor Cycle News* race report shows, this was only part of the story: 'Highlight of the 500cc final, won by Tom Phillis, was a photo-finish between Selwyn Griffiths (Matchless) who took second place from Dave Downer (Norton twin) by a tyre's width. Downer, riding his Paul Dunstall ex works Domiracer, made a poor start but came right through the field.'

At Mallory Park on Sunday 28 April 1963, Downer finished third in the 500cc final behind the winner Phil Read and Joe Dunphy (both mounted on Manx Singles). Again with excellent riders like Griff Jenkins, Chris Conn and John Cooper behind the Domiracer, it was a good showing.

That Fateful Day

Two weeks later, on Sunday 12 May 1963, came that fateful day at Brands Hatch and the race that was to claim Dave Downer's life and leave Derek Minter seriously injured, described by *MCN* as 'a race which no-one who saw it will forget. A tragic outcome to a most tremendous dice.'

In his report, Charlie Rous went on to say: 'Tragedy struck the most terrific race I have ever seen ... On the last lap of what was possibly the fastest and closest, and certainly the most tremendous race ever at the track, Dave Downer crashed fatally in a pile up with Derek Minter, who sustained head and back injuries.' The two riders, in company with Phil Read (Norton), had stormed away from the rest of the pack in the final fifteen-lap 1000cc event. Read had led to start with, but with Downer and Minter right on his heels. Downer then exploited the full potential of what Rous described as 'Paul Dunstall's incredibly fast 650 Norton' and went ahead. Still nothing separated the three riders. Although Downer led the race at the end of each subsequent lap thanks to the Norton twin's superior acceleration, the lead changed constantly.

For ten laps this fierce, no-holds-barred battle raged until Read retired. As the race approached its finale, the two remaining riders were spurred on to even greater efforts as they sped round the full 2.65-mile (4.26km) Brands Hatch GP circuit, literally neck and neck.

With the Dunstall Norton twin constantly blasting past Minter's 500 Manx Norton to lead the race at the conclusion of each lap, Minter's only hope of victory was to shake the 650 rider off on the corners. Charlie Rous described the moment:

> As they rocketed around on the final circuit he [Minter] took the lead at Druids Hill Bend and was still in front when they arrived at Dingle Dell Corner and – as he cranked over for the turn – his machine slid out from beneath him and Downer, who was still very close behind, was unable to avoid the crash.

Another commentator had this to say of the incident:

> What an absolute tragedy it was that the most marvellous race I have witnessed at Brands, or anywhere else, should have ended in the death of 23-year-old Dave Downer, the young engineer from Belvedere, Kent. He was riding Paul Dunstall's 650 Domiracer superbly and every time he passed the press box on the finishing line he had snatched the lead. I think that all the many friends of Dave Downer would like it to be said that this was his finest hour.

Never was a truer word spoken.

Dunstall Returns

In late June 1963 Paul Dunstall confirmed that he had decided to continue his race effort. His new rider would be Tom Phillips, who had been putting up impressive performances on a new Greeves Silverstone 250 and his own Norton single that year. Tom's first entry was scheduled at Cadwell Park, riding the ex-works 500 Domiracer. The six-fifty was to be used for the first time at Brands Hatch on Sunday 14 July.

It was to be a winning debut for the new pairing, because at Cadwell Park Tom won the 500cc final, although it had been halved in distance to only four laps owing to torrential rain.

Tom Phillips didn't feature at Brands Hatch on 14 July, but he most certainly did six days later when he scored a double at Castle Combe, winning both the 250cc (Greeves) and 500cc events, the latter on the Dunstall Domiracer. He also set the fastest lap in the 500cc race at 86.94mph (139.9km/h).

The Phillips/Dunstall partnership, however, did not last. *Motor Cycle News* carried a report on 21 August 1963 that: 'Joe Dunphy will be racing Paul Dunstall's 650 Norton at the next Brands Hatch meeting on Sunday [August 25]. Dunphy has arranged to ride the Dunstall "Domiracers" for the remainder of the season in addition to his own machines.'

Despite this, Joe Dunphy didn't race the Dunstall 650 Domiracer at Brands Hatch after all, since, while warming up the machine in the paddock, Paul Dunstall spotted an oil leak in a rocker oil feed pipe. So Joe used his own Manx Norton for the 1000cc race. Syd Mizen rode the 500 Dunstall Domiracer in both the 500 and 1000cc classes and was quoted after the race as saying that he would probably use the bike in the future – not surprisingly, since he gained two second places in the 500 and 1000cc races, behind Dunphy!

Racing at Brands Hatch for the first time since his crash there back in May, Derek Minter returned to the Kent circuit with what *Motor Cycle News* said was 'all his old dash' on Sunday 22 September to win both senior races on a works Gilera four and set a new race record of 88.11mph (141.79km/h).

In the 1000cc race the main opposition was expected to come from Joe Dunphy and Syd Mizen, both riding Dunstall 650 Domiracers. However, as the *Motor Cycle News* race report dated 25 September 1963 reveals, 'Dunphy ... was unable to make any great challenge, but came home in third place, while Mizen's machine went sick while he was in fourth place.'

A Dismal End to the 1963 Season

The 1963 season ended on a dismal note for the Dunstall équipe. Paul's two six-fifty models were to have been ridden by John Hartle and Joe Dunphy, but as Paul commented, 'John didn't ride because his hands were weak, and Joe didn't wish to change his own 500 Norton for the older 650.' As for the 500 Domiracer, this was ridden by Syd Mizen, but even this didn't go well, as he was knocked off at the start. When he did finally get going he retired after the engine went onto one cylinder.

And so a year that had begun with such optimism ended on a particularly low note. However, if observers thought this was the end of Paul Dunstall's team, they would be proved supremely wrong.

Customers could order a truly custom-built Dunstall Norton twin. This one is the ultimate road model. Built in 1966, it was basically a 650SS engine kitted out with various Dunstall goodies, plus an earlier wide-line frame, Manx rear hub and Italian Oldani front stopper.

New Year, New Hopes

Paul Dunstall had new plans and hopes for 1984. Ever the publicist, he was pictured together with sidecar star Colin Seeley in the 12 February issue of *Motor Cycle News*, together with a news story entitled 'Seeley's Dommy'. Essentially the plan was for the two to join forces by building a new outfit, powered by one of Dunstall's by now famed 650 Norton twin engines.

But the real Dunstall news story of early 1964 was his new range of Dominator Customizing Equipment. Typical was an illustrated advertisement of a mouthwatering Dunstall Dominator, kitted out as a café racer, that began to appear regularly in the motorcycle press. The components listed included:

Alloy fork ring nuts 40s pair
Chromed fork springs 40s pair
Rev counter instrument £5
Chromed head lamp brackets 30s pair
Chromed clip-ons 45s pair
Five gallon tank £13
Domiracer seat £4 10s
Chrome battery box lid £1
Exchange chromed chainguard 35s (rear)
Complete rear set footrests £8 10s
Exchange chromed chaincase (primary) £3
Domiracer exhaust pipes £7 10s

Readers were advised to 'Send stamped addressed envelope for our Illustrated Leaflet'.

Although the advertisements were headed 'Paul Dunstall', there was still the Eltham Motor Cycles name, with the address as 156 Well Hall Road, Eltham, London SE9.

The Custom King

By April 1964 not only were component parts being advertised, but complete Dunstall bikes. A typical period advertisement states: 'A Complete Custom service is available for Brand New Models. Machines are supplied completely fitted out with any equipment at only £25 above list price.' Customers had the choice of choosing the 88SS, 650SS or the 750 Atlas.

Together with the sale of individual components, the 'Genuine Paul Dunstall Domiracer' sales programme had begun in earnest. And, with the café racer and rockers culture just beginning to take off, so did Dunstall's sales of

A Dunstall 750 Atlas seen in October 1966, with all the latest Dunstall customizing parts, including a full dolphin fairing, racing tank and additional chromeworks.

both bits and bikes. A new cottage industry had been born. And of course, and highly relevant to this book, it was based around the Norton Dominator.

More news about the complete Dunstall bikes came at the end of July 1964, when *Motor Cycle News* carried a news story headlined 'Dunstall special Nortons join sports market':

> Eltham (Kent) dealer and tuning specialist, Paul Dunstall, is now marketing new sports special Nortons with £70 worth of fitted extras – at only £30 above list price. Because of difficulties in obtaining the 500cc and 750cc models, Dunstall's main trade is in modified 650s. He estimates to sell approximately three of these specially prepared machines a month.

The extras included a 5½ gallon alloy tank (worth £20 alone), 'Manx'-type external telescopic fork springs, rev counter, rear-set footrests, shortened pillion seat or racing seat, plus clip-ons and modified headlamp brackets.

The entire exhaust system was also a Dunstall speciality. Coupled with various specially chromed components (listed previously) these additions, as *MCN* commented, 'bring the Dominator's looks up to scratch for the out and out sportsman.'

While these changes had little or no effect on performance, it was also possible, for an additional £25, to have a Dunstall engine tune, which it was claimed would give a top speed in the region of 130mph (209km/h).

Business Comes First

If 1964 had seen Paul Dunstall move into the customizing and tuning business at the expense of racing, this theme continued in 1965. In February Paul announced an increased range of extras for the Dunstall Nortons. This totted up to a total of twenty-one items for the fully equipped model, which now sold for £35 above list price, an increase of £5 over the previous year. If purchased separately these would cost £76, so the customer could still save a considerable amount by purchasing a machine already converted.

The engine tune now cost £30. For this the purchaser gained larger bore carburettors, enlarged and polished ports, lightened and polished rockers and followers, high compression pistons and double-speed oil pump. Delivery on the complete customized bikes was quoted as being four weeks.

King of the Road

In testing one of the 650 Dunstall Dominators for the 16 June 1965 issue of *Motor Cycle News*, Robin Miller called it the 'King of the Road'. He began the test by saying:

> Britain may lag behind in the space race, her brightest ideas for jet fighters may get the chop, but when it comes to producing big, beefy, mile-eating motorbikes she is supreme … I have been riding a Daddy among big bikes – the 650 Dunstall Dominator. A more magnificent, but less mean, monster I have yet to come across, in captivity that is! It took me up the A1 at a steady 100mph [there were no speed cameras then!] yet trickled through stop-start Whit holiday traffic showing a dove-like side to its character which, quite honestly, I never expected.

Tested around the Brands Hatch short circuit by Dave Degens, this actual bike had been timed at 60 seconds dead, and Paul Dunstall claimed that Degens had 'taken great delight in zooming past Manx Nortons blowing the horn'. It was claimed that Degens' quickest time on the 650 racer was only slightly faster.

On collecting the bike from Paul Dunstall's shop at Eltham, Robin Miller had been 'immediately plunged in the Whitsun holiday traffic and had to endure a journey, not quite to the centre of the earth, but almost it seemed, through the dreaded Blackwall tunnel.' He was pleased with how the Dunstall machine 'behaved magnificently' in city traffic: 'Bottom gear is a little high for traffic crawling, but not once did the clutch protest and it was always easy to find neutral. On the one occasion when I didn't and the engine stalled, one hefty swing on the kickstart and the motor roared into life.'

Cold starting, however, as the test revealed, was a slightly different matter: 'The 10.5:1 compression pistons made their presence felt and too often the engine rebelled with uncomfortable results.'

As for acceleration, this was described as 'breathtaking! … From 4,000 to its claimed peak power figure of just under 7,000rpm, it was as brisk, if not slightly sharper, than a Manx Norton. But a handful of throttle in the lower range and the motor pinked in protest.' The author wonders, though, about this last point – was the tester using the manual advance/retard control for the racing magneto?

The bike tested by *MCN* was fitted with straight bars, which replaced the clip-ons, rear-set footrests and a more 'luxurious' racing-type seat. Miller found that this 'gave a compromise riding position which was just right for cruising at 80mph', but 'anything above this and clip-ons would have been an advantage because you were more or less hanging on.'

Achieving 100mph was 'not so much an effort, more of a moment of surprise, as you glanced at the speedometer.' Miller also commented that 'the gearbox and linkage were positive and easy to use. Third and top gears were beautifully close and made riding through fast swervery bends particularly enjoyable.' Much the same enthusiasm applied to other aspects of the machine: 'Being a Norton, handling was superb and it was temptingly easy to throw the machine over until the exhaust scraped on the left and the footrest on the right, even though everything was well tucked away.'

Probably the biggest accolade, however, was reserved for the braking department:

1965 Dunstall 650 Dominator (roadster)

Engine	Air-cooled ohv twin with vertical cylinders, alloy head and cast-iron barrel, two main bearings, 360-degree, 3-piece crankshaft, split con-rods and shell big-end bearings, coil valve springs, vertically-split aluminium crankcases
Bore	68mm
Stroke	89mm
Displacement	646cc
Compression ratio	10.5:1
Lubrication	Gear pump; dry sump
Ignition	12-volt with alternator, manually operated Lucas racing magneto
Carburettor	2 × Amal Monobloc 389 1⅜in
Primary drive	Simplex chain
Final drive	Chain
Gearbox	AMC 4-speed, positive stop, foot-change
Frame	Norton Slimline Featherbed, full cradle, twin front down tubes, welded-up sub-frame
Front suspension	Norton Roadholders, with Manx external fork springs
Rear suspension	Swinging arm, with oil-damped, Girling twin shock absorbers
Front brake	8in full-width drum, SLS*
Rear brake	7in full-width drum, SLS*
Tyres	Avon 3.00 × 19 Speedmaster front, 3.50 × 19 GP rear
Wheelbase	55.5in (1,410mm)
Ground clearance	5.5in (140mm)
Seat height	30.5in (775mm)
Fuel tank capacity	5gal (22.7ltr)
Dry weight	359lb (162.8kg)
Maximum power	52bhp @ 7,000rpm
Top speed	119mph (191.5km/h)

* Some machines 2LS

> Stopping anything from 100mph needs better than average brakes, and the front stopper was a rather special twin leading shoe job which Paul Dunstall has dreamed up. Like many of his 'goodies' it sells over the counter and while Norton brakes are among the best anyway, this mod brings them up to racing standard.

The *MCN* test recorded a maximum speed in top of 119mph (191.5km/h); speeds in other gears were: bottom 45mph (72.4km/h), second 70mph (112.6km/h) and third 100mph (160.9km/h). And the price? £416 0s 10d, including the UK purchase tax.

BSA and Triumph

In early October 1965 came news that, for the first time, anything other than the Norton Dominator series was to come under the customizing King's banner: 'Paul Dunstall, the man with the silver touch, has waved his wand over BSAs. From now on the 1966 range of BSA big twins will be available in "Dunstallised" form, and he will shortly be marketing Triumphs fully kitted up with Dunstall goodies.' As before, both complete customized bikes and individual components were to be marketed. There was also, for the first time, a Dunstall fairing. Priced at £10, this would be available for Norton, BSA and Triumph.

So why was there this change in policy? For one thing the Dunstall organization was an ever-expanding operation by this time. For another, Paul Dunstall, with his close contacts with the marque, would have been fully aware that the AMC group, which controlled Norton, was by now in serious financial trouble (*see* Chapter 13). As events were to prove, however, Paul's personal enthusiasm for the Norton twin was undiminished.

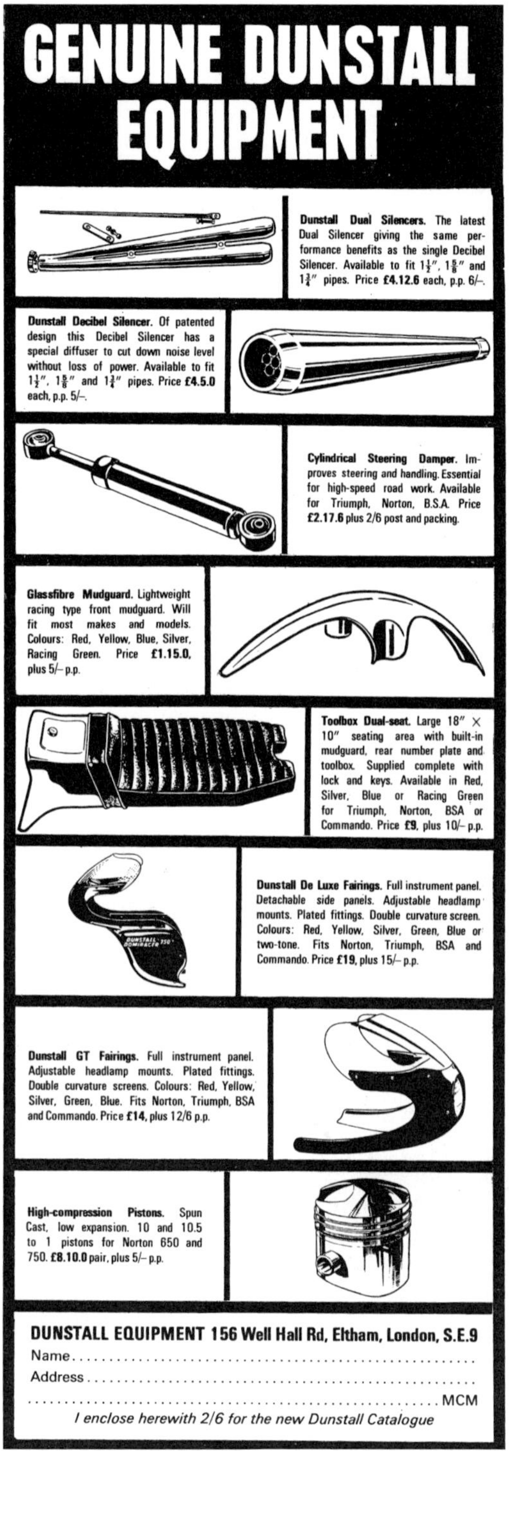

A late 1960s Dunstall advertisement showing some of the special Norton components.

The Metisse Connection

The next big Dunstall news story was on the racing front and came in the spring of 1966, with the arrival of the brand new 750 Atlas-engined Dunstall Metisse. To start with it was planned to race a prototype bike, which had already been completed, followed by what Paul Dunstall described as a replica costing £625.

When he built his first seven-fifty racer (to replace the six-fifty models campaigned since 1962), Paul had fitted the engine into what he considered would be the best frame. This was an ex-works Lowboy Featherbed of the type specially developed by Reynolds Ltd for the original works 500 Domiracer, on which Tom Phillis lapped the Isle of Man TT at 100.36mph in 1961 to finish third (*see* Chapter 7).

However, something of a shock awaited Dunstall. With the near 70bhp 750 engine fitted into this chassis, the machine was what Paul described as 'no compliment to the "World's Best Roadholder" slogan.' Quite simply, with the additional power, acceleration and speed, the front end became decidedly 'feathery' at high speeds and something of a confidence downer on fast swervery. As Paul went on to relate: 'This was a strange and unexpected phenomenon. The same machine fitted with its original 500cc engine, steers and handles perfectly – as was intended and achieved. But it begins to waver when a 650 unit is substituted and is worse still when the 750 is slipped in.'

Paul Dunstall built this prototype 750 Dunstall Metisse racer in 1966.

The answer, he realized, lay in solving the relative problems of weight distribution, power-weight ratio, suspension ... and what Paul described as a host of other headaches. All this would have taken time, a commodity that he did not wish to waste.

This was where the brothers Rickman came in. The New Milton, Hampshire, factory of Don and Derek Rickman built, though perhaps 'rebuilt' is a more apt description, the Dunstall 750 Domiracer in just over three (yes, *three*) weeks! The first time Paul Dunstall spoke to the Rickmans about the project was when Charlie Rous introduced the Rickmans (by telephone) to Paul Dunstall on 14 March 1966 – and the bike was delivered back to him on 6 April. It then ran for the first time in its new frame the next day and it was on the start line for its first race at Brands Hatch on Good Friday, 8 April.

The Debut

Griff Jenkins was by now Paul Dunstall's rider and, although he didn't score any fairy-tale victories during the debut meeting at Brands Hatch, the future potential of the new Dunstall Metisse was clearly evident.

Jenkins made a slow, second-from-last start in the main race of the day, the prestigious 'King of Brands' event, but carved his way through to sixth place seemingly without effort. What Griff soon discovered was that the new-found steering and handling qualities allowed him at last to use the power in what he described as 'huge handfuls'.

However, this brought a new problem; braking power, or lack of it. The brakes (as used from 1962) were a Manx Norton conical rear hub and an Italian Oldani at the front. Quite simply, as Griff explained, they could not stand the pace. This failing had never occurred previously and showed that the machine was certainly being driven harder.

Serious brake fade caused Griff to retire from the race, but anxious to get in as much track time as possible on the new Metisse, he raced it again, this time in the shorter distance supporting 1000cc event.

In this race Griff got a much better start and went straight into a wheel-to-wheel battle for the lead with Dave Degens (650 Dresda Triton). *Motor Cycle News* described what unfolded: 'Clearly the Dunstall-Metisse was the fastest machine in the race – it is also quite possible the fastest road racing machine in this country. But with its blistered brakes, Jenkins could not exploit his speed advantage by holding position around the corners, and Degens beat him.'

Disc Brakes

The next modification was to improve the brakes by fitting Rickman-Lockheed disc brakes, together with Rickman front forks.

Although everyone in the racing game was by now switching to 5- or in some cases even 6-speed gearboxes, it was tried on the Dunstall 750 and found to actually *slow* lap times.

Here's how one tester of the period summed up the 750 Dunstall-Metisse:

> The power from the engine is colossal. Megaphonitis is non-existent as such and things begin to happen from about 4,000rpm onwards. The engine capacity of 745cc probably helps provide torque with the leverage of Tower Bridge, eliminating the need for more than a four speed gearbox. The machine is no more difficult to drive than a super-sports roadster – except that there is a lot more power.

Although the Rickman-framed bike weighed some 25lb (11.3kg) more than the Lowboy version, Paul Dunstall was 'not bothered' thanks to the handling benefits. Also Dave Degens showed how impressed he was with the Metisse chassis by putting his six-fifty Triumph engine in one of the Rickman frames.

The Monza Record Attempt

In October 1966 Paul Dunstall made his first attempt at international records, the chosen venue being Monza, Italy. This didn't get off to a good start, however, when there was a mix-up between the ACU and the FIM, the latter claiming that they had not been officially notified of the attempt.

Backed by Castrol, this was to be an attempt on the world one-hour record for 750cc machines. Paul Dunstall planned using one of his own fully equipped special road machines, the rider being Griff Jenkins. Once the officials had finally agreed, the attempt was made on Saturday 29 October 1966.

Much of the 'backroom' preparation for the project had been undertaken by Ken Curley, who had not only worked closely with Dunstall for some time, but had previously been employed in the AMC race shop.

As the bid began, rain was sweeping the Italian autodrome, but soon Jenkins was reaching 140mph (225.3km/h) down the straight on his dolphin-faired machine and, as *Motor Cycle News* reported, 'he was brave enough to be able to hold it on round the banked curves, merely lifting his head to deal with the bumps.'

This valiant effort, however, was dashed after 52 minutes 23 seconds, when Jenkins was forced out having completed forty-one laps. This was because in the rain the barrels were being cooled unevenly and distorting; eventually one split.

The annoying thing was that, had Jenkins completed the lap, he would have set a new record, for at that stage he was averaging 124.3mph (200km/h) and therefore would

A page from the 1967 Dunstall Dominator catalogue showing bikes and special tuning available.

have passed the number of miles set up in an hour by George Catlin on a BMW R69S six-hundred at Montlhéry in 1961. This record stood at 111mph (178.6km/h), whereas Jenkins's fastest lap was over 127mph (204.4km/h)

Another attempt later that day with the pukka racing 750 Dunstall-Metisse also ended in failure: the machine first misfired badly and was later put out when the Atlas-based engine seized.

At the conclusion of the attempt, Paul Dunstall said, 'We are certainly going to have another go. The roadster was going really well. We were using a balance pipe on the exhausts and I reckon this gave us an extra eight mph.'

Earls Court

Only a few days after returning from Italy Paul Dunstall had a stand at the London Earls Court Show. Five machines were featured: a Dominator 750, Triumph Bonneville, BSA Spitfire, Metisse 750 (Atlas-powered) road model (all four with Dunstall equipment) and what was described as a 'special lightweight 500 Dunstall Domiracer'.

The complete Dunstall range of equipment for 1967 was also on display. An example of this was the Dunstall exhaust system, which, it was claimed, incorporated a new principle in exhaust pipe design, giving superior engine efficiency on twin-cylinder machines, improved acceleration and a higher top speed. This new exhaust system was available for not only Norton twins, but also for BSA and Triumph, and was supplied complete with cooling ring nuts, balance pipe clamps, alternative silencer mounting brackets and adjustable polished alloy shields.

A complete new 28-page catalogue was now available – the price of 1s being refunded with the first purchase, however small. The stand was staffed by Griff Jenkins and Rex Butcher, with 'Paul helping out at busy times.'

Onwards and Upwards

Even though AMC had gone into liquidation during 1966 (*see* Chapter 13), the Paul Dunstall empire continued to expand. A Norton connection was maintained via the new Commando during the late 1960s but, as the Japanese began their takeover of the big bike market during the early 1970s, Paul Dunstall moved with the times, eventually switching to Honda and Suzuki. By the end of that decade Paul, however, had seen the writing on the wall and moved into the property market.

One could almost describe Paul Dunstall as the Barry Sheene of the motorcycle marketing world – someone who was great at capturing the press and public imagination – and setting new ways of doing things in the industry. Certainly Dunstall, largely via the Norton twin, built himself a niche in motorcycle folklore.

Index